FROM THE STAGE TO THE STUDIO

From the Stage to the Studio

HOW FINE MUSICIANS BECOME
GREAT TEACHERS

Cornelia Watkins and Laurie Scott

OXFORD
UNIVERSITY PRESS

OXFORD
UNIVERSITY PRESS

Oxford University Press, Inc., publishes works that further
Oxford University's objective of excellence
in research, scholarship, and education.

Oxford   New York
Auckland   Cape Town   Dar es Salaam   Hong Kong   Karachi
Kuala Lumpur   Madrid   Melbourne   Mexico City   Nairobi
New Delhi   Shanghai   Taipei   Toronto

With offices in
Argentina   Austria   Brazil   Chile   Czech Republic   France   Greece
Guatemala   Hungary   Italy   Japan   Poland   Portugal   Singapore
South Korea   Switzerland   Thailand   Turkey   Ukraine   Vietnam

Published by Oxford University Press, Inc.
198 Madison Avenue, New York, New York 10016
www.oup.com

Oxford is a registered trademark of Oxford University Press

Library of Congress Cataloging-in-Publication Data

Watkins, Cornelia.
    From the stage to the studio : how fine musicians become great teachers /
Cornelia Watkins and Laurie Scott.
        p. cm.
    Includes bibliographical references and index.
    ISBN 978-0-19-974052-9 (hardcover : alk. paper)—
    ISBN 978-0-19-974051-2 (pbk. : alk. paper) 1. Music—Instruction and study.
2. Music teachers—Training of. I. Scott, Laurie. II. Title.
    MT1.W37 2012
    780.71—dc23   2012021037

1 3 5 7 9 8 6 4 2

Printed in the United States of America
on acid-free paper

To Max, Danny, Jeremy, and Michael for their support and endurance.

C.W.

To my son Martin, who undoubtedly has been one of my best teachers.

L.S.

Contents

Acknowledgments

FIRST, WE WOULD like extend a very special thank you to Stephen Clapp for his input and support of this book.

We would also like to acknowledge the following individuals who directly or indirectly contributed to this book: DeAnna Adkins, Melissa Becker, Chelcy Bowles, Tom Burritt, Elizabeth Chappell, Winifred Crock, Robert Duke, Carol Kelly Duncan, Delaine Fedson, Marianne Gedigian, John Geringer, Bonnie Goodrich, Amy Harris, Judith Jellison, Kristi Manno, Penelope Meitz, Leslie Nail, Amy Reddoch, David Small, Scott Stewart, Randal Swiggum, Tim Washecka, and Darlene Wiley. We thank each of you for your unique perspective and generosity with your ideas.

Laurie Scott: I would like to thank my former violin teachers, Richard Gill, Homer Garretson, Robert Emile, and Vincent Frittelli. I am honored to extend their legacy of thoughtful and optimistic teaching. I am also very grateful to my colleague Kristin Jensen for her insight and ideas related to this manuscript. I would like to acknowledge my professional colleagues in the division of Music and Human Learning, whose inspiration and intellectual vitality continually energize my thinking and teaching. In addition, I extend my thanks to the outstanding faculty of the University of Texas String Project, in whom I optimistically see the future of music education. In particular, I express heartfelt gratitude to Yvonne Davila, and Andy Strietelmeier for their understanding and support during the completion of this project. A very special thank-you goes to William Dick, my teaching partner and dear friend. His ingenious ideas have inspired my life and every aspect of my teaching for the past thirty years. Finally I thank my family, particularly my sister, Mary Smith, for unfaltering encouragement and inspiration.

Cornelia Watkins: I am sincerely grateful to Kenneth Goldsmith, who has gone out of his way to support my teaching and this project. He is a model of magnanimity in the music profession, and I am proud to call him my friend and colleague. I want to thank Ray Dillard and Richard Lavenda for taking the time to read the manuscript and offering their invaluable suggestions; and gratitude to David Wells for the same, and as always for being my great and compassionate teacher of cello, music, and life. I also owe a debt of gratitude to my good friends of the Wisconsin Comprehensive Musicianship Project who have taught me so much about teaching with breadth and depth, and whose wonderful ideas are embedded in many of these pages. And even after writing thousands of words about music, it is still hard to find words that are sufficient to appreciate my wonderful husband and best friend, Max Dyer.

Foreword

THE FACT IS, YOU *will* teach, unless you vigorously resist invitations! As a performer in the community where you settle, you will be visible—there won't be that many of you. So rather than having your resistance worn down after months or years of prospective students' requests, and stumbling into teaching encounters based only on your own experience from years ago, good and bad, *From the Stage to the Studio* will help you to feel good about starting well and continuing effectively.

The greatest string performers of the past century, among them Heifetz, Feuermann, Piatigorsky, Primrose, and Perlman, became passionate teachers, eager to assist the next generation with the benefit of their own heritage and development. We are all beneficiaries of that heritage.

I find that teaching helps my performing because the necessity of putting observations into words for students helps me to clarify observations about my own playing, leading to an improved result. After all, practicing is the process of hearing something in my playing that I wish sounded better, figuring out the problem's cause, organizing solutions, and making a habit of accuracy that becomes automatic. Good teaching applies the principles of our own practicing to someone else's playing—hearing something in a student's playing that could be better and giving the student a way to incorporate the solution.

The book begins by focusing on your own artistry, allowing you to become more effective in your practicing and communication of music, this wonderful language of emotion and spirit. The book then continues with sensible, practical tips to save you from the hazards that ensnare some teachers, and explores many great concepts, suggestions, and teaching situations that will benefit musicians of any age and experience level.

From the Stage to the Studio is the first book of its kind to create a comprehensive overview of a performing musician's world and expand it toward the art of teaching. It fills a most important gap in our professional literature. My own thinking and teaching have been challenged and improved through the ideas contained in these covers.

As a passionate performer and teacher, I strongly commend this book to your attention. Its contents will enhance every aspect of your musical life!

Stephen Clapp
Violin Faculty Member and Dean Emeritus, The Juilliard School

Preface

MUSIC MAJORS ARE traditionally offered one of two choices: performance or education. We, the authors, both earned degrees in performance, and have experienced the dedication that is necessary to become a performing musician. We both also have strong ties to the world of teaching, through training, experience, associations, or all three. We are aware of stereotypes associated with these two music degree "camps," and are very familiar with the biases, why they exist, and how they are perpetuated. We know teachers who are definitely not performers, just as we know performers who are definitely not teachers. It is our firm belief, however, that the vast majority of musicians really can and should know how to do both quite well.

Our primary concern now is with the performers who will teach yet haven't been offered any teacher training in their degree programs. We hear from former performance majors, like the violinist who is thrilled that her interview and recital had helped her secure a university position but is now panicked because she'll be responsible for teaching a string techniques course and doesn't know what to do; or the capable young cellist who has yet to win an orchestra audition, is teaching private lessons at a middle school to make ends meet, and is at a loss when it comes to teaching vibrato. We have conversed with and surveyed hundreds of performance majors who wish they had known that it is simply not realistic to base a career in music solely on their performance ability.

Because the division between teaching and performing has dictated the training of musicians for so long, the goal of bringing these partner professions closer together has become a high priority. We have devoted ourselves to writing proposals, articles, and books; designing syllabi; and, of course, teaching. At music conferences, our presentations that connect the best of both worlds have been enthusiastically received by many college faculty and administrators. Even so, the status quo hasn't changed much over the years. Not long ago it became obvious that it was time to take this mission to the next level: to write a book that would offer practical guidance to any musician who wanted or needed pedagogical training, while demonstrating vital connections between teaching and performing.

We began by outlining all the reasons, real or imagined, why pedagogy has not been a well-defined component of many performance degrees:

- The prevalent misconception that learning to teach runs counter to learning to perform, and will therefore distract performance majors from their studies.
- The concern among applied teachers that a pedagogy instructor might muddy the water with conflicting ideas about the "best way" to play or teach.
- The highly impractical notion that schools, in order to offer music pedagogy, must provide a separate course for each performance area.
- The challenge that applied teachers face when required to offer pedagogy to their students, with rarely the time or the background to provide a comprehensive overview of teaching.

This book was written to provide real answers and solutions to these issues:

- Musicians who examine and translate the best of what they do into what they teach will quickly find that it enhances, rather than diminishes, their performing abilities.
- A course in pedagogy need not put the instructor between the applied teacher and the students. Instead, a well-conceived pedagogy class can provide a framework for each musician to examine the best of what he or she does, and involve the applied teacher's expertise in the process.
- A heterogeneous class of outwardly unrelated instrumentalists, singers, and conductors will begin to see themselves as a unified group of fine musicians with very similar goals, who can benefit from considering each other's approaches.
- Applied instructors required to teach pedagogy will now have a resource for their students, hopefully making the subject far easier to teach as an independent or interactive study class.

Part I guides you, the performer, to think about, talk about, clarify, and reinforce the aspects of your personal approach that make you a strong, confident musician. You will be asked to explore what you believe defines artistry, and how you make great music; how you listen, and ways to cultivate listening as a well-refined and useful skill. You will examine virtually every aspect of your technique from a universal perspective, from the fundamentals such as balance and breathing to the variety and complexity of specific techniques on your instrument. You'll be encouraged to explore your approach to practicing, and to examine the ways you prepare and deliver your best performances—all the while considering how the chemistry between these essential elements makes you the musician you are.

Part II will help you transform what you know into what you offer your students. You will look at your own life as a student for valuable lessons about what works and what doesn't. You will be guided through the principles of good teaching and ways to create a thoughtful sequence of skills, musicianship, and repertoire. You will consider the value of nurturing independence in your students, and approaches that offer students a comprehensive basis for their musicianship. As your priorities and deeply held beliefs become more evident in your teaching, they will be further clarified and defined through a guided process of creating a personal philosophy statement.

Part III explores a variety of teaching situations you are likely to encounter and offers suggestions to help you be successful in each one, while alerting you to common problems and possible solutions. Finally we look at the cyclical nature of the teacher-student relationship, what it means to grow personally and professionally while making a positive and lasting impact on those around us.

This book presents goals for performers at different places in their careers. Students who will soon graduate can still benefit from their applied teachers' expertise while taking a big step toward their own musical independence. Performers who are already "out in the world" can take a self-guided tour through their performing expertise and develop ways to translate their best playing into their best teaching. Performers of all levels can become more aware of their lives as musicians along a continuum of learning and teaching. From a broader perspective, we are better able to see how the teaching we received powerfully influenced our lives, and how we can do the same—and perhaps better—for new generations of musicians and music lovers.

There is another unexpected benefit of exploring your best self as a musician and a teacher: you'll start to say things you didn't know you knew, and draw on wisdom you didn't know you had. As you focus on those areas of greatest importance to *you,* your own performing will become more refined, more personal, and more meaningful in ways you might not imagine right now. We hope you enjoy the process.

Introduction

When Your Calling in Life Is to Perform, Why Learn to Teach?

You are a performing musician. In playing, singing, or conducting, you have found your life's calling. Perhaps you've won competitions, performed as a soloist, landed a job with a top orchestra or opera company, or are touring with a successful chamber ensemble—or perhaps you aspire to such goals. You are single-minded and passionate about your art. So what does teaching have to do with your chosen career?

Scenario 1: *Just a year ago you landed a first violin position with a full-time orchestra—your dream job. But when recent contract negotiations failed, they announced that the next season would be cut back from forty-eight to thirty-five weeks. Even though you had no plans to take on students in the near future, that recent vacancy at the music school's preparatory division now seems like a necessity—not just to you but to every violinist in the orchestra. Why would they choose you over all the others who will undoubtedly apply?*

Scenario 2: *You have just earned an artist's diploma from a prestigious opera studio, where you sang lead roles in several operas. You've won some competitions and have secured a few professional bookings for minor roles. Still, as you continue preparing for more competitions and the possibility of a big break, you have bills to pay. Now the opera studio is looking to fill a one-year position while one of the coaches is on sabbatical, and they have invited you to apply. You have the chance to do what you love and still pay the rent, rather than taking a day job as a secretary. However, all candidates must teach a master class to be considered for the job, and you've never taught a lesson in your life.*

Scenario 3: Despite making it to the final round in numerous auditions, the clarinet position you were sure you would have by now hasn't materialized. You've been managing with a little saved money, but all the traveling to auditions has your reserves drained. Now teaching after-school lessons at the local middle school seems like a necessity. Oh well, how hard can it be? Then the first student walks in, band music in hand ("Starship Jubilee"), can't count a measure, or play two notes without a horrible squawk. What now?

Scenario 4: You completed your DMA in cello performance and joyfully accepted a job at a small liberal arts university. You signed a real contract, you're making a real salary; you have health insurance and your own studio, and look forward to performing in faculty recitals. You just received your studio roster: four music majors and four minors, and two liberal arts majors who, to fulfill their fine arts requirement, have elected to take cello lessons—as beginners. You will also be responsible for teaching two bass students in the university orchestra who need help with basic technique, orchestral excerpts, and repertoire. "Hold it!" you say. "I'm not a bass teacher, and I have never taught a beginner in my life. Where are all the students playing Saint-Saëns, Dvořák, and solo Bach?"

This is a just a small sampling of possibilities that your future as a professional musician might hold for you. In the professional world, even if your artistic success exceeds your highest expectations, it is not likely that you will only perform for a living. The world's premier musicians are frequently asked to share their expertise at master classes, and discover it is necessary to translate their musicianship into words and approaches to be effective. Studio positions at universities and conservatories— which come with status, salaries, and benefits—are offered to and kept by performers who play well *and* teach well. Accomplished freelance musicians find themselves in a pool of other fine musicians, but those who distinguish themselves as skilled teachers have added career and income opportunities.

So whether the reason is to answer a genuine calling, simply to generate more income, or something in between, there is a good chance that teaching will be a part of your career. Here are some other considerations that might encourage you.

Teaching is a worthy profession. Some music school environments engender the attitude that "those who can, do; those who can't, teach," perpetuating the notion that teaching is inferior to performing—something you would do only if you couldn't play, sing, or conduct very well. But take a moment to consider who played a huge role in helping you become the performer you are? It was your teacher, of course—an accomplished and established musician whom you recognized as someone who could guide you toward becoming the same. Even if you were too close to the situation to see what was happening, the process that allowed such invaluable performance expertise to be passed to you is the act—and at its best, the art—of teaching.

You are responsible for your own continued growth. Music schools offer the best curriculum and faculty possible to help their students achieve their performance goals, but students can't be dependent on their teachers forever. No matter your level of playing or substantial repertoire list at graduation, no musician is ever "finished" learning and growing. Your success is dependent on your ability to flourish as a musician *independent* of the support system on which you have relied for so long. Since you must ultimately be your own teacher, you'll want to be a good one.

Learning to teach will deepen your own understanding. As students, musicians allow their teachers full access to shaping their skills—perhaps to the point of suspending personal ideas and beliefs. Yet it is musicians' ability to comprehend and apply concepts that carry them forward into their careers. Therefore an integral part of every musician's development is to think about the why and how of musical development: How does this technique work? Why does it make a difference? Is it really the best way? Teaching requires you to explore concepts more deeply, and understand much more than if you simply do something because someone told you to do it.

You can make a difference in students' lives. Think about the best teacher you've had in your life—any teacher, no matter the subject or level of study. What was special about that teacher that makes you still think about him or her? How did that teacher bring out the best in you? When you combine your vision of a wonderful teacher with the skills, information, and musical experiences you have defined and clarified, you have the potential to be a memorable teacher yourself.

You can have a positive impact on the future of music. The quality of your teaching directly influences the world of music, whether your students become musicians by profession or the concertgoers and arts patrons of the future. It's also important to remember that your students will become the parents of children who could be encouraged to participate in music. The experience you offer—meaningful or superficial, positive or negative—can affect whether the music you love withers in a generation or is extended into perpetuity.

Great teachers leave legacies. Many great performers have made a significant impact on the world of music through their pedagogy. Some are well known and respected within their discipline; others have had such distinguished careers that they are revered not just by those who play the same instrument, but by the wider world of musicians, including Ivan Galamian and Josef Gingold, violin, Himie Voxman, clarinet, François Rabbath, bass, Marcel Moyse, flute, Pablo Casals, cello,

Alice Chalifoux, harp, Arnold Jacobs, tuba, and such pianists as Carl Czerny, Franz Liszt, and Rosina Lhevinne. Many of these musicians have composed etudes and concert literature for their instrument, founded schools and festivals, or have been pioneers in unlocking previously undiscovered potential in their instrument's technique and artistry; all have shared their passion and insights with outstanding and appreciative students who carry their vision into the future.

While perhaps teaching may not have been part of your original plan, just like anything else you do in life, you will get out of it what you put into it. The higher you value your contribution toward the success of your students, the more rewarding a profession it will be for you. "The Best Teacher" can be someone you not only sought as an emerging performer, but an esteemed vocation to which you aspire.

Personal Inventory: Take ten minutes right now and write down as much as you can that pertains to everything a student of your instrument to learn—from the beginning through the completion of high school—in order to perform at a level that would allow the student to choose music as a major in college. Include fundamental physical setup, techniques they should master, and literature they should play, including scales, exercises, and etudes. (See table AI.1 in Appendix I.2.)

That's quite a list, isn't it? And did you remember to include some instruction on how to practice? Count rhythms? Sight read? How to both lead and follow while playing? The more you think, the longer the list becomes.

Now let's figure out how much time a teacher has to help a student learn all of this.

- *A fifth-grade student has an average of thirty lessons during a school year and maybe five or six lessons in a summer. Even if these are hour lessons, together they total barely as much as an average work week!*
- *A student who studies from age ten to age eighteen might have two months of guided instruction—total!*

Of course these are spread out over many months, so there is time in between for students to practice, right? But will they? Did *you*? (This is separate issue, but you'll need to keep it in mind as you look at the overall process.) Go back to your big list and consider how it might be possible to divide these skills, repertoire, and experiences into feasible units of study. How will you fit it all in?

If you teach at the university level, it's your job to prepare the music majors (with or without the benefit of good preparatory training) for a professional career in a very compressed amount of time.

- *Undergraduates get approximately 115 lessons (three work weeks) to complete a four-year degree.*
- *Master's degree students receive around 55 lessons (barely a week and a half!).*
- *Doctoral candidates might get eighty or ninety lessons (. . . you do the math).*

No matter the equation, the answer is the same: time with your students is precious. You simply must know what they need to learn and have efficient ways to get the job done—all the while sharing the thrill of learning a fabulous instrument and wonderful music.

You're about to embark upon a process of examining what is significant to you as a performing musician, then turning your approach into a substantial and meaningful offering for students. The best teachers have a multi-level understanding of what they do and why they do it; and they can express it all in a variety of ways: with words, images, sounds, gestures, and of course, music. If until now you've not needed to explain what you think and do as a musician, this is the time to start. Challenging questions will arise, such as "Does this really work the way it should?" or "I've been told this all my life, but do I believe it myself?" or "Why does this matter?" As you answer these questions you will strengthen who you are, both as a performer and a teacher. Those seemingly random bits of information you've acquired over the years will begin to coalesce into a unified, organized body of knowledge—in a sense, a blueprint of your life as a musician. Even though you will almost certainly modify this blueprint over time, it can serve as your guide to successfully nurturing and enriching the lives of many future musicians.

Because to answer that cellist's earlier question—where *are* those students playing Saint-Saëns, Dvořák, and solo Bach? They'll be right in front of you—they just won't be playing those pieces *yet*. That's your job.

I The Performing Musician

1   Musicianship

THE FINAL CHORD lingers over spellbound silence. Warm, appreciative applause slowly swells and fills the hall. A few hoarse shouts of "Bravo!" ring out as some audience members rise to their feet and others wipe away involuntary tears. The artists reappear on the stage for another bow, and ultimately everyone is standing. As the sustained ovation brings the musicians back for a third time, one musician puts a hand to his heart in gratitude, the other smiles warmly, making eye contact with audience members in each section of the hall. As the applause subsides, the crowd files out almost reluctantly, not wanting to disrupt the connection they feel with the music, the musicians, even one another.

What just happened? The concert every musician wishes to perform, yes—but how and why did this happen? Why was the audience so responsive? What was the connection between the musicians and the audience that made this kind of event possible? Was it sheer technical brilliance, or something more?

Exploring, Defining, and Communicating Musicality

Refined technical ability can certainly be inspiring, and musicians spend countless hours practicing to perfect their technique. On the other hand, we are musicians, not technicians, and the most revered artists in our field are rarely lauded only for their technical accomplishments. We know what expressive playing is, because we hear it every day from concert artists, our colleagues, and our teachers, and we demand it of ourselves. We can easily identify a truly musical performance over one that is not—even choose the "better" of two musical performances. So what does this "musician" title actually mean? Beyond the obvious ability to play an instrument or sing, is it possible to explain in words what makes a performer or a performance "musical"?

> **Personal Inventory:** Before reading on, think for a few minutes about how you would define musical playing, and jot down a few ideas. You might want to first consider what is unmusical—and then change it to a positive statement. Consolidate your ideas into a single sentence.

It's a real challenge to create any kind of definition of musical playing—let alone a precise one—not only because musicianship has many components but also because it is difficult to put into words something that is communicated primarily *without* words. Yet a large part of what musicians do when they teach or practice is to communicate with students or themselves about areas of their playing they seek to improve and refine. Technique is easy to talk about because there is a vast and workable vocabulary that is regularly used to describe technical issues: "The sixteenth note passage is uneven because the fingers aren't lifting at a consistent height over the keys," or "The bow needs to be placed farther outside the balance point for a freer bounce." But how do musicians communicate what is needed to improve in the area of musical performance? If a teacher says to a student, "You need to play more musically," it's probably true, but such a statement does not offer any specific direction as to how the student might make changes for the better. To be effective, musical directives are typically framed in more practical language, such as "The subito forte needs to be more dramatic" or "Find a way to pace the ritard more naturally." "That phrase isn't going anywhere—can you shape it more meaningfully?" or "Make a different sound in the minor section."

These directives would be specific to a particular piece and a particular performer, and therefore too limited to define musicality, but they do infer broader categories of musicianship, such as these:

- The ability to perform with a variety of dynamics, articulations, and tone colors

- A well-developed sense of timing, pacing, and tempo
- The ability to connect a group of notes into a single, unified shape that completes a musical idea
- The ability to respond to changes in harmonies and other compositional elements in a meaningful way

These are important aspects of musical performance, and a student would need to examine, refine, and nurture these concepts over many years in order to establish mature musicianship. Still, these thoughts are limited in scope because each identifies only one specific component of musicianship. A musical performance has many levels of complexity and interacting components. Consider the following definitions of musicianship:

- The unification of musical expression and technical skill so that the technique disappears and the listener is only aware of the meaning and beauty of the music
- The integration of well-developed instrumental technique with music history and theory in order to create a performance that is stylistically appropriate to the period, the composer, and the genre
- The ability to "speak" to an audience with music-making, to "connect" with them, or to "tell a story" with a piece of music.

These definitions take into account some important interactions: between the physical realm and the art, between various aspects of musical language, and between the performer and the listener. While these statements describe more of what musicians actually do when they perform, it remains virtually impossible to capture the full meaning of musical performance in a single statement. In fact, the broader the statement, the more difficult it is to determine how such a thing could be accomplished.

> Music is an outburst of the soul.
>
> FREDERICK DELIUS
>
> The notes I handle no better than many pianists. But the pauses between the notes—ah, that is where the art resides!
>
> ARTUR SCHNABEL
>
> Music is your own experience, your thoughts, your wisdom. If you don't live it, it won't come out of your horn.
>
> CHARLIE PARKER

The art of interpretation is not to play what is written.

PABLO CASALS

To study music, we must learn the rules. To create music, we must break them.

NADIA BOULANGER

Simplicity is the final achievement. After one has played a vast quantity of notes and more notes, it is simplicity that emerges as the crowning reward of art.

FREDERIC CHOPIN

> ### Consider This
> Reflect on these statements of well-known artists, as well as others you have heard. What "big picture" element of musicality is implied in each statement? What would a musician actually be doing in performance to manifest the concept inherent in each of these statements?

Such definitions are thought-provoking, perhaps even profound, but none of them gives us a complete picture of musicianship. Even more to the point, these broader statements presume that the performer has already mastered a full vocabulary of musical elements, and it is not likely that anyone could learn to play expressively if suggestions like these were the only guidance offered.

The whole problem can be stated quite simply by asking, "Is there a meaning to music?" My answer would be, "Yes." And "Can you state in so many words what the meaning is?" My answer to that would be, "No."

AARON COPLAND

Can Musicality Be Learned?

The teacher listens to his violin student play through her piece. The rhythm is correct, the notes are mostly in tune, and her tone is decent—but the performance is so mechanical that the teacher interrupts. "I'm sorry, but I had to stop you. First of all, you need to vibrate every note, not just one every now and then. Also, this melody needs to be forte when we first hear it—but when it is repeated in the minor you need to play much softer." The teacher circles the dynamic markings in the music. "This fermata needs to be held much longer before you go on. Save your bow, OK? Start again, please." The student begins again, and wanting to please her teacher, she vibrates every note, plays the dynamics as she was told, and holds out the note at the fermata as long as she can before going on. "The vibrato is better, and I could hear your piano that time, but the fermata is too long now," says the teacher. "Something in between would work better." So the student plays again, and the fermata errs on the short side again, but it's longer than the first time. The lesson is almost over, so these fixes will have to suffice for now. "OK, that's better," the teacher says, and offers a smile of encouragement, but inside he wonders how it's possible for someone to do all the right things and still sound so unmusical. Perhaps, he muses, she just doesn't "have it."

Have you ever been in this teacher's place? Was this student ever you? This lesson had some ingredients of musical instruction. Each of the teacher's suggestions were aimed at fostering good musicianship in order to help the student produce a more musical-sounding performance—and with limited success, it worked. The unfortunate truth is that it is quite possible for a musician to play with great dynamic contrast, use vibrato, and sustain a long fermata yet still sound unmusical. The problem in the scenario is that the technical directives alone simply did not connect the student to any expressive meaning. Technique only allows the *possibility* of a musical performance. Without an expressive purpose, a technical approach to teaching musicality can result in dutifully executed but inexpressive performances.

Most music students are taught technique before musicianship so that the skills are well-established when it is time to create a musical sound on an instrument. These skills can be as basic as increasing the height of drumsticks for a crescendo or varying the speed and width of vibrato to change the intensity of sound. When a phrase demands more expressivity, musicians—even ones with apparent innate musicality—are frequently coached via their technique in order to access more musical playing. Certainly one must know about breath support or arm weight to help create dynamic contrast, how to produce a good vibrato, and what a fermata is and how to sustain a sound. But technique cannot be the sole pathway to expressive performing. Musical comprehension—the *reason* a musician would play with contrast, use vibrato, or hold a fermata so that it "feels right"—has to be part of the equation. Consider now some expressive approaches that might help nurture the musicianship of a student with similar issues:

TECHNICAL DIRECTIVE: Play (or sing) loud there, then very soft here.

MUSICAL EXPLORATION: How does the minor version of the melody feel different from the major one? Can you feel that emotional experience in your body? How does that mood swing alter the tone of your voice? Does the change happen immediately or is there a pause or hesitation?

TECHNICAL DIRECTIVE: Use vibrato on every note.

MUSICAL EXPLORATION: What is the music trying to express . . . passion, warmth, joy, excitement? What does that sound like in your voice? When the phrase reaches its peak should the vibrato sound different? What about the minor phrase? Can the kind of vibrato you use be an extension of how your body feels?

TECHNICAL DIRECTIVE: Wait longer at the fermata.

MUSICAL EXPLORATION: How much time would it take for normal life to resume after a dramatic event? Or the dust to settle after a sack of flour has been dropped? Or consider how long it takes for a ball to come back to you after you've thrown it into the air?

The question "why" lies behind these musical explorations. The answers supply a musician at any stage of development with a reason to further refine technique. Most important, however, such explorations open two significant pathways to musical expression: (1) they help a performer become more aware of the connection between written music and personal expression, and (2) they reveal the possibility of many ways to play musically.

Consider This

There is an adage about being musically talented: that people "either have it or they don't." Of course there will be prodigies who exude innate musicality from the moment they begin, others who learn only with great effort, and everyone in between. But does this mean that someone who is initially challenged to play or sing musically cannot become an expressive musician?

Perhaps the students who seem to have innate musical sensibilities are like children learning their native language, having heard it all their lives. The most vital and basic communication comes first: the sounds and artic-ulations of the language are cultivated, the meaning of words and phrases are experienced. All this happens without formal lessons, and long before rules of grammar and intellectualized definitions are ever imposed. Compare that to the way most people learn a second language: in a class, where vocabulary and pronunciations are learned, followed by sentence structure and grammar; combinations and variations are explored; and more sophisticated vocabulary, inflections, and nuances are developed and integrated over time. When students can barely pronounce the new words they're learning, it's a lot to expect that they can immediately speak with meaningful inflection. However, this does not rule out the possibility that the second language cannot develop into a deeply expres-sive form of communication. The ability to express emotions, needs, and desires are at the core of every human being, but learning to express those through a secondary form of communication—especially when it involves an unfamiliar object like an instrument—takes time to develop.

Musicianship Based on Musical Knowledge

There is still more to musical performance than personal expression and effective technique. The vast body of knowledge pertaining to music has a substantial influence on musical interpretation. This information is gradually acquired as you learn your instrument and the repertoire, but some of it is learned primarily through special classes in music theory, history, and performance practice. When deliberate connections are not drawn between the information and how it affects performance, this knowledge seems irrelevant to becoming a performing musician. It can take years, perhaps decades, for musicians to become fully aware of the relationships between performing and what they learned in music history and music theory. In the interim, that information tends to lie dormant, but it still serves as an unconscious component in effective musical performance.

> **Personal Inventory:** Before you read further, take ten minutes to list as many aspects of music history, composers, theory, and composition that help to inform your musicianship, leaving a few lines between each. Then go back through the list and ask "Why?" and "How?" questions of each—as in "Why does this matter?" or "How does this influence the way I play?"—and write your answers beside each component on your list.

Your list is probably quite long, even if you didn't take the time to detail each aspect fully. The point is that you know a tremendous amount about music, and readily utilize much of that knowledge when performing. In fact, some of this information may be so well integrated into your musical sensibilities that you aren't consciously aware of it. For instance, you immediately change your stylistic approach when switching from a piece by Mozart to one by Tchaikovsky, even when sight-reading; and despite a forte dynamic marking in either score, you know not to play or sing louder than your colleague who has the melody. Such musical responsiveness might seem too obvious to consider, but the more you are aware of your well-conditioned choices, the more intentional your musicianship can be, and the better prepared you will be to guide students.

Understanding the Context and Language of Music

When preparing for a performance, artist-level musicians learn background information about the composer and study the compositional details that make the work a masterpiece. This comprehensive preparation is essential to making a performance as meaningful and artful as the piece was intended.

THE COMPOSER'S LIFE AND TIMES

While it is possible to perform music without knowing the context from which it came, any interpretation of a composition is more meaningful when the musical understanding includes factors related to the composer's personal, social or political circumstances, as well as an awareness of the compositional style and performance practice of the day.

Background information. Knowledge of a composer and the history of his or her composition can offer valuable insights for interpretation. This essential background information is likely to include the age and experience of the composer (often gleaned via a publishing or cataloguing number) and specific life events or occasions that inspired the work. Beyond this, it's important to remember that composers did not live in isolation: they were influenced by teachers, social status, employment, health, politics, and personal relationships, just as people are today. Learning about these influences can offer unexpected insights for interpreting a composer's music. While much can be learned from historical and analytical publications, anything written by a composer him- or herself, especially articles and letters, can help the performer feel significantly more connected to the composer and the composition.

Attributes of compositional periods and performance practice. Whether a composer utilized previously established traditions or broke new stylistic ground, understanding the compositional techniques of the period give context to an interpretation. It is also important to learn how the instruments of the time were different from modern instruments: how they were made, what materials were used, tuning differences, and so forth. Typical performance venues of the day, whether outdoors, at a church, in a small chamber, or at a palace, can offer clues to sounds and techniques that are closer to the composer's original intentions. Musicians make choices about to what degree these factors influence their performances: substantially, so as to be as true as possible to the sounds that may have been heard in the earliest performances, or subtly, with the assumption that the composer would be glad for modern changes in instruments, tuning, and acoustical settings.

COMPOSITIONAL ELEMENTS

Before the twentieth century, the only way composers could make their creations permanent and available to all was to put ink marks on a page. Even with modern recording equipment and computerized notation programs, the manuscript is still a crucial part of the art of composition, and the study of a composer's score is essential to a meaningful interpretation. Performing musicians are trained to understand this rich and complex language; they also learn unwritten rules of interpretation: some that apply to Western music in general, others that are specific to eras of composition, and still more that are idiomatic to certain composers.

The following are some of the compositional elements that influence musical choices. While some might seem almost too obvious to mention, try to imagine how a performance would sound if a musician lacked such understanding. This is how great teachers pinpoint important teaching elements and work to heighten their students' musical expression, and how great performers are able to demonstrate such command of their musicianship.

Genre. The kind of piece being performed influences the stylistic approach, whether it be a solo suite; solo piece with accompaniment; sonata, trio, quartet, or other chamber music combinations; or concerto. The musician's role in the context of the piece also influences interpretation: as part of a section in an orchestra, as a soloist in a concerto or opera, as an equal partner in a sonata, or as the continuo underpinning in a Baroque composition. Songs, dances, and marches—whether labeled as such in the music or interpreted as such by the performer—all require different stylistic and articulation approaches.

Form. While trained musicians might easily take this aspect for granted, forms such as rondo, ternary, minuet and trio— even through-composed forms—have a distinct feel to the performer and influence many choices made in timing, tempos, dynamics, color changes, and so forth.

Meter, tempo, rhythm, and timing. When a musical performance is described as having "the right feel," it can likely be attributed to the interpretation of tempo, rhythm, and timing. This area of musicianship is much easier to identify when it is *not* working rather than when it is, from infractions of the most basic rules to a subtle faux pas of interpretation. The fundamental premise is that all notes are given full duration and space—whether subdividing the long ones or not compressing the short ones. Certain musical conventions help us recognize and interpret various

> **Consider This**
> Think about how you perform a piece in sonata form: the different musical responses you have, whether finishing the exposition to repeat it or moving on to the development; how it feels to arrive at the recapitulation; the sounds you would use as you enter the coda section, feeling the momentum or repose that completes a musical journey. How would your musical interpretation be affected if this understanding was not in place?

components of meter and rhythm—such as understanding the difference in rhythmic groupings between 3/4 and 6/8 meters, or knowing to identify and draw attention to a hemiola in a composition by Handel or Brahms. Conventions are much less useful when determining how long to hold a fermata or how much rubato is enough. Musicians must take into account that rhythms (as well as many other aspects of written music) are really only a reasonable approximation of any composers' initial inspiration. It would be a mistake to consider all rhythms and tempi to be as absolute as they appear on the page (for instance, dotted rhythms in Baroque music, the early placement of the second pulse in a Viennese waltz, or eighth notes that are "swung"), so the reinterpretation of such notation is essential to a meaningful performance.

Melody. This is probably the most recognized element of music, and the one most taken for granted by the casual listener. Yet of all the components of music, shaping a melodic phrase is perhaps the most demanding skill required of any musician. Furthermore, as challenging as it is to play a perfectly phrased melody, it is even more difficult to describe in words how it's done. However there are certain factors that influence musical phrasing, even if they are infrequently verbalized. Here are a few commonly accepted guidelines.

Parameters for Shaping a Musical Phrase

- All melodies have a beginning note, an arrival note, and an ending note—all other notes serve to move the music toward or away from those notes, with the possible exceptions of a secondary arrival or deceptive ending.
- Dynamics and timing are used to enhance the contour and direction of a phrase, whether or not notated by the composer.
- Notes of shorter rhythmic value usually move toward longer notes.
- Large leaps are often more expressive than stepwise movement; chromatic notes often serve to create expressive harmonic tension, delay an arrival note, or both.
- Tension and release in a melody is usually supported by the harmonies, so it is always advisable to work on phrasing with an awareness of the harmonic underpinnings.

A performance lacking in just one of these parameters could be noticeably less expressive. While this list is hardly complete, these ideas at least begin to define the basis for creating a well-shaped melody.

Articulations. Slurs, dots, and lines over notes are indications from the composer (or sometimes an editor) of length, shape, connection, and stress, but they are only the beginning of interpreting a piece. Since the symbols are limited but the variety of sounds are not, legato, portato, brushed or pointed staccato must be considered through the conventions of compositional periods or the composers themselves, and of course through the implicit meaning of the music.

Tonality and harmony. Knowing key signatures and chords is a significant step toward understanding how the harmonic structure of a piece helps us interpret music, but it's really just the beginning. Composers often use tonalities to give their pieces structural and emotional arch, in a sense like a very large-scale melody, and use "false" tonal centers to fool or surprise the listener. Musicians learn that key signatures can also be significant to interpreting the music, as some composers heard particular characteristics in tonalities, like Beethoven's "heroic" key of E-flat major. Modalities of all kinds, including blues and pentatonic scales, color the expression of a composition. Chord progressions within keys also create varying degrees of tension, resolution, or surprise, and the frequency of chord changes, otherwise known as harmonic rhythm can affect the sense of pacing, whether or not the actual tempo is altered.

Terminology. Expressive terms and directives in the music offer important clues toward discovering the mood, feeling, and spirit of a composition. Some of a performer's most creative explorations emerge from a dedication to realizing those expressive markings— through the voice, the instrument, or the baton.

> **Consider This**
> What other ways do tonality and harmony influence musical interpretation? Consider chord inversions, altered chords, and suspensions, among other possibilities. How should the historical period of the composition be a factor when interpreting harmonies for performance?

Dynamics and accents. Dynamics are the volume indicators of music, but without understanding the range of contexts and expressive possibilities that exist, dynamic changes can be as dispassionate as changing the volume on a machine. To a mature musician, dynamic markings and accents say at least as much about quality as quantity. For instance, a forte is not just loud—questions must be asked: Why is it the music forte? Is this the predominant voice, or are all the parts equally loud? Is the forte the culmination of a crescendo or the beginning of a new section? Is it powerful? Expansive? Robust? Angry? Warm?

Other Compositional Elements. Instrumentation, ornamentation, counterpoint, ostinato, motifs, fugue subjects, and appoggiaturas: such a list could continue to grow almost indefinitely. There's not really any more need here to speculate about the specific effects each element can have on a musician's interpretation. While some influence an interpretation more than others, each needs to be considered as a potentially meaningful part of musical performance. These essential components of musical understanding can be viewed in two ways:

1. The lack of awareness or understanding of an essential compositional element can cause a performer to play unmusically, or cause a piece to sound uninteresting. Imagine performing Vivaldi without understanding a sequence, or Beethoven's Fifth Symphony without knowing about rhythmic motifs, or Bach without understanding the concept of a bass line.

2. The better musicians are at identifying significant compositional elements of a piece, the better they are able to enhance the music's substance and meaning, and highlight its unique character in performance. Digging deeply and taking nothing for granted is the performer's imperative.

Exploring Expressive Musical Performance through the Human Experience

While understanding compositional devices gives musicians a substantial basis for meaningful interpretation, a performance would likely feel incomplete without the musician's ability to play the music with his or her own personal sense of expression. When it is said that a performer "plays with feeling," what are we talking about? Conveying emotion through musical sound is certainly part of it, but a performer's senses and life experiences also contribute to his or her sense of timing and responsiveness to the music: what one has experienced in nature, in relationships, through verbal expression, breathing, gestures, and so forth. Consciously or not, musicians draw on these experiences to help convey musical meaning.

> **Personal Inventory:** Before reading further, list your five senses, and then consider descriptive words commonly used to elicit musical expression that fall under each of those sensory experiences.

SENSORY EXPERIENCES

Sight. Visual imagery is used constantly when describing music. Performers refer to quantity and quality of light, such as when they call sounds "bright" and "dark." These descriptors usually refer to the harmonies in the music or overtones in a sound. (The brighter the sound, the more upper overtones are audible.) The word "color" is often used, though not everyone envisions an actual color when using that term. Musicians do speak of sounds that are transparent or dense, up close or far away, and large or small, often in reference to dynamics. Shapes, such as rounded or angular, are frequently used to describe articulations. The beauty of communicating about music through such familiar images is that visual references tend to be self-descriptive, so fewer words are needed to convey the meaning.

Images from nature can have a powerful effect on music-making. A pianist might envision a long, complex phrase as the contour of mountains on the horizon. The delicate perfection of a small flower might inspire a flautist to create a sound of similar exquisiteness. The vast power of a great landscape frees a baritone to produce his most open and powerful sound. A cellist searching for just the right tone quality for the coda of a Brahms sonata envisions the final glow of a sunset. While such imagery will not always provide the same inspiration to everyone, sharing potent images with students or colleagues can encourage them to discover their own personal connections. Therefore, even the most esoteric or obscure associations are more valuable shared than kept to one's self.

Touch. Smooth, silky, soft, furry, feathery, rough, coarse, are all tactile approaches to describing sounds in music. Musicians also use temperature as descriptors, such as "warm" or *con fuoco*. References to cooler or even frigid temperatures are less common but offer great possibilities for color and contrast. "Sharp," "rounded," or other shaped sounds, while discussed as a visual reference in the previous section, might offer some performers more to work with in the way of a physical, tactile approach.

Hearing. Music is an aural art, so comparisons to other sounds are the most obvious. Any variations of articulation, tone colors, intensity, volume, and sustain or decay can be used to imitate spoken or sung words, sounds in nature, or qualities of other instruments. Even the sounds of machines, like an approaching train, can be effective in evoking musical creativity.

Taste. Musicians don't necessarily think about taste when they experience a sound, yet *dolce* is one of our most common markings in music. What does "sweet" sound like? What about "bitter"? Certainly some of the compositions of Dmitri Shostakovich invite an acerbic quality in the interpretation. *Secco* is another common interpretive marking, but what about its opposite, "juicy"? Considering the variety of flavors and even textures experienced by the palate, this is perhaps an under-employed inroad to describing music.

Smell. The olfactory sense is probably the least used as a musical descriptor, though some musicians connect the music they hear, compose, and play to olfactory experiences.

> **Consider This**
> Think of images and experiences that express cold, such as glassy ice, tree branches laden with snow, icicles slowly dripping, or shivering against the wind. Are there gestures and sounds inspired by these images that could be expressed in your music-making?

Scriabin, for instance, liked to waft smells into the concert hall to enhance performances of his music. Perhaps the potential inspiration lies in our physical responses to a smell—such as the spontaneous repulsion from the pungent odor of ammonia versus the comforting allure of fresh-baked bread.

HUMAN EMOTIONS, CHARACTERISTICS, AND STORIES IN MUSIC

Besides dynamics, emotions are often the first expressive elements that young musicians explore—such as the simple contrast of a "happy" piece in a major key and a "sad" piece in a minor one. Of course these adjectives are fairly superficial, barely addressing the diverse and complex variations that exist within either emotion, from pleasant to ecstatic, from melancholy to anguish—beyond which there is a whole world of human feeling and expression: anger, pride, compassion, sarcasm, tenderness, reluctance, and so forth. The musical expression of these emotions requires a wide range of tone color, and can influence the choices of tempo, timing, and articulations. Some musicians physically embody each mood like an actor in order to create a convincing performance.

More specifically, here are some areas and examples of human expression:

Vocal or verbal expression. Musicians explore the sounds of questions, answers, laughing, crying, exclaiming, scolding, whispering, and so on by listening for inflection, qualities of tone, and vowel and consonant sounds. Singers must learn the pronunciation and meaning of lyrics in a foreign language, but instrumentalists can also explore qualities of sound in the native language of a composer to learn the sounds that were part of his or her everyday life.

Physical expression. Gestures are also used to convey a variety of moods and emotions. Consider what kind of body language suggests pride, and compare it to the kind that communicates anger or the kind that soothes. Such movements, or sometimes simply the posture that embodies an emotional state, can be used to create expressive sounds on an instrument.

Stylistic differences are also readily expressed with gestures: a rustic dance might evoke swinging, swaying, or bouncing; a march encourages straight-line, up-and-down movements; the smoother, more connected sounds of a song evoke a similar smooth and extended gesture. These movements can be transferred via hands, bow, baton, or breath to create a satisfying musical parallel on an instrument, with the voice, or in communication with an orchestra.

Character and storytelling. Operas are the epitome of story-telling in music. To perform in an opera, a singer must identify with the character's personality and his or her interaction with other characters; those performing in lead roles must understand that character's psychology and personal evolution within in the story.

All this must be portrayed not only with gestures and actions on stage, but through expressive musicianship and great technical command. While opera offers us the most overt example of character and storytelling in music, other genre invite musicians to dig deeply to convey personalities, stories, and imagery. To perform art songs like Schubert's *Der Erlkönig*, programmatic music like Strauss' *Don Quixote* and Prokofiev's *Peter and the Wolf*, or even Robert Schumann's piano works assigned to his alter egos Eusebius and Florestan, musicians assimilate the distinct personalities and traits of one or more characters and explore ways to portray them by varying the tone, articulation, and style. Similar approaches can be used to enhance the embedded imagery in pieces like Vivaldi's *Four Seasons* or Debussy's *La Mer*, but a composition needn't be programmatic to benefit from the musician creating characters and "telling a story" in any performance.

MUSICAL PACING BASED ON EXPERIENCES

> **Personal Inventory:** Think about an accelerando that creates the perfect transition to a quicker tempo, or a rallentando that leads into a well-timed final cadence. What factors or parameters do you use, consciously or unconsciously, to determine what feels right?

While musicians must have a working understanding of meters and tempos, as well as all the markings and conventions that require altering those in performance, there is no quadratic equation for rubato, nor a tried-and-true formula for pacing a ritardando. Yet timings explored through common images or experiences have a universally familiar feel. Cause-and-effect timings, especially those that produce varied results, cultivate flexibility and interpretive spontaneity in musical performance. Consider these possibilities:

- Pacing an accelerando: Drop a ball and watch it bounce faster and faster.
- Rubato: Picture a roller coaster, a swing, or waves on a beach.
- Timing a fermata: Envision a ball thrown in the air with varying amounts of thrust: more means the balls takes longer to return, less means it comes back faster.
- Ritardando and caesura: Under what circumstances might you coast to a stop, pull back quickly, or stop abruptly?
- Stretching notes into the peak of a phrase: When biking up a hill, you're slowest right near the top and going over the crest before picking up speed again.

Consider This

The word "moving" is commonly used to describe an effective performance. Emotionally something shifts inside the listener, giving the sense of feeling "transported," "lifted up," or "carried away." Composers' melodies are sometimes described as "floating" or "soaring," but of course not all renditions actually "get off the ground." What qualities in music-making allow a melody to feel weightless or soaring? What kind of performance draws the audience in, or sweeps them away?

Humor. It is probably true that good joke telling is an art form like any other: as soon as it has been defined, it defies its own definition. Nevertheless, jokes are told in music, and it helps to ponder the sense of timing that makes people smile, even laugh out loud. The setup is important, because listeners need to anticipate the next probable musical event. In music sometimes the composer supplies us with the punch line—the unexpected "answer." But even the most predictable musical moment placed just a little later than the audience expects it makes them laugh when the joke is on them. Sometimes the answer comes quicker than expected, catching listeners off guard, before they've had time to predict it. Subtle and slightly unexpected shifts in pacing can keep an audience enthralled, as if they are being taken on a marvelous joy ride.

Consider This

Victor Borge was both a masterful pianist and a comic genius. His exquisite timing was evident in both his humor and his musicianship, and the sparkle and spontaneity of his performances are as inspiring as they are entertaining. If you've never seen one of his archival performances—or haven't watched one in a long time—be sure to do so soon.

RELATING MUSIC TO RELIGION AND ART

Religion and spirituality have long been a source for inspiration in musical composition and performance. Themes of forgiveness, reverence, redemption, resurrection, immortality, purity, and exaltation provide interpretive approaches that can be both personal and universal.

Art. Painting, sculpture, architecture, and literature provide further inspiration for musicians who experience a connection between a work of art and their musical interpretation. For instance, the cultural significance of great architecture recently inspired a youth orchestra conductor to offer a concert series to teach the relationship between architecture and music. One of Picasso's angular paintings can provide interpretive insight for the performance of a twentieth-century composition; and the balance and strength, of Michelangelo's *David*, with the statue's exaggerated large hands, could embolden a performer to trust his more heartfelt and impassioned interpretations at his upcoming recital. Such artist-to-artist connections are usually very personal and subjective yet they have the power to provide tremendous creative inspiration.

> There is no excellent beauty that hath not some strangeness in the proportion.
> FRANCIS BACON

RELATING MUSIC TO MATH AND SCIENCE

The scientific and mathematical world, like music, has a way of both amplifying and defying rational thought. Even areas that seem absolute can have a powerful impact on expressive music making. Here are some possibilities:

Science. Chemistry, biology, and other studies of nature can offer inspiring images for musical interpretation: chemical reactions, metamorphosis, symmetry, patterns, and even chaos in nature. Astronomy offers images: shooting stars, black holes, the mysterious vastness of the universe, and so forth. Physics is a great source for analogies related to gravity and weightlessness or time and timelessness. Even surface tension, which allows a glass of water to be overfilled, can be used as an analogy for expressive notes that seem too full to fit within a given tempo.

Math. Numbers have been used for centuries to create patterns and symbolism in musical composition. Bach's love of numbers and numerical symbolism has been an intriguing part of compositional analysis of his music. Some composers have studied the "Golden Ratio" (a proportion based on the Fibonacci series 2:3:5:8:13, etc.) for application in their compositions, just as architects have used it for their designs, and a performer's awareness of this ratio can shed light on interpretations. Crescendos based on an addition (2 + 2 + 2) offer a terrace effect; an exponential equation (2 × 2 × 2) produces a bell-shaped crescendo that is powerful, almost explosive.

In the most literal sense, "feeling the music" is our ability to connect music to life experiences. Words and images, while not always sufficient, have the potential to explain the relationship of music to life, create pathways toward meaningful expression, and, at best, offer inspiration for transcendent performances.

Ideas for Further Exploration

1. Choose one interpretive element in the section *Context and Language of Music*. Select a phrase from a piece which, in order to be played musically,

relies on the integration of that element. Perform the phrase with an interpretation that lacks the chosen element, and let others guess what is missing. If need be, perform a second time, adding the element to the interpretation to help identify the missing ingredient. Be creative and have fun!

2. Review the list "Parameters for Shaping a Musical Phrase." Do you agree with this list? Is there anything you would you add, take away, or reword? Jot down your thoughts, and then refine your words to create your own guidelines. If possible, share it with a fellow musician, and continue to refine and clarify your ideas.

3. Choose one piece (or movement of a larger work) that you are currently preparing. Imagine that a friend who cannot hear wants you to describe your piece to him or her. Write a full description of the piece with moods, storytelling, sensory experiences, and so forth to help your friend understand as fully as possible the essence of the music.

4. Listen to a CD of movie music without watching the movie, and jot down ideas about feeling or character is being portrayed in each. Watch the movie, listening for these themes. How well do the music and the performance convey the meaning? How closely did your descriptions come to the actual use in the movie?

5. Choose a piece from your repertoire (recently performed work or one you are currently preparing). Write a sentence or two about what is most meaningful to you about the piece. Now research the composer and the background of the piece. Dig deeply—find out what was happening in the composer's life at the time the piece was written, any information that's available about the circumstances or reason the piece was composed. Describe how this knowledge could enhance your understanding and performance of this selection.

Recommended Reading

Blum, D. (1977). *Casals and the Art of Interpretation*. London: Heinemann.

Cone, E. T. (1968). *Musical Form and Musical Performance: A Lucid and Penetrating Study of the Nature of Musical Form and Its Presentation in Performance*. New York: Norton.

Farkas, P. (1976). *The Art of Musicianship: A Treatise on the Skills, Knowledge, and Sensitivity Needed by the Mature Musician to Perform in an Artistic and Professional Manner*. Bloomington, Ind: Musical Publications.

Green, B. (2003). *The Mastery of Music: Ten Pathways to True Artistry*. New York: Broadway Books.

O'Toole, P. A. (2003). *Shaping Sound Musicians: An Innovative Approach to Teaching Comprehensive Musicianship through Performance.* Chicago: GIA.

Thompson, W. F. (2009). *Music, Thought, and Feeling: Understanding the Psychology of Music.* New York: Oxford University Press.

Werner, K. (1996). *Effortless Mastery: Liberating the Master Musician Within.* New Albany, Ind: Jamey Aebersold Jazz.

2   Listening

LISTENING IS A COMPONENT of our lives that simply must be—without it we would simply cease to be musicians. We spend many years of our lives learning to recognize precise intonation, excellent balance, fine phrase shaping, and impeccable timing. We use these highly cultivated listening skills to perform with others, to offer constructive criticism, to teach, to judge competitions, and of course, to cultivate and elevate our own performance abilities.

Not all listening is the same. Musicians might listen one way when they attend a concert, another way when they listen to a recording, and differently still when they are the ones performing, practicing, or teaching. Listening becomes so acute that even at the grocery store it can be difficult to ignore a familiar melody played on the PA system. While others might hear it peripherally, hum along, and still focus on the vegetables, musicians' minds are often sidetracked, identifying the composer, the instrumentation, and speculating whose arrangement it might be. A pop tune might start one musician making mental recreations of the singer's unusual inflections, and wondering how her voice might sound if she used her diaphragm. Another musician with studio experience might be so distracted by the excessive use of digital pitch correction that he can't decide what kind of cereal to buy. For better and for worse, it is a challenge to turn off active listening once we have learned to do it so well.

Learning to Listen

Musicianship is built on awareness and recognition. Recognition is the most rudimentary level of listening, such as hearing and identifying a melody or an instrument. With minimal training, musicians become adept at identifying a sound and putting a name to it. The more familiar that sound becomes, the more sensitive the listener is to it, and the easier it becomes to distinguish that sound even when it is surrounded by other sounds. For instance, the musician who can identify the instrumentation of a symphony just by listening to a tutti section is like the chef who can name all the ingredients in a recipe after a few tastes, the perfumer who can distinguish the essential oils used to create a fragrance, or the bird watcher who can detect one particular bird call from what sounds to most like chaotic chirping. Training develops the ability to discern specific flavors, aromas, and of course, sounds.

Still, recognition and identification are only the beginning stages of true expertise. If a dish didn't taste good, a perfume smelled odd, or a performance wasn't wonderful, most people could tell you they didn't like it, but few could explain why. Artists and connoisseurs of any discipline must learn not only to identify the components, but to intimately understand how the combinations, balances, quality, and variations of those components create a work of art.

With training, conductors, composers, and arrangers become very adept at, among other things, creating colors through combinations of instrumental voices, while merging those voices with their compositional skills to convey mood and character. These musicians can often work in isolation, "hearing" in their minds the sounds that are yet to be realized.

While performers develop similar skills to varying degrees, instrumentalists and singers tend to focus their listening skills on more performance-oriented qualities. These include aspects of musicianship such as tone and projection, phrasing, rhythm and timing, and intonation. Awareness of the highest levels of technique and musicianship takes years to recognize and cultivate. If you listen to a recording of yourself performing your best at a younger age, you would probably hear a lack of refinement that was, at the time, indiscernible to you. While it's quite possible that your technique might not have been developed enough to create the sounds you wanted to hear, it is also likely that you simply couldn't hear how to play that piece better than you did: more sophisticated levels of musicianship were still not in your aural vocabulary.

Only when you could hear and recognize further refinement could you elevate your performing to the next artistic level.

Many musicians are, from early in their lives, very sensitive to sounds. Even so, the best teachers spend a great deal of time training their students to listen. Teachers know that even the most technically capable students will be severely limited as musicians if their listening skills are underdeveloped. No matter how many hours students practice, their ability to create refined tone, intonation, rhythm, and musicianship is directly related to how well they can hear and recognize quality. Wise teachers ask their students to compare one sound to another: to distinguish a good tone from a poor one, a well-tuned note from an out-of-tune one, or a well-shaped phrase from a misdirected one. From this aural awareness, students become better equipped to develop technique that allows them to consistently produce high-quality musicianship.

> **Personal Inventory:** Do you remember how and when you learned to listen? What have you been trained to hear? Take five minutes to make a list of everything that comes to mind and, if you can remember, how you learned each aspect.

Here are some considerations that might be on your list:

- Tone—clarity, focus, richness of overtones within a sound; colors and textures to convey character
- Articulation—how a sound begins and ends, and quality and inflection of the duration, to imitate, match, or contrast with others; musical effectiveness of articulation choices
- Pitch—recognizing higher and lower; pitch memory; precision in adjusting intonation and matching pitches; hearing intervals and their acoustical characteristics; recognizing chords and progressions
- Dynamics and projection—the ability to recognize dynamic levels in relative volume as well as the perception of dynamic qualities and contrast conveyed through sound characteristics; projecting tone
- Appropriate stylistic conventions—listening for and modifying interpretations according to the style of music, the genre, and the performance setting
- Ensemble—listening and responding to fellow musicians in ensembles to project, support, blend, or balance; coordinating sounds and tempos, and responding to subtle changes

Modes of Listening: Objective, Critical, Selective, and Subjective

Not all listening is the same. Whether conscious or not, the reasons we listen influence the way we listen.

Objective listening is nonjudgmental listening, simply being aware of the sounds being made without being influenced by reactions or negative comparisons. This is especially helpful for practicing, when it is essential to be unemotional about a recurring problem in order to understand why it is happening. Such objectivity helps musicians and teachers recognize and prioritize the work that is still needed for development and mastery.

Critical or discriminative listening is not criticism per se but the ability to recognize qualities of tone, articulation, intonation, tempo, and timing, and to determine how these qualities could be improved. Critical listening is used to make comparisons of better and worse as in judging a competition. For the same reason, this kind of listening is crucial to a musician's ability to practice effectively.

Selective listening allows a musician to focus exclusively on a single aspect of a performance or one section of an ensemble. This can be deliberate and helpful,

> **Consider This**
>
> Some performers don't enjoy attending concerts because their critical listening won't turn off—they hear everything they would do differently in the interpretation and find flaws in the performance. What is your listening experience going to concerts and recitals? Has the experience changed throughout your training? Consider the differences between simple and trained listening—if you could choose, would you have a preference?

> **Consider This**
>
> Percussionist and teacher Amy Reddoch, deaf since birth, shares some of her insights about listening: "My 'listening' is something I've had to develop myself, with the help of hearing aids. My mother was told that hearing through hearing aids is somewhat like hearing through a running vacuum cleaner. When I am in a rehearsal or ensemble situation of any kind, I do have to listen pretty hard, consciously and purposefully, to separate out what I call the flak from the good stuff." Reddoch likely listens far more carefully than the rest of us, yet every musician must screen out certain noises—both externally and internally produced. How much do you find yourself listening carefully to "separate the flak from the good stuff"?

as when a conductor chooses to ignore a wrong note that occurs inadvertently while rehearsing the pacing of a rallentando. Selective listening allows a teacher or practicing musician to acknowledge an accomplishment in one area without dragging down the praise with a caveat: ". . . but this other aspect wasn't good." On the other hand, selective listening can be detrimental to good musicianship if a performer is so focused on one aspect of his or her technique that another is neglected.

Subjective listening is influenced by emotions or biases. A teacher might not be happy with her student's recital performance because the intonation and rhythm were not to her standards, but the parent who loves the child unconditionally will think the performance was wonderful. Subjective listening can cause problems when musicians lose their perspective, hearing only what they want to hear—a "wishful thinking" kind of listening. But it can also be a choice: "The musicians were having so much fun on stage that I didn't mind a few intonation problems—their music made me feel good."

A mature musician can find ways to utilize all four modes of listening, and often multiple modes at the same time depending on the circumstances.

The only difference between a flower and a weed is judgment.
ANONYMOUS

Personal Inventory: Consider how each of the modes of listening might have both helped and hindered your development as a musician. What is your most productive mode of listening?

Inner Listening

Many musicians discover that having an aural "vision" of the music they make is essential to creating a great performance. They are aware that knowing what they want to say and how they want it to come across is essential to their ability to communicate effectively. This kind of inner hearing might entail using the voice, both internally and aloud. Composers often talk about listening to the music inside and writing it down; conductors must have an internal sense of the quality, character, and balance that is needed for a fine interpretation; and performers, whether playing well-rehearsed music or improvising, are aware of hearing music inside just as—or immediately before—those sounds are created.

I have to keep reminding my students, asking them, "What is your experience of listening to this? Don't tell me about the notes you see on the page, tell me about what you hear."

JAMES TENNEY, COMPOSER

One thing that becomes obvious to performers is that if we don't know what we want to express—whether it is a tone quality, the pitch of a note, or the direction of a phrase—it is not likely that quality musicianship will emerge. This connection between the inside aural ideal and the outside manifestation is vital: we listen from the inside and ask ourselves what we want to hear. Then as we produce the sound, we compare this ideal to what we just heard. At best, especially if the aural concept was well conceived, that sound is realized.

But suppose the realization wasn't wonderful: what then? In performance, we don't have the luxury to stop and reflect: we must quickly adjust to give full attention to upcoming notes, and continue to listen ahead. When practicing, we have many more options: we are able to analyze why the outer manifestation didn't sound like the inner ideal; or we might come to the realization that the original concept wasn't so marvelous in the first place. In this case, we use our inner and outer singing to continue developing our ideal; we can even use our instrument to create a fabulous sound, listen to it, and then go to work on our inner vision, expanding that sound into a complete musical idea, both inside and outside.

INTONATION

It is not possible to have a full conversation about listening without bringing intonation into the discussion. Musicians who generate their own intonation must rely on a well-cultivated internal sense of pitch in order to sing or play in tune.

The ability to control pitch in the voice also plays a major role in whether musicians (singers, instrumentalists, or conductors) can anticipate how a pitch should sound. Some people might claim to be "tone deaf," but this is not an untreatable physical condition, as the phrase implies; most who have pitch problems simply have untrained

Consider This

Have you ever heard someone play or sing who obviously didn't have an inner ideal for the sound being produced? Was it a student, perhaps? This kind of oblivious approach is perhaps the main reason why students tend to sound like students: they blow or bang or saw away, emitting sounds that they might reconsider only afterward (if they were listening at all, that is). Learning to activate and listen to one's inner voice is essential to a musician's ability to develop and refine technique and musicianship.

voices, ears, or both. Intonation problems are almost immediately re-solved when students learn to match pitches with their voices. Once they can do this, they can "sing inside" first, then sing on pitch through the voice or generate it on the instrument.

The study of Western music requires complete exposure to its conventions. In order to play in tune, the brain must have a strong memory of the next correct pitch and how to produce it on a particular instrument. Western music is mostly dependent on A440 and equal temperament as a starting point to tuning, and classical musicians have well-trained ears to hear those precise intervallic relationships as well as extremely small deviations. This must be our basis for good intonation.

The closer the notion of "correct intonation" is examined, however, the more elusive the meaning of the phrase really is. Before the eighteenth century, Western music was based on pureness of perfect intervals, and Just intonation was the norm. Most music of the last three centuries is based on a system of equal temperament, precisely even intervals of one hundred cents per half step. This system is well suited for keyboards and fretted instruments, as well as triadic harmonies and modulations, which have been the basis of Western composition for the last few centuries.

However, the sanctity of pure perfect intervals was compromised when this change occurred, because equal temperament required the slight alteration of some of the most fundamental perfect intervals (namely fourths and fifths), and the perfect thirds and sixths of Just intonation were lost. Many musicians are desensitized to the problem, but if you're a string player, you might notice the difference when you tune your instrument with your ears compared to utilizing an electronic tuner. In addition, while a "perfect sixth" is not even in our working vocabulary, that's the highly resonant, easy-on-the-ears interval you are likely drawn to when playing or listening to solo Bach—about sixteen cents flat to equal temperament "correctness."

So the truth of what is really "in tune" lies somewhere between the absolute of

> **Consider This**
>
> Western musicians are so steeped in our own language and a sense of correctness about intonation that it's difficult for many of us to conceive of a musical language where "correct intonation" is quite different than our own. The classical Indian scale, for example, has incremental divisions of the shruti, and the music utilizes both a three-shruti "whole step" and a four-shruti "whole step." The ability to recognize "well-tuned" intervals in traditional Middle Eastern and classical Indian music requires expansion and retraining of the Western ear.

electronic tuners and the ability to listen and respond to the prevailing tonality, while being flexible to surrounding notes and expressive variables. The more musicians learn about tuning, the more acutely they are aware of the need to listen for what sounds best in the context of the music at the moment it is produced.

> **Personal Inventory:** How have you developed your inner singing and listening skills? Can you explain the importance of this ability, and how it relates to your musicianship?

The Perception of Sound: Listening with the Senses

HEIGHTENING AURAL PERCEPTION

When musicians listen carefully, we often instinctively close our eyes. Because visual stimulation is one of the biggest distractions, shutting down this sense tends to heighten our aural awareness. Even when the visual input is generally useful, such as reading notes on the page, or observing technique in the mirror, this extra input detracts from the ability to listen. More difficult to ignore are physical sensations, such as noticing how much tension is in our hands, and cognitive processes, like reminding ourselves of a note correction. Audio recordings remove us from those distractions and allow us to listen objectively to the sounds that were actually produced. This process can reveal how well aligned the inner and outer listening experiences really are.

Well-developed listening skills are so important to musicians that we go to great lengths to isolate and nurture that sense; yet in reality, there are few life situations when listening to music is a purely aural experience. Although we perceive music primarily as sound in our ears, our other senses add information to the experience. Sitting in a concert hall, for instance, we listen with more than just our ears—we see and interpret physical gestures and emotional countenance; we feel the vibrations not only in our eardrums but in our entire bodies; and we are aware of the more subjective nature of listening which sometimes evokes personal associations and emotions.

> **Personal Inventory:** In your opinion, how do live, videotaped, and audio-recorded performances differ? Does your experience change when you to sit close to a performer as opposed to sitting far back in a hall? Would you rather watch a close-up video recording of a concert or be in the hall, even if seated far away?

HEARING WITH SIGHT

We've already acknowledged that heightening our aural skills is important, but since we pride ourselves on increased sensitivity, should we not work to heighten our other senses as well? One sense that we cannot easily shut down—nor would we choose to shut down—is our ability to hear, yet Dame Evelyn Glennie, a hearing-impaired percussionist, offers an intriguing perspective that can help us become aware of how the other senses help us listen.

At a lecture-demonstration sponsored by Technology, Entertainment, and Design (TED), Glennie hovers over her marimba in utter silence and high anticipation, her sticks quivering a millimeter above the bars. "Can you hear anything?" she asks the audience. "Exactly. Because I'm not even touching it. But yet we get the sensation of something happening. In the same way that when I see a tree move, then I imagine that tree making a rustling sound. Do you see what I mean? Whatever the eye sees, then there's always sound happening. So there's always, always that huge . . . kaleidoscope of things to draw from."

If you consider music-making as a form of communication, physical expression truly *is* huge. How a performer walks out on stage, the gestures and breathing used to start a piece, facial expression and other body language during the performance, even the release of the final note—all communicate to an audience and influence what they "hear."

As musicians, we might want even more visual information than the average concert attendee because of our desire to know more about how a great musician sings or plays the same instrument. But does watching actually enhance our ability to listen, or detract from it? Not everyone agrees on this topic. Composer Leo Ornstein is quoted as saying: "Actually, if you're visually watching the performer, probably a good deal of your attention has now been diverted from the very thing that your attention should be on, and that is listening to the music, listening to the combinations that are being performed for you right there."

> ### Consider This
> Performers often explore how their physical gestures can affect their ability to express meaning in the music, but do you believe those expressive movements can be "heard" on an audio recording when the visual aspect is removed?

> **Personal Inventory:** What do you believe about listening with your eyes? Is it a benefit, a distraction, or both?

HEARING WITH THE SENSE OF TOUCH

Again, let's consider what Glennie has to say about listening via the sense of touch. Here she explains how her heightened sense of touch—with the guidance of her teacher, Jimmy Blades—helped her learn to tune the tympani:

> And so we began our lessons every single time tuning drums to such a narrow pitch interval. And it's amazing that when you do open your body up, and open your hand up to allow the vibration to come through, that in fact the tiny, tiny difference can be felt with just the tiniest part of your finger. . . . I would put my hands on the wall of the music room, and together we would listen to the sounds of the instruments, and really try to connect with those sounds far, far more broadly than simply depending on the ear.

It is indeed a rare musician who is so dependent on his or her sense of touch, especially to the very high degree of refinement Glennie has achieved. However, any musician who has played or sung in a large ensemble has likely experienced that very disconcerting inability to hear oneself. In those moments, musicians learn to rely on the sensation of the instrument vibrating for feedback on the quality and quantity of sound, perhaps even using those vibrations to identify the pitch being produced, as Glennie has learned to do. This suggests that increasing one's sensitivity to the sense of touch can further the experience of both listening and performing.

Many performing musicians are sensitized not just to their instrument's vibrations but to feeling the vibrations of the room. A resonant hall certainly contributes to an instrument's sound; a "dead" room gives very little back, and sometimes makes the least attractive elements more obvious. Musicians are aware of the different qualities of resonance between a concert hall made primarily of wood and a church made of stone; or the difference between a large room and a small one. All sound is generated by physical vibration, whether it strikes our eardrums or our skin or we "feel it in our bones." Sensitizing ourselves to the vibrations music produces can heighten our experience and elevate our awareness far beyond passive listening.

> **Personal Inventory:** Are you physically aware of the vibrations of your instrument? Do these vibrations aid your ability to listen, adjust, and respond to the sounds you are making? Do they heighten your musical sensitivity?

Engaged Listening

As rich as listening with a full sensory experience can be, there is still one more way we "listen"—and that is an engaged and responsive kind of listening when our imagination, memories, emotions, or spirituality become part of the experience.

Consider first any great orator, whose speeches are deeply moving. It is not just the choice of his or her words, but the inflection, timing, and delivery that profoundly convey a message and its meaning. Martin Luther King Jr. had a powerful voice that brimmed with emotion, but others who speak with a quiet, calm voice can have a profound impact as well. The same is true in great musicians, many of whom seem able to project their personalities and life perspectives into their music-making. Pablo Casals was known for the depth of humanity he portrayed through his performances, and Vladimir Horowitz's powerful musicianship projected a very personal fervor. Other performers seem to lose themselves in the composer's music, giving us the sense that they are able to "channel" or embody that composer's work—the composer seems more present than the performer.

> Music is the effort we make to explain to ourselves how our brains work. We listen to Bach transfixed because this is listening to a human mind.
>
> LEWIS THOMAS, PHYSICIAN AND WRITER

Personal Inventory: Do you believe it is possible to "hear" characteristics such as joy, spirituality, commitment, confidence, or intelligence in a musical performance? Think about some of your favorite musicians: what do they project in the way they conduct, sing, or play that attracts you? How do you sense that you can hear those qualities?

Neurological studies have revealed interesting evidence of "mirror neurons" in the human brain. Rather than a person's direct action or involvement being necessary to stimulate the brain, mirror neurons apparently allow the brain to be stimulated in virtually the same way when simply *observing* a movement or emotion. This area of research has intriguing implications for musicians—not only to help us better understand how we learn, but to suggest a hypothesis for the formerly inexplicable emotional exchange between performer and audience. This empathetic response is an indication of another way humans "hear" music: a kind of perception that cannot be attributed to any of the conventionally accepted senses.

Despite these fascinating ways to listen, most musicians would choose to sing or play over attending a concert, and it's no wonder: musicians can listen *while* they create the sounds, be moved by what they hear, and use that inspiration to create the next musical moment. When this wonderful feedback loop starts to happen, any performance has the potential to spiral into something extraordinary. With such a thrilling possibility waiting in the wings at every concert, performers know that when it comes to listening, the best seat in the house is truly the one they have on stage.

> ### Consider This
> Few musicians need convincing that audiences receive more from a great performance than excellent technique and impeccable phrasing—but if proof was needed, this mirror neuron research might offer it. Do you think this mirroring concept only goes one way, or does an audience reflect back emotions that the performer can feel?

Ideas for Further Exploration

1. Think about a recent concert or recital, either one that you attended or in which you performed. Write a few sentences about your experience using objective, critical, subjective, and selective listening. Consider the pros and cons of each.

2. How have you been guided by a teacher to develop your listening skills? Have you made your own discoveries about listening, in particular ones that include other sensory approaches?

3. If you sing or play an instrument with pitches that are generated by you, make a list of how you learned to listen for excellent intonation, what you listen for, and how you continue to refine your intonation skills.

Recommended Reading

Campbell, M., & Greated, C. (2001). *The Musician's Guide to Acoustics.* Oxford: Oxford University Press.

Loubriel, Luis, E. (2011). *Lasting Change for Trumpeters: The Pedagogical Approach of Arnold Jacobs.* Chicago, Ill.: Scholar Publications.

Pratt, G. (1998). *Aural Awareness: Principles and Practice.* Oxford: Oxford University Press.

Ross, Alex. (2008). *The Rest Is Noise.* New York: Farrar, Straus, and Giroux.

One must understand that the purpose of technique is to transmit the inner meaning, the message, of the music.

PABLO CASALS

3 Technique

THE LONGER MUSICIANS live and work in the world of music performance, the more refined, sophisticated, and integrated their skills become. At its best, the resulting technique becomes an automatic, almost intuitive approach to playing or singing: there is no separation between the envisioned expression and the real one—whatever the performer wants will simply be there.

However, the more automatic a musician's skill becomes, the more challenging it can be to remember how it was learned initially or developed over the years. How did your technique come to be? Certainly with guidance from your teachers, plenty of practice, trial and error; but also perhaps from some experimentation, or a lucky accident when you discovered that something—holding your hand just so, or standing in a new way, or feeling a certain sensation in your body—made a particular technique just "click."

No two musicians are the same, even if they play the same instrument and appear to have the same technical approach What works for one might feel entirely wrong to another. On the other hand, no matter what instrument we play, or whether we sing or conduct, all musicians are unified in that our technique needs to be stable, reliable, accurate, flexible, and immediate.

Consider This

If there is some aspect of your playing that feels so easy and automatic that you can't remember learning it, or can't fathom it being awkward to someone else, have a first lesson on an instrument unrelated to yours, or try reversing hands on your own instrument—now that's a shock. The utter unfamiliarity is what any new student will experience, and is very likely the way it felt when you first started taking lessons.

Exploring Technique through Universal Elements

Most musicians tend to think of their technique through the specific requirements of their instrument. Your list of necessary skills from the introduction likely reveals your performance area, even if you never mentioned your instrument by name. If your list primarily consists of left hand and bowing techniques, you are a string player. Organists, pianists, harpists, and percussionists write about fingering, hand coordination, voicing, and pedaling. Wind players master skills related to embouchure, breathing, and fingering. Singers focus on the use of the diaphragm, the larynx, and other parts of the anatomy, as well as breath support, phonation, and diction. Conductors list posture, beat patterns, expressive gestures, and cueing. Yet as distinct as these specific skills are, there are certain goals common to all musicians' technique. This universal approach is what we will use to explore what each of us do as musicians, and how we establish the most reliable and accessible technique for ourselves and our students.

Two ubiquitous principles should be considered throughout this discussion of technique, both of which have been discussed in the previous two chapters. The first principle is that all technique exists to serve the music. The second is that all musicians must listen. Aural feedback is what tells us whether our technique is doing what it is supposed to do. No matter the attention a musician gives to his or her physical approach, if the music doesn't sound the way it was intended, something is wrong.

The Essential Physical Attributes of Technique

We will now look at basic requirements that are a significant part of every musician's technique. These are factors that directly or indirectly affect the physical skills necessary to play an instrument, sing, or conduct. For our purposes, they are organized into five categories—the topics of the five sections that make up the remainder of this chapter: (1) the physical components of technical stability; (2) instrumental acoustics and the mechanics of sound production; (3) movement and accuracy; (4) the cognitive processes that support effective physical technique; (5) musicians' health and injury prevention.

At the end of the first, second, third, and fourth sections of this chapter, you will find tables (tables 3.1–4) that list each technical element, with columns that give you places to jot down your notes related to three general areas of consideration:

1. What are the physical and/or aural manifestations of this particular element's presence? (In other words, what does it sound like, look like, and feel like when a musician is good at this?)
2. How does the lack of this attribute affect performance on my instrument? (What does it sound like, look like, and feel like when this area is undeveloped or poorly managed?)
3. How is this technical element established and developed?

As you make notes in the tables, review your master list (from the introduction) for the necessary skills that are related to each component. Add skills as you think of them. You might find that certain techniques are related to more than one category. For instance, a wind instrumentalist or a singer might find that "intonation skills" belongs both in lift/support and accuracy. This is not a problem. On the contrary, it suggests two essential elements requisite for intonation development.

The technical development (third) column is a place to make note of the images, exercises, and practice techniques you have used to develop this area. When the discussion turns more toward teaching in Part II, you will revisit this column and consider how to create a developmental sequence for each element, starting with an exercise or position that can create a foundation from which to build related techniques. If you already have thoughts about sequencing these skills now, by all means make note of them—otherwise, one or two basic exercises in each area will suffice.

Physical Components of Technical Stability

Like a beating heart, the following core elements of technique are easily taken for granted; yet when these are lacking, the musician and the music-making suffer.

Posture/positioning (of instrument to body). Your posture as you play your instrument, sing, or conduct should maximize physical stability and allow free movement of your limbs over the needed range of the instrument: the spine aligned in the most natural position, and the weight of the head balanced over the spine. Minimal twist and contortion of the body is considered optimum.

Breath/breathing. Breathing is a core component of vocal or wind instrument technique. While much less critical to strings, keyboards, percussion, or conducting, the lack of natural breathing while performing can cause undue tension and stifle the possibility of natural musical phrasing and timing of any musician.

Balance. Physical balance frees a performer to move easily and stay focused on the music. Lack of balance can directly affect a musician's overall sense of well-being, in part because so much energy is tied up in trying to hold the body up. Balance (or lack thereof) affects not only the physical realm but also the musician's sense of mental and psychological stability and centeredness.

Muscular release. The appearance of balance and proper positioning is not a guarantee of physical freedom if any extraneous muscle tension is held in the body. Even well-trained musicians are not always aware of unnecessary tension in their playing or singing, including in seemingly unrelated muscles, such as tight leg muscles in string players. If not entirely debilitating, the familiarity of excess tension makes it challenging to diagnose and release. Musicians often find it helpful to explore the least amount of muscle activity needed to create a sound, gradually adding back only that which is absolutely necessary to resume more normal playing or singing.

TABLE 3.1 Physical Components of Technical Stability

Physical component	Obtainable qualities and techniques when this component is present	Problems that can result from a deficiency in this component	Fundamental method(s) to establish this component
Posture and/or positioning			
Breath/breathing			
Balance			
Muscular release			
Other			

Instrumental Acoustics and the Mechanics of Sound Production

Technique on any instrument is necessarily based on how that instrument produces its sound, and the performer's ability to optimize its resonance. Instrumental acoustics involve many interrelated factors. Knowledge of the materials that make up your instrument and how these vibrate to produce sound allows direct access to understanding optimal technique.

> **Personal Inventory:** Describe the acoustical properties of your instrument (which includes your body if you sing or your ensemble if you conduct), and the way you interact with it to create sound. Include obvious facts about how your instrument works, as well as those subtle variances of quality or quantity that can affect the sound. For instance, compare the differences between nickel, silver, or gold head joints on a flute, gradations of thicknesses carved into the quadrants of a bass, or the hardness of a clarinet reed. Use the questions below as a guide.

1. How does the instrument respond? In other words, what vibrates and what allows the sound to be amplified and emerge from the instrument? Describe its unique timbre or distinctive qualities that distinguish it from other instruments, including those in the same instrument family.

2. Describe the best materials for each part of the instrument.

3. Since the best instrument can sound poorly if not well set up, what adjustments are important for optimum resonance, quality of sound, and relative ease of technique? Consider all aspects of setup on your instrument: the instrument itself and essential parts (such as mouthpieces, bows, drum heads, and reeds); adjustable components (key or valve action, string height, bow tension, and reeds); and essential items that need replacing (strings, pads, corks, and . . . reeds). How does each affect responsiveness, quality, and ease of control?

4. Describe any advantages or disadvantages of new, seasoned, or aged parts of the instrument. In other words, which parts need breaking in (are best if not new); which need replacing (best if new or lightly used), and which seem best when fully aged, if any?

5. How much do you actively create the sound as opposed to allowing the instrument to resonate? In what ways might a performer inadvertently inhibit the sound of the instrument?

This last question focuses on the all-important working partnership between you and your instrument. Every time you set your instrument vibrating with your hands, your breath, or your feet, you merge an understanding of your instrument's acoustics with a technique that is honed to meet its unique requirements. Keep this in mind as you consider each component in the following discussion of the mechanics of sound production.

Optimal resonance. Based on what you know about the acoustics of your instrument and what you do as a performer, describe the optimal physical action of the performer and optimal reaction of your instrument that creates the most resonant sound possible. What positions or actions might inhibit optimal sound?

Articulation (onset). How do you start a sound on your instrument? What ways do you vary your approach to produce different kinds of articulations for a variety of musical and stylistic affects?

Sustaining and/or shaping a sound (duration). Some instruments are capable of not only sustaining a sound, but shaping it (either a bowed instrument or one that uses air to control the sound). Describe how to sustain, increase, and decrease sound on your instrument, including how you do so through bow changes or a retake of breath. If your instrument is plucked or hit and is not capable of sustaining a tone, describe how the initial attack influences the sustain, and how it is possible to create the illusion of continuous or increasing sound.

Stopping or releasing a sound (completion). Musicians stop their sound by releasing their active role in making the sound or by blocking the vibrations in various ways. Each method creates its own particular quality. Describe the techniques used on your instrument, as well as any kinds of stopping that are considered wrong or inappropriate.

Dynamics. How do you increase and decrease the volume of your instrument? Is there more than one way to do this? Are there ways that are considered better or worse?

Tone color. From subtle to extreme, color changes are often made by deliberately choosing to highlight or purposely manipulate one or more properties of an instruments' optimal acoustics. Consider how you do this to create particular sounds on your instrument. Are there other ways to create color changes on your instrument? If the use of soft pedals, mallet changes, mutes, or other modifications are standard practice for your instrument, how do these mechanisms work, and how do they affect the tone color?

Movement and Accuracy

Now we will explore the movements musicians use to produce sound. Most of the movements addressed in this category are created by the smaller joints and muscles

TABLE 3.2 Instrumental Acoustics and the Mechanics of Sound Production

Mechanics of sound production	Specific techniques or technical approaches for excellence	Evidence of deficiencies related to this component	Fundamental method(s) to establish this component
Optimal resonance			
Articulation (onset)			
Sustaining and/or shaping sound (duration)			
Stopping or releasing a sound (completion)			
Dynamics			
Tone color			
Other			

of the extremities, though at times they are initiated by larger muscle groups for efficiency and to avoid straining. We'll also look at how these actions become accurate and consistent, and how they coordinate with other movements.

Weight and gravity. Musicians can work with body weight and gravity to achieve power and resonance more effortlessly by utilizing passive gestures such as dropping, bouncing, hanging, and swinging. For instance, the weight of a bass drum mallet is moved upward by a series of muscles; then the percussionist allows gravity to take over most of the downward force to strike the drum. The muscles then regain control of the mallet after the rebound.

Lift and support. This category refers to the movements of the torso and large muscles to aid posture and allow freedom of movement in the limbs. Singers also use lift to open the resonance cavities in their bodies, facilitating breath support. Lift could be considered the opposite of weight and gravity, as these elements seem almost contradictory; yet musicians often integrate lift, weight, and gravity in their physical setup or in specific techniques.

Strength and stamina. Larger muscle groups in the torso, referred to as core muscles, must be strong and stable to support basic positions; other muscles need strength to create sounds and change notes. The act of playing will help develop smaller muscles, but strengthening larger muscles often requires more traditional exercises away from the instrument. What kinds of strength and stamina are needed to play a concerto or perform an opera from start to finish? Are the muscular requirements different when performing a short but intense perpetual motion piece or virtuosic aria?

Efficiency. Using only necessary muscles with as little effort as possible is a sign of an efficient approach to technique. Musicians need to be aware of using large muscles for large gestures and support, and smaller muscles for smaller movements, since overworking smaller muscles to create powerful gestures can cause fatigue and overuse injuries. The idea of efficiency can be extended to other considerations, such as the need for percussionists to move fluently from instrument to instrument in performance, or an organist to change stops and switch hands to another manual.

Freedom, fluidity, and flexibility. All musicians, regardless of their performance area, seek ways to perform with physical movements that are free of restrictions. Even when maximum athleticism is required, most musicians discover that more exertion can actually limit their technique, and that trying harder to play or sing better often produces the opposite effect. What ways do you achieve maximum freedom and mobility at your instrument? Are stretches or warm-up exercises essential to this area of your technique? Besides strictly physical movements, consider ways that mental and psychological states can influence physical freedom.

Control. The physical freedom discussed in the previous category will not be hampered by the beneficial kind of control considered here. Control allows a musician to know, for example, exactly how much breath can be used at any given point in a phrase, or how much weight is needed to strike the keys of a piano to produce a particular dynamic, or how much to vary the bow weight, speed, and placement without squashing the vibrating string. Knowing exactly how much to do, and the precise moment to do it, is the kind of control all musicians must cultivate.

Agility and speed. What positions, states of readiness, and movements allow maximum velocity? Are there any unique aspects of your instrument's technique that require special consideration when it comes to performing with agility and speed?

Coordination and dissociation. Not only do musicians have to coordinate body parts, such as tongues and fingers, feet and hands, arms and fingers, but they must also learn how to dissociate, like the conductor who cues with one hand while maintaining a beat pattern with the other. String players must master the ability to coordinate actions of the left and right hands and arms, while directing each movement using an entirely different set of parameters.

Accuracy, precision, and reliability. The ultimate goal of any musician's skill development is the certainty that technique will be accurate, precise, and reliable at a moment's notice. But paradoxically, in order to achieve this end, accuracy, precision, and reliability must be the guiding principles from the beginning, with each mastered technique as an installment toward these artistic standards. Consider how the need for accuracy, precision, and reliability is essential to every component of your technique, and how you work to develop this in your performing.

Cognitive Processes Essential to Technique

Since technique is a primarily physical process, examining it through the physical realm is essential to understanding how and why it works. Still, if we only look at the physical we ignore a significant and obvious connection, which is that all movement originates in the brain. The clarity and timing of those directives, and even the musician's state of mind, can substantially influence performance ability.

Sequential preparation (anticipated physical and mental readiness). From the outside, music production can seem to be a spontaneous event; however mental and physical readiness often precedes the execution of any technique. For instance, harpists prepare the string by squeezing it with the finger prior to the attack. Singers and wind instrumentalists must hear the next note "inside," while allowing time to breathe and prepare the body for the quality and quantity of the tone, and dynamic desired. While this kind of preparation might be so well integrated that it

TABLE 3.3 Movement and Accuracy

Technical component	Obtainable qualities and techniques when this component is present	Problems that can result from a deficiency in (or overuse of) this component	Fundamental method(s) to establish this component
Weight and gravity			
Lift and support			
Strength and stamina			
Efficiency			
Freedom/fluidity/flexibility			
Control			
Agility and speed			
Coordination and dissociation			
Accuracy, precision, and reliability			
Other			

is automatic, there are countless situations and techniques in which sequential preparation plays a significant role, from the spontaneous way we prepare our bodies to sing or play untold times daily to the thoughtfully nuanced approach we develop to execute a challenging passage.

Bundling. Musical performance is such a multilevel process that it is often necessary for our brains and bodies to bundle a series of movements into a single prompt. When a series of movements or notes are contained in one signal, the mind and body are freed for other input that requires more conscious attention, such as watching a conductor for a cue, or following a colleague's rubato phrasing in a chamber music performance. Bundling can also be a conscious choice in the practice room, working with a group of notes as one element rather than several, or incorporating a crescendo into how a run is practiced so that the dynamic becomes as integral to the phrase as the notes themselves.

Trust. Musicians are most aware of trust when it suddenly goes missing, like the passage that flows easily in practice which becomes difficult in front of a teacher or colleague. Lack of trust creates situations in which an established movement is questioned or blocked in performance, and a new movement—often not as fluid—must be created on the spot. When this self-doubt is pervasive, even practicing can be more laborious than necessary, and performance ability is seriously hampered. Musicians are freest and usually most accurate when they can trust the learning process and allow well-practiced gestures to be realized.

TABLE 3.4 Cognitive Processes That Support Effective Physical Technique

Cognitive processes	How this process positively influences performance	Problems that can result from deficiency of this component	Fundamental approach to establish this component
Sequential preparation			
Bundling			
Trust			
Other			

Musicians' Health and Injury Prevention

Besides being artists and skilled technicians, musicians are athletes, and need to find a healthy physical approach to sustain their careers. All musicians need to be aware of the vulnerabilities of their particular performance areas and implement important countermeasures to avoid injury problems. Most musicians stand or sit in one place and in one posture when practicing or performing; and any position that is static is potentially problematic, especially if a balanced posture is not well established. Repetitive-use injuries are very common for musicians, and unless care is taken, long hours of practice and performing can lead to debilitating injury. Hearing loss can be a devastating health issue and is of particular concern for wind players, whose embouchures put high pressure on their eardrums.

It's not just what musicians do that can lead to injury; the environment can also create potential problems. Instrumentalists who sit in front of instruments that produce high-decibel sounds; and conductors who stand in front of an entire orchestra for multihour rehearsals. Cramped spaces like orchestra pits can be especially hazardous to hearing, and can also cause muscular issues for players who must look in one direction to see the music and another to watch the conductor.

Learn which factors are of particular concern for your instrument or in your performance environment, and explore possible ways to avoid such potential problems, such as a healthy posture and positioning habits, proper chairs, and exercises and stretches that target vulnerable areas. Make your own physical health as important a goal as excellence in your performing.

Ideas for Further Exploration

1. Give a lesson to a colleague or fellow student who has never played your instrument before. In fifteen minutes or less, teach the basic setup, including posture and positioning of the instrument, and one basic technique.
2. Learn about your instrument from the inside out. Research your instrument's acoustics via books and online resources, and talk with instrument makers about their approach to creating a superb instrument.
3. Talk to at least one bodywork specialist (orthopedic surgeon, audiologist, weight trainer, massage therapist, physical therapist, Feldenkreis, Pilates, or Alexander specialist) about how you sit or stand, how you hold your instrument, what repeated movements you do, and any issues that have come up for you in the past. Make an annotated list of pitfalls of your instrument and ways to avoid injuries. Also note any particular techniques that, if learned well from the beginning, would help players avoid injury problems over the course of their careers.

4. Choose one technical element and observe (on YouTube, on videotape, or at a live concert) how a virtuoso of your choice utilizes it in performance. Also observe a performer who lacks this element (a younger student or fellow colleague—no names!) and note the effect on technique when this element is lacking. Write a short report comparing the two, being as specific as possible about what you observed.

5. What technical components reviewed in this chapter represent your strengths? Which need the most attention? Are you aware of why your best is the best, and why your most challenging area is problematic?

Recommended Reading

Explore classic treatises and contemporary books related to technique in your performance area. Oxford University Press performance studies and applied music books could be a way to start your search; ask your applied teacher for recommendations. Selected books on musicians' health are listed below.

De Alcantara, P. (1997). *Indirect Procedures: A Musician's Guide to the Alexander Technique.* New York: Oxford University Press.

Horvath, J. (2002). *Playing (Less) Hurt: An Injury Prevention Guide for Musicians.* Rev. ed. Minneapolis, Minn: J. Horvath.

Kempter, S. (2003). *How Muscles Learn: Teaching the Violin with the Body in Mind.* Miami, Fla: Summy-Birchard.

Klickstein, G. (2009). *The Musician's Way: A Guide to Practice, Performance, and Wellness.* New York: Oxford University Press.

Paull, B. & Harrison, C. (1997). *The Athletic Musician: A Guide to Playing Without Pain.* Lanham, Md.: Scarecrow Press.

4 Practicing

Do We Have to Practice?

It is common knowledge that consistent and extensive practice is required to become an accomplished musician: several hours per day on a near-daily basis for years on end. This is not just to train and develop as a student but also to maintain and improve skills and learn new repertoire throughout one's career. For centuries, musicians have accepted this as a way of life, and have developed sophisticated approaches to practice that have been passed down through generations of musicians, from teacher to student. Entire books have been devoted to the subject of music practice. So it probably comes as no surprise to any accomplished musician that research has suggested that a person will probably log a minimum of ten thousand hours of practice to achieve mastery of any subject or skill—or about three hours a day for ten years (Ericsson, Krampe, & Tesch-Romer, 1993). Based on most musicians' experience, at least to be ready for a performing career, this sounds about right.

Of course it's easy to think that not everyone needs all those hours. What about a genius like Mozart, who wrote symphonies at age nine? Taking a closer look at what is known about the composer's young life, however, it may come as some relief to the rest of us that he still needed the same long hours of work to fully realize his potential. Despite the stories of his prodigious talent, we do know that Mozart's father, Leopold, pushed his young son very hard, so by the time Wolfgang was in his early teens, it's very likely he had logged many thousands of hours already, practicing, studying, and composing. Thinking about this timeline, it's worth noting that while Mozart's early compositions are fascinating, because they show the developmental path of one of the most renowned and brilliant musicians in history, his later compositions are the ones that demonstrate his true genius—the result of more practice and study, one could surmise. While his talents could also be attributed to other qualities, such as unusual creativity and analytical intelligence, perhaps all musicians really do share the same lot in life when it comes to practice.

If ten thousand hours seems like "all in a day's work" to performing musicians, a significant caveat should be noted: it is *not* a given that simply logging in those hours will invariably lead to mastery. According to research, the

> ### Consider This
> Experience with your instrument along with trial and error have helped you discover some of your most fruitful approaches to practicing. What you may not have considered is that besides your instrument and your commitment to learning, there is a third partner in the practice room: your brain. Understanding what is known about how the brain learns and functions can help musicians work more efficiently and productively. Look for sidebars throughout this chapter to consider some of the neuroscience that supports our work.

development of expertise entails approximately ten thousand hours of *systematic and goal-directed practice*. This raises important questions for aspiring musicians: what defines effective practice? How clear are the goals, from the most immediate to the long term? How is it possible to make the most out of every minute? If *quantity* of time alone isn't enough, then anyone with ambitions toward mastery must consider the *quality* of practice time, because what happens during those hours really does matter.

> **Personal Inventory:** Begin making a list of your best practice techniques—strategies and systems that you regularly use to improve technical basics like coordination, tone, intonation, speed, accuracy, and so forth. In addition, make notes on any systems or processes you use in the practice room (such as how you determine the number repetitions needed, or how you reintegrate an isolated section back into a piece), how you make best use of your time, and what you feel is your optimum state of mind for practicing.

Purposeful Practice Goals
INCREASING AWARENESS

Without awareness, practicing would have no value. What would be the point if musicians couldn't notice irregularities in a rhythm, or hear that a passage was out of tune, or recognize that a piece necessary more dynamic contrast? From the most universal areas of musicianship to the most instrument-specific techniques, practicing requires performers to observe, make necessary adjustments, and observe again. Complete awareness—and the immediate feedback that allows the possibility of improvement—is the most fundamental premise of any practice session.

Warming up. Musicians often use the beginning of their practice time to warm up—to ready their bodies physically, as well as to heighten their awareness of sounds and sensations. Such stimulation can include physical warm-ups, both at and away from an instrument, or more cognitive ones, like reviewing annotations from the previous lesson or listening to recordings. All can awaken the mind and heighten a musician's readiness for practice.

Sensory awareness. Musical awareness comes from hearing, seeing, and a kinesthetic sense of touch or movement. Sensory awareness can be a purely *internal* experience, such as how a position or gesture feels; or an *external* experience, that involves listening and watching the results of the internal processes. When practicing, external aids such as mirrors, metronomes, tuners, and recording equipment—even constructive criticism from teachers and colleagues—can increase external awareness through increased objectivity and feedback.

Personal Inventory: In what ways do you use a variety of senses and approaches during practice? Review your completed tables from Chapter 3, *Technique*. Choose any challenging aspect of your performance area and create practice techniques that utilize aural, visual, and kinesthetic approaches. Which of these depend on external awareness? Internal awareness? Add these practice approaches to the third column of your table.

Cognitive awareness. Mental focus is essential to having full awareness. The musician is the only one who can know what is happening in his or her mind while practicing—there are no mirrors or recording devices that can lend objectivity to this area. As a practicing musician you must be self-aware: to know whether you are counting, anticipating the next gesture, pitch, or musical intent, or remembering to relax a habitually tight muscle. You alone can know whether you are utterly absorbed in your own practice process or are too aware of the person practicing in the next room. Practicing is not just a physical process—it includes trial and error with mental directives in order to discover how cognitive awareness influences performance. Specific instructions like "smooth connection," "vibrate before the shift," or "cue the flute" can help focus attention where it is most valuable.

Distractions. Distractions come in many forms. They can be external—when there's a knock at the door—or internal—when you remember mid-phrase that you need to reschedule your trio rehearsal. Mental preoccupations, even if they are related to the task at hand, can keep musicians from being fully aware. For instance, a performer can be so focused on an audition that's two days away that he can't get specific about the areas he could still be improving The goal of making a huge sound might cause a singer to unwittingly stress her vocal chords. Ironically, the music itself can be one of the worst distractions: a musician stares at the page to read the notes when in fact watching what he's actually doing or closing his eyes to better hear the sounds that are emerging would be much more beneficial to his development.

> **Consider This**
> Musicians often isolate an aspect of their technique for focused practice, which helps keep the short-term memory from being overloaded with or distracted by too much information. Once the technique is better established, it is bundled by the brain, and more easily combined with other techniques and concepts.

> **Personal Inventory:** Awareness is crucial to effective practice, yet distractions and preoccupations are common. Besides the obvious external distractions like a knock at the door, what are the distractions that happen within your practice routine? How do you stay focused?

FOSTERING EASE THROUGH REPETITION

The goal of internalizing a new technique or mastering an unfamiliar set of notes is to make it as easy as possible, allowing complete freedom to make music. Repetition is the most common way musicians achieve consistency and dependability in performing. To that end, musicians have developed a vast assortment of practice techniques and processes to keep themselves repeating—rhythms, practice loops, even games—whatever it takes to be sure the desired behavior is so thoroughly learned it requires almost no thought—what many call "muscle memory."

> ### Consider This
> Repetition with variety is essential to mastery: not just how many times we repeat, but our awareness of what it looks like, sounds like, feels like, how we describe it to ourselves, and how we compare it to other things we know. Results of related research also suggest that repetition in a variety of settings can help memory—so practicing in a different space each day could help you develop and internalize skills more deeply than always working in your favorite place (Smith, Glenberg, & Bjork, 1978).

Muscle memory is something of a misnomer, since the muscles themselves cannot "remember" anything—only the brain can. However, once a movement or position is well established, the brain signal and the muscle response are so quick as to be virtually simultaneous; and because it is impossible to notice the brain signal happening first, the memory seems to be in the muscle itself. At the beginning of the learning process, however, the disconnect is often very obvious: a new position or movement must be consciously, even laboriously controlled by the learner and is likely to feel awkward or ungraceful. This initial stage passes when, after several repetitions, the brain creates a more straightforward pathway for the behavior, and the learner needn't think consciously about every detail. Still, at this stage, the position or movement is not fully integrated as a permanent part of the brain. After several days of repetitions, the learning enters a more automatic stage, when an efficient pathway has been established for this behavior. Now the behavior or passage feels easy—the musician has finally "got" it. In order to make the muscular habit permanent, however, the repetitions need to continue over a period of months, perhaps even years.

Almost inevitably, there are times when musicians need to discard a behavior and replace it with a new one. This can be a considerable challenge, however, since ingrained habits are not simply "the way we're used to doing something"—they are well-embedded neural pathways in the brain, made more or less permanent by multiple repetitions over a long period of time. The only way to shed an unwanted behavior is to consciously start a new behavior and use it in place of the old one as often as possible. Awareness is an important key during this time of transition, since a distracted performer is more likely to use the old pattern than the new one, and the default connection in the brain will continue to be reinforced. Because of this, experienced musicians often choose an "off-season" time to establish a new habit, when they are the least distracted by concerts and other demands on their attention.

Consider This

As the results of our practicing efforts begin to take hold, we've probably commented, "It's beginning to come together." These words hold more truth than we might realize. When the conscious stage of learning moves toward becoming more automatic, it is because the information has been bundled into groups. When the brain is asked to recall this information, the information is retrieved in a "chunk." These information bundles are exactly what the musician can trust during performance. But when a moment of doubt suddenly overrides one of these automatic movements, the gesture that was once free, unencumbered and highly accurate will suddenly be none of these (Masters, Poolton, & Maxwell, 2008). "Getting in our own way" may be a more astute assessment of the problem than we might have realized.

While we deliberately use repetition to learn new music or behaviors, it is worth noting that there is at least one other level at which repetition helps musicians learn. This is the repetition that happens when we transfer established skill or knowledge to a new piece or situation. When the behavior is applied in a different situation, that skill or information is not only reinforced but given a new frame of reference in the brain. The more skills and information are transferred and linked to other reference points, the more readily our brain can access them. This kind of repetitive learning is often not conscious, but musicians can choose to make it an active part of the learning experience by recognizing patterns in the notes, rhythms, or articulations; by consciously noting when a particular technique or musical gesture is being utilized in more than one situation; or by "borrowing" a particular quality in our performing that happens easily in one piece, and "sharing" it with another piece lacking that quality. Even seemingly unrelated information and images can be applied to develop and reinforce our musicianship and skills. For instance, a musician who feels connected to nature might apply a familiar image of mountains fading into the distance to create a diminuendo; a chess player could utilize the concept of planning ahead as an important way to improving his sight-reading skills. The transfer of any familiar concept or skill to a new situation helps musicians learn music and techniques more quickly, while it reinforces both the cognitive understanding and the desired behavior.

INCREASING ACCURACY AND CONTROL

Reliability and consistency of precise movements and measurement are essential to a musician's development. In this context, control does not refer to muscular restraint in order to "be in charge"—it has to do with the balance of both tension and relaxation in the muscles and the consistency and accuracy of a musicians' gestures and measurements.

Much of what we do while singing, conducting, or playing an instrument entails repetitive use of isolated parts of the body that must work in association with other isolated areas, such as the coordination of tongue and fingers or feet and hands. It also can mean that certain muscles that normally work together might need to be dissociated. For example, normal usage of grasping and lifting an object requires firm muscles in hand and arm together, but a string player must learn to keep many muscles in the arm, wrist, and hand relaxed while holding and maneuvering a bow. Because of such unconventional usage, musicians must be creative to find ways to practice muscle differentiation, and integrate in minute detail consistency of the speed of movements, the amount of air used, the angle of the bow, and the spacing between keys on a keyboard or notes on a fingerboard.

One of the biggest mistakes a musician can make in the practice room is to practice inaccurately, especially when using repetition as a practice technique. Humans are remarkable in their capacity to learn—including unwanted tension, poor posture, wrong notes, even a subtly out-of-tune note. If the goal is to increase the odds that the correct behavior will be repeated, then it's not "how many repetitions" that count, it's "how many *accurate* repetitions." Even mixing faulty information with good information confuses the issue—which is the brain supposed to remember? The best learning comes from a very high "success rate" right from the start.

> **Consider This**
> Musicians can practice with virtually no mistakes if they are willing to start slowly enough to be correct from the start. Once accuracy is established, multiple repetitions at a variety of tempos strengthen the synapses, and the technique becomes so well integrated that it doesn't need full conscious attention. Neuroscientists call this "automaticity"—Burton Kaplan (author of *Practicing for Artistic Success*) refers to it as "useful boredom." Whatever you call it, musicians must be willing to tolerate a certain amount of short-term monotony for the big-picture gains.

One practice technique that supports the high-success-rate ideal is based on volleyball scoring, where one team cannot accrue points unless they are serving, and the only way they get the ball to serve is by winning one volley. In this process, the first accurate attempt doesn't count: it just gets the ball in your court. Now you might choose to accrue a given number of points to "win"—that is, finish this round of repetitions. If a mistake happens, you lose your serve, and have to get a correct one to get the chance back to finish your reps.

> **Personal Inventory:** Practicing slowly and carefully is one way we can increase the opportunity for accuracy at the beginning stages of learning. However, a slow tempo or movement does not always translate to fast or automatic. So while the words "practice slowly" are common in the music world, the meaning behind the phrase is not necessarily literal. How else would you define "slow practice"? What practice techniques do you use that create accuracy yet are not slow notes or movements?

INCREASING TRUST

For musicians, the concept of trust is as much psychological as it is physical. What does it take to "just know" you will hit that high note or nail that run? How do you practice trusting yourself? Obviously all the practice goals discussed to this point move musicians toward the reliability they depend on, but for many musicians there is more to trusting themselves than the practice techniques they use.

Despite our best efforts, mistakes can and will happen. Are they not proof of untrustworthiness? Perhaps—but any performer will tell you how slippery a slope that kind of thinking is. "I missed the high note once, so I might miss it again" can be disastrous, whether on stage or in a practice room. Mistakes that happen during practice are in a sense a gift because they offer the opportunity to make adjustments *before* problems happen on stage. Rather than viewing mistakes as proof that the body is not trustworthy, an experienced musician uses them as useful indicators of areas in the music that need more attention and internalization. Since the pressure of performing—needing to be perfect at one critical moment—can compound even the smallest lack-of-trust feeling, experienced performers allow themselves ample opportunity during the practice process to test the "trust factor" as a way to determine how internalized and reliable the behavior has become.

Trusting cannot guarantee perfection, but even in the earliest stages of learning a new piece or developing a new technique, musicians who trust both the practice process and themselves have the best opportunity for reliable, accurate, and trouble-free performances.

> **Personal Inventory:** Are there particular techniques in your area of study that are more vulnerable to lack-of-trust issues than others? How do you practice developing trust in your performance skills?

DEVELOPING A MUSICAL VOICE

Obviously, the mastery of technique alone does not automatically make anyone a musician in the fullest sense of the word. If technical skills are disconnected from life experience—such as emotions, characters, or stories—the instrumentalist, singer, or conductor runs the risk of being simply a good technician. Well-integrated skills provide immediate physical access to sounds and qualities that help create musical expression, but putting musical development on hold until technique is fully developed makes expression seem more like a decorative addition rather than the central reason to play music. If musical expression is at the core of what musicians do, then it must be central to the ongoing practice process.

Many musicians have an intuitive sense of musical expression, so much so that they often find it challenging to be consciously aware of ways they practice musicianship. On the other hand, there are those who are naturally expressive in everyday life, yet find it difficult to transfer their emotions and experiences through their instruments. The most direct link that connects human experience to musicianship (and vice versa) is the voice. Singing—even if only inside—helps the musician explore dynamic shaping, natural pacing, or quality of tone. This "practice technique" of creating music on the inside first is often the best way to know what the music needs, even if it takes many attempts to find that musical quality.

> **Consider This**
>
> Some practice techniques combine technique with musicianship. Backward add-a-note is one example of this approach: find the desired quality of sound for a climactic note and play or sing only that note several times to feel comfortable with the physical, mental, and even psychological approach needed for your optimal performance. Begin to add notes that move toward that arrival, starting with the penultimate note and working backward until every note becomes a meaningful step toward that arrival. The result is not only well-practiced notes, but a passage that has been technically developed from its musical meaning.

Musicians make both conscious and unconscious choices about musical meaning and expression, but practicing is usually the time to be conscious. As discussed in the chapter on musicianship, conscious musical decisions are often based on historical or biographical information about a composer or a time period, the harmonies, or other compositional elements. Since depth of understanding can transform a good performance to a great one, part of a musician's "practice time" might be well used studying scores to get under the surface of a piece. Hearing or attending performances of great musicians can offer a vision that enriches a performers' musical expressivity. Such inspiration combined with deliberate development of a wide variety of tone qualities and colors, speed and width of vibrato, and flexible sense of timing all contribute to a musician's ability to create meaningful sounds—as well as be spontaneous when inspiration strikes. Being more aware of our musical choices in practice can help musical development become as intentional and well founded as the technical development that helps it come to life.

Consider This

Results of studies related to the presence of "mirror neurons" in the brain suggest that when one watches another person performing an action, one's brain activates as though it was performing the action oneself (Rizzolatti, Sinigalia, & Anderson, 2006). Perhaps this is why it helps students to watch their teachers, attend concerts, and participate in studio repertoire sessions or master classes. While watching and listening cannot replace a real practice session, our brains apparently can "rehearse" without actual physical activity. For this same reason, a mental practice session is an excellent choice when an actual practice session is not possible.

Personal Inventory: Which specific approaches in your practice routine help you develop your musical voice?

Practice Processes

No matter what practice techniques musicians use, they often apply them within an overall process to be sure that the improved area is well integrated into the piece for which it is needed. Within the context of working on a piece, for instance, a practice process might contain these basic steps:

- Isolate the problem
- Strategize possible solutions
- Create the desired result as efficiently as possible
- Repeat until the desired result is the norm
- Combine with other aspects of the passage or technique, repeating as needed
- Reintegrate the resolution into the context of the piece

A practice process might also involve a practice cycle or checklist to be sure all aspects of playing have been observed and refined. This may be an unconscious process for many musicians who work with a well-developed sense of priority and flow, and might run something like this:

- Check for correct notes and rhythms
- Analyze physical coordination issues
- Explore dynamics, tone, and other expressive factors
- Combine all factors below performance tempo, making necessary adjustments
- Test technique and plan for physical requirements at performance tempo
- Repeat as needed until all aspects are integrated and reliable at full tempo

Such a roster of necessary musical elements creates a thorough approach and keeps a practice session moving forward, and might also include other specific instrumental factors that could find their way onto that list, such as hands alone, pedaling, breathing, or bow distribution. Putting each passage "through the paces" in a consistent way gives musicians parameters for knowing when their work is complete.

Personal Inventory: What process do you routinely use to learn new music? What processes do you use to resolve problems when working on a piece?

Physical and Mental States for Optimal Practicing

Our techniques and processes for practice are a big part of what we do, but they don't offer a complete picture of life in the practice room: musicians must also consider their physical conditioning and state of mind.

PHYSICAL WELL-BEING IN THE PRACTICE ROOM

In your early life as a musician, when it was time to practice, you probably just started to sing or play. But the more hours you spend practicing, the more like an athlete you become. Your physical conditioning is vital to your health and longevity as a musician, and has likely become an integral part of your routine, from important adjustments you make during practice sessions to exercise and therapy outside. You do what is necessary to stay comfortable, relaxed, and physically trouble-free for the long term.

> **Personal Inventory:** What parts of your practice routine involve physical conditioning—strengthening, stretching, or balancing—away from your instrument? Are there specific stretches or warm-ups you do at your instrument to get your muscles ready for a practice session?

Balance. Musicians' passionate desire to make great music can easily pull them "off center" physically, or block their awareness of how they use their bodies. Yoga, Alexander Technique, Feldenkreis, and Pilates are some of the more widely accepted practices that can help a musician reengage the ability to be physically aware while performing. Musicians who practice optimum posture and movement through such approaches report that they not only are physically freer, but have access to more deeply expressive musicianship.

Strengthening. The act of practicing certainly strengthens the muscles of the extremities, but musicians who need stamina must develop the strength of large muscle groups, particularly those known as the "core muscles" of the body. Lung capacity and breath control needed by singers and wind instrument players can be enhanced through cardiovascular exercise, such as swimming or running. Sometimes strength also needs to be developed to counterbalance a group of overworked muscles; for example, cellists tend to have strong but contracted muscles in the chest and need more strength in the muscles of the upper back and shoulder blade area to avoid back problems.

Stretching. Any activity that requires repeating the same movements, especially within a limited range of motion (which certainly describes what most musicians do) can cause muscles and tendons to "bunch." When musicians practice for extended periods of time, or play or sing in a room that is too cold, the soft tissue fibers contract and become restricted. This can be especially problematic in the tendons, the fiber that connects muscle to bone. When a tendon contracts and rubs against its surrounding sheath, the tendon becomes inflamed, causing the painful and debilitating condition known as tendinitis. Stretching and warming the muscles eases constrictions, lengthens and narrows the tendons, and helps minimize the risk of problems.

Professional care. Musicians almost instinctively stretch and rub overused muscles, but to optimize the body for long practice hours, professional physical care can be important to health and longevity. Body specialists who watch musicians perform can often suggest exercises that will enhance physical conditioning. Musicians tend to wait until they have a problem before they visit a masseuse, chiropractor, or physical therapist, but seeking advice and treatment from health care professionals *before* a crisis can prevent more debilitating issues from arising in the future. Besides supplying physical care, any of these specialists can offer advice on staying healthy, strong, and better able to endure extended hours of practice.

STATE OF MIND

What is your best mental state for practicing? Most musicians find that a calm, observant, and attentive state is most conducive to learning. Such a mindset allows for objective observations in making adjustments and corrections toward optimum performance, without cluttering the work with judgmental or emotional reactions. Like a teacher observing and guiding a student, such an approach makes it possible to be aware of which areas need the most work, and even to see a hierarchy of necessary adjustments that will effect changes most significantly.

Caring about what you learn can significantly heighten memory as well. This is due to the chemical composition of the brain when pleasurable emotions are present. Perhaps every musician has experienced this—a piece we're excited about learning comes to us much more quickly than one that we learn simply because we must. With this awareness, musicians are wise to find beauty and joy in all pieces, even those they're averse to learning, thereby benefiting themselves, the learning process, and the music.

Mistakes—and reactions to those mistakes—can also make or break a practice session. Mistakes offer musicians the possibility to weed out what works from what doesn't; too many of them can lead to frustration and work against the learning process. Repeated mistakes usually means the musician is taking on too much, and the first step is to cut back: fewer notes, slower tempo, one component, or one hand. But sometimes doing so leads to still more frustration: "I should be better; I shouldn't have to slow down so much; I should be able to do this already." If this is you, remember that successful people actually have many more failures than unsuccessful people: undeterred, they see mistakes in the big picture of the process, and are willing to make more attempts to achieve success. Staying detached and objective allows a musician to calmly determine the cause of the problem, make the correction deliberately and efficiently, and then reinforce the desired behavior.

There will also be days in all musicians' lives when they can barely drag themselves to the practice room. But even when the passion is lacking, a little focus can go a long way. Some musicians find that limiting their first half hour to a single parameter helps them get past their initial resistance to practicing. Such focus doesn't always have to be scales or the same warm-up routine: exploring tone colors, improvising, singing or playing a favorite piece, or even choosing to practice in a different space can help get musicians over the proverbial "hump" toward productive practicing.

> ### Consider This
>
> Chemicals in the brain are connected to mood, which can affect our ability to learn. The pleasure chemical dopamine is released when the brain is stimulated and starts to learn. The feelings of enjoyment when we settle into a practice session are, at least in part, caused by the dopamine. It has also been demonstrated that some acute stress (such as at a lesson or master class) can enhance learning due to the way the brain functions when alert. However, when a person is chronically nervous, stressed, or frightened, the negative emotions produce chemicals that actually repress the development of new connections in the brain, making it more difficult to learn.

Optimal Use of Time

Time is something that every musician must come to terms with, whether it's not enough time to prepare for a lesson, rehearsal, or performance or too much time waiting to be called to perform at an audition (when it seems the choice is to either wear yourself out, or sit around and get cold). How we manage our practice time can make a huge difference in our ability to achieve our goals.

> **Personal Inventory:** Acknowledging that there will always be time constraints, how do you use time most effectively? Consider how you prioritize your work, and how you make the most of your shortest practice sessions. Add these ideas to your list of practice techniques.

UTILIZING SHORT AMOUNTS OF TIME

Busy musicians have to grab practice time when they can. Ideally there are still days with two- or three-hour blocks of undisturbed practice time reserved in the schedule, but not every day allows that kind of time. Professional engagements, teaching, and important family obligations can mean available practice time as a professional is a fraction of what it was as a student, and every minute of practice must be used efficiently. Some musicians claim that although they practiced untold hours in music school, they learned to practice effectively only after they graduated.

When there's ten minutes before rehearsal time, what can be accomplished besides simply warming up? Probably the worst use of a short amount of time is to take on too much while accomplishing little—or spending the time being more aware of the clock than anything else. Experienced musicians often find that focusing on only one issue is critical to short but productive practice sessions: focusing intonation, clarifying rhythms in a tricky passage, or developing any single aspect of tone production or musicianship. When learning a new piece in short bursts, it's possible to memorize one line of music per day so that in the next two weeks that movement of Bach will be well in hand. Highly focused practice sessions have the potential to allow very deep practicing, no matter the length. Many musicians have had the experience of a kind of time warp when they become so involved in one aspect of their practice that one minute or one hour could have passed—they would be challenged to tell the difference.

OPTIMAL PRACTICE TIME

At some point in their lives, musicians discover an optimal "rhythm" for their day's work. For some, mornings are best spent stretching and singing through music in their heads; for others, it's the best time to tackle the most challenging areas of playing that might go unpracticed if saved for later. One musician might prefer technical exercises in the morning and work on her pieces in the evening when her expressivity and creativity seem highest, avoiding practice in the afternoon when she feels sleepy. Of course, the same musician will have to adjust that a new approach when she's told that her time for the concerto competition is three o'clock in the afternoon.

Other optimal practice times might be right after a lesson, when ideas are fresh and beg to be reinforced. Practicing immediately after attending a concert, observing a master class, or hearing a great recording can be significant to the growth of a musician. When a musician wants to discover *that* piece, or *that* sound, inspiration calls for an immediate response, and the moment simply cannot be saved for later.

MENTAL PRACTICE

Mental clarity is a large part of performing well, and a surprising amount of progress can be accomplished via the mind. In the previously mentioned situation, if the instrument isn't available or physical practice is simply impossible, mental practice can be an excellent substitute. Mentally rehearsing what you just learned, envisioning yourself making the incredible sound you just heard, or replaying that piece in your mind with you as the soloist makes the new possibility more accessible when you are finally able to practice again.

Seasoned musicians know that the results of physical practice become more secure through frequent mental rehearsals. Mental practice can be as routine as counting a rhythm or envisioning your fingers navigating a particularly gnarly section; it can also be as rich as a full choir rehearsal, "hearing" magnificent sounds, impeccable phrasing, and a glorious climax. Mental practice can even be utilized over an extended period of time while recovering from an injury; and habituated physical approaches can be reworked through mental practice without lifting a finger. Entire pieces can be memorized on transcontinental flights; and auditions and performances can be envisioned in their entirety, helping performers be undistracted by the sights, sounds, and feelings of the actual situation.

> **Personal Inventory:** How have you used mental practice to help yourself practice and prepare? Have you found it to be valuable? What are the challenges?

KNOWING WHEN TO REST

Just as important as knowing how to practice is being able to recognize when it's time to take a break or stop for the day. This requires musicians to listen not just to the music they make, but to what their bodies are telling them. Some musicians wait to feel mental or physical exhaustion before they consider stopping. However, when the body feels overloaded, a walk, eating a healthy snack, drinking water, stretching, deep breathing or a short nap can help release the intensity of work and rebalance the mind and body. Knowing when to stop for the day is critical to the health and longevity of the ambitious and relentless artist.

> **Personal Inventory:** What are your personal requirements for effective practice? How do you know when to take a break or stop for the day? When you're not having a great day in the practice room, how do you decide whether to persevere or call it a day? Do you let yourself take a day off?

Trusting the Process

Part of the drive to perfection is that need to achieve significant results *today* during *this* practice session. While it's important to examine how to get the most out of a practice session, it's also important to see practicing in the big picture. Practicing is a process, and it's not possible, nor is it necessary, to sort everything out in a day. There will be times when body, mind, and spirit are not aligned around practice, and calling it a day is the best option. The ability to acknowledge when enough is enough is significant to the practice process and to your own well-being. Some musicians even advocate scheduling a day off on a regular basis to allow the body a full day of rest and maintain a sense of perspective.

Thousands of practice hours toward mastery take years to accumulate, and even when they are behind you, there is always more to learn. As musicians mature, they often find that other factors influence their development, sometimes with fewer hours devoted to physical practice and more to score study, research, travel, teaching, physical conditioning, other arts and disciplines, or spiritual fulfillment. All can contribute to deeper artistry in the practice room and onstage. Practicing, in all its guises, will always be a process. It is a journey with destinations along the way, but never a final arrival—made one dedicated hour at a time.

> **Consider This**
> Before you push yourself to your physical and mental brink in the practice room, consider research that has also shown that sleep is a significant factor in the learning process (Walker, 2005). Sleep quiets the brain by dissipating the mental clutter of random experiences, while bundling recently learned information, and moving it toward more automatic access. These processes clean out the conscious brain, leaving it more ready to learn again (Simmons & Duke, 2006).

> Success is not final, failure is not fatal: it is the courage to continue that counts.
> WINSTON CHURCHILL

Ideas for Further Exploration

1. Create a glossary of practice techniques, referring to your completed tables from Chapter 3, *Technique*, to be sure nothing important has been omitted. Include an optimal practice process that could apply to virtually any practicing situation (see the *Practice Processes* section in this chapter for ideas).

2. What criteria do you use to decide when a passage or your work on a specific issue is "good enough" to let it go for that practice session?

3. Have any of your teachers addressed practice techniques or processes in your work with them? Are you or would you have been glad for this guidance?

4. Choose one aspect of your technique or musicianship that you would like to improve. Create a plan for your work (consult your applied teacher if you are in school) and journal your progress over the course of eight to ten weeks.

Recommended Reading

Coyle, D. (2009). *The Talent Code: Greatness Isn't Born, It's Grown. Here's How*. New York: Random House.

Duke, R. A., Simmons, A. L., & Davis, C. (2009). It's Not How Much; It's How. *Journal of Research in Music Education* 56 (4), 310–321.

Ericsson, K. A., Krampe, R. Th., & Tesch-Romer, C. (1993). The Role of Deliberate Practice in the Acquisition of Expert Performance. *Psychological Review* 100 (3), 379, 384.

Gallwey, T. (1974). *The Inner Game of Tennis*. New York: Random House.

Gladwell, M. (2009). *Outliers: The Story of Success*. New York: Little, Brown.

Green, B. (2003). *The Mastery of Music: Ten Pathways to True Artistry*. New York: Broadway Books.

Green, E. A. H. (2006). *Practicing Successfully: A Masterclass in the Musical Art*. Chicago: GIA.

Iacoboni, M. (2008). *Mirroring People: The New Science of How We Connect with Others*. New York: Farrar, Straus, and Giroux.

Johnston, P. (2007). *Practiceopedia*. Pearce, Australia: Practice Spot Press.

Kaplan, B. (2004). *Practicing for Artistic Success: The Musician's Guide to Self-Empowerment*. Morris, N.Y.: Perception Development Techniques.

Klickstein, G. (2009). *The Musician's Way: A Guide to Practice, Performance, and Wellness*. New York: Oxford University Press.

Levitin, D. J. (2006). *This Is Your Brain on Music: The Science of Human Obsession*. New York: Penguin.

Masters, R. S. W., Poolton, J. M., Maxwell, J. P. (2008). Implicit Motor Learning and Complex Decision Making in Time Constrained Environments. *Journal of Motor Behavior* 40 (1), 71–79.

MENC (ed.). (2004). *Teacher to Teacher: A Music Educator's Survival Guide*. Reston, Va.: MENC: National Association for Music Education.

Ormrod, J. E. (2008). *Human Learning*. 5th ed. Upper Saddle River, N.J.: Pearson Prentice Hall.

Rizzolatti, G., Sinigalia, C., & Anderson, F. (2006). *Mirrors in the Brain: How Our Minds Share Actions, Emotion and Experience*. New York: Oxford University Press.

Said, E. W. (1991). *Musical Elaborations*. New York: Columbia University Press.

Simmons, A., & Duke, R. A. (2006). The Effects of Sleep on the Performance of a Keyboard Melody. *Journal of Research in Music Education* 54 (3), 257–269.

Smith, S. M., Glenberg, A. M., & Bjork, R. A. (1978). Environmental Context and Human Memory. *Memory and Cognition* 6 (4), 342–353.

Walker, M. P. (2005). A Refined Model of Sleep and the Time Course of Memory Formation. *Behavioral and Brain Sciences* 28 (1), 51–104.

Watkins, C. (2008). *Rosindust: Teaching, Learning and a Life from a Cellist's Perspective*. Houston: Rosindust.

Wilson, F. R. (1986). *Tone Deaf and All Thumbs? An Invitation to Music-Making*. New York: Vintage Books.

Wulf, G. (2007). *Attention and Motor Skill Learning*. Champaign, Ill.: Human Kinetics.

5 Performing

IN THE PREVIOUS CHAPTER, we discussed the ways musicians develop and maintain a high level of artistry. However, musicians do not play and sing only in the safe confines of their practice rooms—they perform for others. Whether the situation is formal or informal, in low-pressure situations or high-stakes auditions, performing can be an entirely different test of any musician's ability to play his or her best. As much as this is the most public part of what musicians do, it is probably the most personal when it comes to how each individual experiences and deals with the intensity of performance. From threatening to thrilling, every musician must prepare to make the best of it, because performing is a substantial part of our chosen career.

> **Personal Inventory:** What has been your best experience performing? To what can you attribute this peak performance?

Certainly, practice should not only raise our ability to play a piece to the highest level possible, but should also prepare us for the performance experience itself. Any disconnect between practicing and the performance experience can create a very disconcerting shock to the unseasoned musician who assumes the piece that sounded great in the practice room will automatically be the same on stage. Preparation without full cognizance of the performance is likely to wilt in the spotlight.

Consider This

Performance coach Don Greene suggests that practice should feel as close to performing as possible and performing is best when it feels like another practice session.

Personal Inventory: Make a list of various issues you've encountered that make performing different from practicing: internal experiences such as rapid heart rate, sweaty hands, dry mouth, or external ones, like the shock of unexpected acoustics, the annoyance of a bad page-turner, the presence of a person who made you nervous, and so on. What processes or techniques do you use to be certain these issues are not problematic during performance? If one area is recurrently difficult for you, can you think creatively about possible solutions to resolve that problem?

Performance-Oriented Practicing

As we already discussed in the previous chapter, a performance-ready skill is one that has become automatic and immediately accessible. It is different from the kind of learning needed for typical test-taking, when it is usually sufficient to remember the material in any sequence, with arbitrary pacing, and where mistakes can be erased and corrected without consequence. In music performance there are a great number of precisely timed events that must happen, often in extraordinarily quick succession, and there is no possibility for a mishap to be corrected once it has occurred. Since the conscious mind simply cannot handle it all, musicians must practice to make each very complicated series of movements as precise, as automatic, and ultimately as reliable as possible.

Therefore, while most practicing consists almost entirely of backtracking, improving, and repeating sections, such habits can be utterly detrimental to performing. Stopping to fix is out of the question; even a fleeting thought about a small stumble could create a chain reaction of several more problems. The ability to think and listen ahead, the capacity to make immediate adjustments, and the wherewithal not to stop for anything—all must be developed to make the transition from the practicing mode to a performing mode.

Consider This

As a performance approaches, some less experienced musicians have the sense that they are getting worse. One possible explanation is their lack of awareness regarding the amount of practice needed to be consistent in performance. Heightened listening (in other words, an increased awareness of what the audience will hear) is another probable cause for this phenomenon. What suggestions would you make to a performer experiencing this problem?

TECHNIQUES FOR PREPARING A PERFORMANCE

Musicians utilize a variety of performance-oriented practice techniques:

- When music must be memorized, musicians must become entirely self-reliant in knowing the next note, the next move, the next sound, the next passage. Experienced musicians realize that having only one system for memorization is not enough, like building a table with only one leg and expecting it not to fall. Three or four approaches to memorization give the performance many legs to stand on. Memorization strategies can be conscious, like studying the harmonic structure of a piece, remembering particular fingerings that help a passage go smoothly, or writing out the piece on blank manuscript paper. Others are more automatic, like the spontaneous retrieval of the "information bundles" discussed in the last chapter, whether they are kinesthetic, aural, or visual recalls—or all three.
- Playing through a piece without stopping for any reason is one of the first steps to move from practicing mode to performing. For some musicians, this works best when a metronome is running as a persistent reminder to keep going. When certain sections are easy to play while others present a problem, a slower tempo overall can allow a more proportionate sense of pacing and flow, both mentally and physically, and provides a significant opportunity to play all the notes accurately in one performance.
- Recording is one of the most tried-and-true methods to add the intensity of performing into a practice session. It helps musicians discover how reliable their preparation really is, and often heightens their listening skills.

Recording can also provide a marker for evaluating the ongoing levels of preparedness. Some musicians avoid recording themselves because its candid reflection can be excruciatingly revealing, but its value to complete preparation is undeniable, and it should be utilized frequently during the preparation process.

- Feedback from a colleague is quite different from that of a recording, given that a person can be emotionally supportive and is also able to offer musical, technical, or psychological insights and advice. What can't be controlled are their reactions and opinions, but this is much closer to the real audience the musician must ultimately face.

- Nothing prepares a musician for performing like a performance. Practice performances, with conditions that are as close as possible to the anticipated conditions of the actual event, can help a musician enormously. Playing in the concert hall or audition room for a recruited or vividly imagined audience can help musicians make final adjustments toward an optimum performance. Detailed mental rehearsals of the entire performance scenario (including dressing, warming up, waiting back stage, and so forth) are also extremely valuable.

Consider This

Musicians set up ideal environments for practicing, as they should: a quiet setting with minimal potential for disturbance, comfortable air temperature, working when feeling strong and focused, and resting when tired. Yet conditions at a performance are often not ideal. Factors outside the performer's control, such as delays, room temperature, and audience noise, can be challenging distractions. Because musicians are still expected to offer great performances in spite of such issues, performers might want to consider practicing under less-than-ideal conditions to improve their ability to focus in a variety of situations.

Personal Inventory: How do you prepare for a performance? How close to a concert date do you transition from normal practice mode to performance mode? Which aspects of performance mode are helpful to incorporate throughout the learning process? What practice routines, such as specific techniques or slow practice, do you use throughout performance preparation?

Performance Issues

EXPECTATIONS AND GOAL SETTING

The desire for technical excellence and profound musical expression are what compels musicians toward ever-increasing heights of artistic achievement. Yet expectations can be a double-edged sword for performers who agonize over falling even slightly short of their highest goals. The first misplaced finger or shortness of breath can negatively influence the rest of the performance. In an ensemble setting, a negative reaction can affect more than just one performer and undermine the spirit of an entire evening of music. Putting mistakes in perspective and thinking more holistically about a performance can keep musicians from "throwing away" hours of musical enjoyment for themselves and the audience. In other words, a cracked note in the French horn solo at the beginning of a Mahler symphony needn't cancel out the next hour of exquisite music.

A performer must also be wary of expectations like "I can't make a mistake" or "This will be my best performance ever." More dangerous still are externalized expectations: "They are going to love my singing" or "I need to win this competition." Goals set in areas that are outside a performer's sphere of influence can be energy drains as well as psychological land mines. No one can control what others think or how well anyone else will perform. It's important for a musician to let go of externalized projections, focusing only on strategies that allow the best opportunity to play, sing, or conduct very well, and build those strategies into a performance plan.

> **Consider This**
> How do performers, whose goal throughout the practice process is to make everything perfect, let go of such an expectation in performance? What mindset might allow the possibility of a great performance without the need for perfection?

PERFORMANCE ANXIETY AND MIND GAMES

Many musicians who experience a high degree of pre-performance anxiety tend to overemphasize their own flaws, or compare themselves to other musicians whose flaws they minimize. Performers who tend toward negative thinking are wise to establish believable and affirming responses to unhelpful messages. In other words, a thought such as "You'll miss the run" can be answered by "No, I've done it hundreds of times, and I can do it again." The next step for the musician is to develop detailed performance directives that are strong enough to push aside any negative thoughts that threaten to derail a performance. (More about this topic can be found in the upcoming section, "Concentration.") This work can be as necessary as practice itself in order to allow the real possibility of a fine performance.

PHYSICAL CHANGES

> **Personal Inventory:** Have you experienced physical changes such as rapid heart rate, sweating, increased tension, or shaking when performing? Do you attribute these to performance anxiety, or something else? Do you have ways to dissipate these symptoms before performing, or do you work through them in performance?

It is easy for musicians to assume that the feelings associated with "performance jitters" mean something is wrong, but such responses to the excitement of performing are physiologically quite normal.

- Adrenaline gives muscles an extra energy boost, and muscles that are primed and ready will start to shake if they aren't able to move adequately.
- Blood, usually occupied with digestion, rushes to your extremities to oxygenate the muscles, which sometimes results in a queasy stomach and a dry mouth.
- Senses are more acute, which heightens the way everything sounds, feels, and looks.

Rather than perceiving these natural responses as indications of a problem, musicians can learn to work with them—at a minimum, so the physical symptoms are not a detriment or distraction, and at best, channeling such a highly charged physical state into powerful performances.

CONCENTRATION

Perhaps every musician has had the experience of making a mistake in performance, responding with the order "Concentrate!" only to make another mistake soon afterward. The problem might be that concentration needs to be focused on a specific action that optimizes a musician's best performance. In other words, directing oneself to "Concentrate!" in performance is too nonspecific—and perhaps too much of a reprimand—to be helpful in the moment. Directives that can put a performer in touch with what needs to happen now, such as "breathe," "smooth shift," or "light fingers" are far more helpful, and push away the "Why did I lose my concentration?" questions until a more appropriate time.

Purposely creating a series of these directives, sometimes called process cues or performance handles, is one way musicians construct a plan for a solid, undistracted performance. In fact, an "inspired" performance on the outside might well be a well-executed performance plan. These tend to work best when they specifically address *actions* that produce the desired outcome. For example, rather than saying "good tone," a process cue might be "connect with the string" or "steady column of air" or "heavy arm"—whatever creates the desired result. To support the flow of the music, these performance handles need to be fairly close together. Like monkey bars at a playground, if a hand slips on one, it's still easy enough to grab the next and keep going.

CENTERING AND FOCUS

Auditions and performances are external by nature. When musicians perform they extend what they do—and, in many ways, who they are—out to others, often in unfamiliar settings. To perform well, musicians must balance their awareness of the hall and the audience with their own internal awareness. Knowing how to become centered and maintain focus is one of most powerful tools any performer can learn to use. The ability to screen out distractions is an important first step, and can be practiced just like any technique on your instrument. Equally important is the ability to regain center when concentration is disrupted, whether the distraction was external, like a sudden loud sound in the audience, or internal, like a technical mishap.

Consider This

Visualized performances are helpful to musicians in a variety of ways. Envisioning the hall, the audience, and the sounds can help musicians experience their reactions to the performing environment. Improvements to any physical or psychological aspect of the performance can be made in the safety of the mental rehearsal. It has also been demonstrated by neuroscientists that the brain responds virtually the same way whether a musician is playing or just imagining playing, making it possible to practice productively for an upcoming performance without risking physical fatigue.

RECOVERING FROM MISTAKES

Allowing for the likelihood—perhaps even the certainty—of mistakes in performance is the first step toward learning how to recover. Musicians performing at a high level of artistry cannot afford to be distracted when mistakes happen: they simply must recover gracefully and immediately focus on what's ahead. Again, those performance handles or process cues are essential to a quick recovery. These offer a way not to dwell on what's already happened but reach instead for the next moment that still has the potential to be excellent.

How musicians frame mistakes in their minds can make a big difference in how they affect a performance. Thinking that it's all downhill after the first slip, or assuming that the only wonderful performance is a perfect one are two examples of troublesome notions about mistakes. Performance coach Don Greene suggests another way of looking at mistakes: "Audition panels and paying audiences aren't looking for perfection; they want to feel the excitement of someone hanging it out on the edge. That's risky. If a mistake happens because of that, though, and you are able to recover immediately and effortlessly, you may earn more than their respect."

> **Personal Inventory:** What is your best way to deal with a mistake or less-than-wonderful moment in a performance?

DETERMINATION

The act of being a musician requires ongoing determination and fortitude, and performing is our most public extension of that commitment. Auditions are probably the biggest test of a musician's mettle, when performance pressure is most intense and the mental game is more critical than ever. Even when you encounter more challenges than usual, and feel the urge to cave in, fighting for effective communication of the music you love is the highest priority. Determination to finish strong—even if the outcome isn't all you dreamed—will yield the best possible performance.

Stage Presence

> **Personal Inventory:** You have attended many concerts. Think about how performers present themselves on stage—what works and what doesn't. Create two columns on a piece of paper: on one side, list the factors that draw you into a performance, and on the other, what distracts you or makes you uncomfortable.

Appearance. Although somewhat superficial, the musician's clothes, hair, and jewelry are often the first thing an audience notices, but that awareness should quickly fade from consciousness, and not be a distraction.

Body language. A performer's physical demeanor can speak as loudly and directly as the music. Audiences can sense if the musician is confident or worried, energized or blasé. While usually sensitive to the stresses of performing and forgiving of initial performance discomfort, an audience that perceives the performer as overly nervous or uncaring will not be comfortable about the performance.

The first sounds. These do not need to be loud to be convincing, but the first note can tell an audience that this will be a performance worth hearing, immediately drawing them into the musical experience.

Connection between performer and audience. There is a full spectrum of the way performers connect with their audiences. At one end, the musician seems to reach out draw the audience into the performance; at the other is the musician who becomes so deeply involved in the music that the audience is mesmerized by his or her intensity. While almost polar opposite in manner, these performers do have a similar affect on listeners, perhaps due to the high level of mastery that is needed to sustain a performance in either mode. This does not mean that musicians must to go to one extreme or another to connect with an audience, but it is worth examining what elements are needed to turn a benign but ineffectual presentation into a more captivating one.

Poise. Defined as a state of balance or equilibrium and freedom from affectation or embarrassment, this is as important to the performer as it is the audience. The performer's ability to maintain stability and composure means glitches, small or large, are quickly forgotten. People come to concerts to hear great music or to support the performer, but when a mistake happens they don't want to be drawn into the performer's angst—they want the beautiful music to resume as quickly as possible.

Graceful conclusion. The polished performer knows how to end with a

---

Consider This

Cellist Gregor Piatigorsky was known for his great performances but terrible, almost debilitating nerves leading up to every concert. One audience member recalls a performance of the Saint-Saëns cello concerto when Piatigorsky's first note came out as a terrible squawk. A palpable shock wave ran through the audience—but Piatigorsky's stage composure was so unshakable and his music making so powerful that, only a few phrases later, the listener began thinking he must have imagined it.

sincere smile, a graceful bow, an inclusive gesture to an accompanist or other collaborators, and a final exit in a poised demeanor. Even if the performance was a challenging event for the musician, the audience's applause deserves to be acknowledged with respect and gratitude.

Expression as the Core Element

> **Personal Inventory:** Is it you or the music that takes center stage when you perform, or do you and the music share the spotlight?

The discussion in this chapter up to this point has been focused on you, the performer—how you prepare, how you react to pressures, how you draw on your strength, how you are perceived on stage. Yet too much self-centeredness, whether it be fretting over fears and concerns or strutting over performance prowess, can overshadow the primary reason to be a performing musician: to make music. Centering on musical expression can be the easiest way to forget about being nervous or needing to impress an audience. When conveying musical meaning is the primary motivation to perform, many musicians find that all other issues fall in line behind it.

COMPELLING PERSONAL REASONS

> **Personal Inventory:** Even when performing is more an external requirement than a choice from within (like a jury at the end of a semester or a less-than-exemplary professional engagement), what is your best motivation to play for others?

Most musicians need a reason inside themselves to perform. Perhaps it's a sense of joy in making music, or loving the sound of the instrument, or the thrill of free and brilliant technique, or the potential for deeper expression than everyday life allows. Pressure from a parent or teacher, or just knowing you're good at something even though you don't love it, are usually not sustainable reasons to be a musician. The most effective and satisfying performances usually come from within, and identifying and connecting with the most personal compelling reasons to make music can deepen and enrich any performing experience.

COMMUNICATING WITH OTHERS

Musicians enjoy performing for audiences who are there to fully experience the music. It is gratifying to offer religious music to worshipers, dance music to dancers, soulful music to mourners, and patriotic music to proud countrymen. Even in a concert setting, when the reason for performing is more generalized, performers can sense that audiences are willing role-players through a variety of moods, characters, and settings. So in an audition situation where those listening almost certainly will be more critical, simply imagining a more receptive audience can make a quantifiable difference to the performer.

> Consider This
> Neuroscientists have proposed that the mirror neurons (which cause the brain to vicariously experience an action that is observed, as discussed in Chapter 2, *Listening*) also play a role in human empathy, as one person experiences another's emotions. This could explain how musicians communicate moods and expression in their music-making, and why an audience can be moved by a performance that is deeply experienced by the musician.

CONNECTING TO THE COMPOSITION

For some, performing is an opportunity to get as close to the composer and the composition as possible, not only by having an intimate understanding of the score, but through learning about the composer's life and experiences to better convey the meaning of the music. Performers can also find inspiration by recreating the sounds through historical performance practice and period instruments, sometimes including costumes to complete the portrayal. Visiting—and if fortunate enough, playing in—the venues of revered composers and performers can bring musicians viscerally closer to the source of the music.

> Consider This
> Musicians can take a cue from theatrical training. Actors are taught not to pretend to be someone but to "become" that person. In order to be in full character for a performance, the actor embodies that person backstage, so that the entrance is in character for the performance. A similar conviction can allow a musician to embody and convey the mood and character of a piece—from the walk onstage to the final note.

Advancing Your Artistry and Expanding Your Influence

At this point we have come full circle and find ourselves back in the realm of what makes music profound and moving, explored in Chapter 1, *Musicianship*. This is the interconnected nature of our development as musicians: as we increase our awareness, we evolve our musicianship, refine our technique, and weave all aspects into profound expression in performance.

Most of our work is solitary and behind the scenes. On stage, however, musicians are no longer alone—we share our passion for music and the pinnacle of our efforts with others. In our audience will be many who love what we do and want to hear more, and others who feel such a connection that they yearn to make music themselves.

Many of our future students are in that second group—these are the people with whom we share our full musical lives. As satisfying the performing life can be, the stage allows us to reveal only the tip of the proverbial iceberg. All that we study, practice, discover, and develop; the thrill of inspiration and creativity, the frustrations, perseverance, and the gratification of successes small and large—the entire process that makes up the vast majority of our lives as musicians—simply cannot be revealed through performance alone. With students, we have the opportunity to show them what we love, and explore why it's meaningful; we can share with them our own struggles and discoveries, help them with theirs, and rediscover music through fresh eyes and ears.

Through teaching, we enrich our own lives while doing the same for our students. We relive our learning process, remember our earliest "goose bump" moments, and realize that our first teacher's previously unfathomable choices now make sense—or not. When we teach, we say things we didn't know we knew—wise and insightful words emerge from somewhere deep inside, guiding our students while reminding ourselves of those things we know to be true, yet might not always do. We become personally invested in our students and their progress, and are prouder beyond reason when they are successful. For these reasons, and many others, teaching is a most wonderful companion profession to a musician's performing life.

Bring everything you love about making music to your work with students. Don't worry that tapping beats and correcting positions means you are compromising your artistic values. Yes, you will do these things, but such duties are always a means to an end: these are the fundamentals that give a new musician a basis upon which to grow. Whether a student becomes a professional musician, a general music teacher, a high school band director, a supporter of the arts, or the next Heifetz is beside the point. When you bring your enthusiasm to every lesson with every student, along with great repertoire, high standards, inspired teaching ideas, and your passion for music—everyone is better for it.

Personal Inventory: Before we move ahead to concepts and principles of teaching, let's reflect on the five significant components of your life as a musician: musicianship, listening, technique, practicing, and performing. In spite of the numerous complexities you have explored, create a statement for each component that captures its essential meaning or value. Here are some words to get you started, but feel free to rephrase as you see fit:

The essence of musical expression is . . .
Listening is vital to musicians because . . .
The purpose of technique is . . .
The most essential ingredient of effective practice is . . .
The essence of performance is . . .

Now finish these statements with

. . . and I will teach my student the importance of these concepts, not just by what I say, but in every way I work with them.

These five themes will be fundamental to your ability to shift effortlessly and uncompromisingly between your music professions: you live by these ideals as a performer, and you live by them as a teacher.

Ideas for Further Exploration

1. Practice a challenging passage for a limited time, to the point that you can play it through without mistakes or stopping (though not necessarily up to tempo). Now play that passage for a colleague, using the same tempo and approach you used during your practice session. Notice any changes in yourself—physically, mentally, technically, or musically—and evaluate your ability to perform at, above, or below your practicing level in each of those categories. Repeat this practice/perform process within twenty-four hours of the first one, preferably for the same person. Compare the two sessions.

2. Choose a relatively short piece to memorize, with both musical complexity and motific repetition, such as an invention or fugue. Decide on three approaches you will use to memorize the piece, and devote at least an hour a day for one week to the process. Keep a running tally on how many times you implement your three approaches, keeping a balance between them rather than leaning heavily on one or two. Videotape your progress each day.

3. Write a description of a performer at a recital with ideal stage presence, using the outline in the *Stage Presence* section of this chapter as a starting point. Be specific about how any descriptor such as "graceful" or "warm" manifests itself in the performer's behaviors, for example facial expressions, gesturing, standing, or bowing. Consider how you can practice and develop your own stage presence.

4. Choose one piece of repertoire that you could easily play or sing in repeated performances. (This could be a piece you are currently teaching.) Schedule three or four performances: a prelude for a church service, a recital for a local school, or your contribution to your own studio recital. Note the benefits of repeating repertoire in subsequent performances.

5. Explore your own ability to convey expression through your music-making. Sit in front of a mirror and notice whether it is possible for you to perform with intensity while maintaining a bland countenance, or with anger when you are smiling, or to convey a dance without dance movements. Next, watch a video recording of a performance. Turn down the volume and observe what is being conveyed visually; then turn up the volume and see how much the musicianship matches the physical manifestation. If the performer looks bland, does he or she sound that way? Do you think it is possible for a musician's demeanor to be either too dispassionate or too animated when performing?

Recommended Reading

Beeching, A. M. (2005). *Beyond Talent: Creating a Successful Career in Music.* New York: Oxford University Press.

Bernstein, S. (1981). *With Your Own Two Hands: Self-Discovery through Music.* New York: Schirmer Books.

Caldwell, R. (1990). *The Performer Prepares.* Seattle: PST.

Gordon, S. (2006). *Mastering the Art of Performing: A Primer for Musicians.* Oxford: Oxford University Press.

Gorrie, J. (ed.). (2009). *A Fate Worse Than Death: A Collection of Articles about Performance Anxiety for Musicians and Public Speakers.* thezonebook.com: Createspace.

Gorrie, J. (2009). *Performing in the Zone.* thezonebook.com: Createspace.

Green, B. (2009). *Bringing Music to Life.* Chicago: GIA.

Green, B. (1986). *The Inner Game of Music.* Garden City, N.Y.: Anchor.

Greene, D. (2001). *Audition Success: An Olympic Sports Psychologist Teaches Performing Artists How to Win.* New York: Routledge.

Greene, D. (2001). *Fight Your Fear and Win: 7 Skills for Performing Your Best under Pressure—At Work, in Sports, on Stage.* New York: Broadway Books.

Greene, D. (2002). *Performance Success: Performing Your Best under Pressure.* New York: Routledge.

Havas, Kato. (1973). *Stage Fright: It's Causes and Cures; With Special Reference to Violin Playing.* Berlin: Bosworth.

Ristad, E. (1982). *A Soprano on Her Head: Right-Side-Up Reflections on Life and Other Performances.* Moab, Utah: Real People Press.

II The Art of Teaching

Principle, n. A basic truth, law, or assumption; a rule or standard, especially of good behavior; a basic or essential quality or element determining intrinsic nature or characteristic behavior [of a teacher].

AMERICAN HERITAGE DICTIONARY

6   Teaching Principles

ONE OF THE BIGGEST surprises to most musicians venturing into the world of teaching is the discovery that having performance expertise will not give them everything they need to become good teachers. Like music, teaching is an art that requires skill acquisition, development, and experience. Whether you have come to teaching by choice or by circumstance, your satisfaction with your role as a teacher will directly correlate with your investment in excellent teaching.

You have just examined in detail your life as a performing musician, perhaps discovering that you knew more than you realized. Now consider how and where you learned all this. Even if your student days are long behind you, there is a good chance that this vast body of information and insight originated from or was influenced by your teachers. There's a good chance they worked harder than you know to offer you the best instruction and guidance—a lot of which they learned from their teachers. What will you pass along to your students, and how you will do it?

There are no absolute rules about teaching: every teacher has his or her own distinctive manner and unique approach. Sometimes we teach the way we were taught because we want to give the same wonderful experience to our students. Sometimes we teach the way we *wish* we had been taught, to make sure our students won't have to overcome similar problems resulting from poor training or callous treatment.

No matter our reasons, there are certain principles that are fundamental to our ability to connect with students, deliver information, and nurture growth in a manner that is meaningful and rewarding. These principles make it possible not just to believe in values such as integrity, sincerity, optimism, and passion, but to make them an integral part of our work, every day, at every lesson, with every student.

> **Personal Inventory:** Think about teachers you have had who you knew cared about you. How did you know? What kind of relationship was it—formal, friendly, warm, nurturing? What did that rapport mean to you, both personally and in your development as a musician?

1. Care about your students as individuals.

Remember that your students are people first, musicians after that. Take time to get to know them, and respect who they are: their intelligence, personalities, and preferences. Know something about their families, their outside interests, and ask about events that occurred during the week. Students need to know we care about them as people.

2. Infect your students with your passion for making music.

"I can't wait for you to learn this piece—it's one of my favorites!" or "Listen to how your instrument just sings when you play beautifully in tune!" Share what you love about making music with your students. Play even the simplest pieces expressively when you demonstrate. Lessons should first be about the beauty, the thrill, and the creativity of making music . . . and then how good technique helps to create those exquisite sounds. No matter how much of the lesson is focused on technique, the attention should invariably be directed back to the beautiful, expressive result.

3. Develop teacher–student relationships based on trust.

By demonstrating honest interest in your students, you begin to nurture relationships based on trust. We know firsthand that learning to be a musician is challenging. Students need to know that the lesson is a safe environment in which to make mistakes, voice concerns, or offer personal descriptions of the music they are making. It's almost impossible for students to be expressive if they are worried about being criticized or belittled for being wrong or thinking differently from their teacher. Other aspects of building trust are essential: that you will be honest with them about their development as musicians; that you are clear and open about expectations in the teacher–student relationship, and promise to uphold your commitments; and that you believe in the student's potential and value the relationship.

4. Teach the person in front of you.

Create a balance between student interests and teacher agenda. Stay aware of what students *want* to learn in addition to what they *need* to learn. Allow students to demonstrate what matters most to them—this will be revealed by what they practice the most. The student in front of you should inform your teaching, so allow what the student brings to the lesson to inspire positive momentum. Speak to the issues of the person in front of you, never in comparison to another student or other players. If comparisons are made, they should refer only to the student's best self, as in "Your tone was so much better the last time—try again."

5. Teach students to listen, to move, and to sing.

Musical expressivity first exists inside us and emerges when the voice and body are free and uninhibited. The issue is not whether musical expressivity can be learned, but how to access it in ways that are most natural and meaningful. Listening to music on the outside gives us an opportunity to respond physically and vocally. Natural movement and uninhibited singing away from an instrument frees expressive possibilities. Lessons should be a safe place to sing and move.

6. Validate the expressive musician in the student.

Most students don't decide to play an instrument only because they want to work on technique—they want to make music. Don't save music-making until students are "good enough." Teach them underlying concepts about musicianship, and then work with *their* vision for a piece, not just yours. Allow them ample opportunity to make personal connections with and create individual interpretations of the music.

Personal Inventory: Look back at some of the expressive explorations about making music in Chapter 1, *Musicianship*. What aspects of musical interpretation can be explored by beginners, even at the most rudimentary level? How can you involve students in performing beautiful music from the first lesson?

7. Give your students honest feedback.

Your students trust you to help them get better. Overlooking wrong notes, a bad tone, or miscounted rhythms—even saying "good" when you don't mean it—compromises the teacher–student relationship. In other words, if something is "a little" out of tune, it's out of tune, plain and simple. Correcting intonation doesn't mean you don't like the student—it means you care about whether or not they play and sing in tune. Give honest, objective, and specific feedback based on what you hear and see: "Your right arm is too high" . . . "The G-sharp was too low." Be sure that you criticize the problem and not the person: flaws are not character defects, only unrefined movements and sounds that can be made accurate through correction and practice.

8. Fix fundamental problems.

Comfort, ease, and freedom of the body with the instrument should be a high priority at all times. Do not overlook bad habits or foundational problems that will inhibit progress. Show the student why the current habit is causing problems, and if at all possible get the student to immediately experience how the new behavior will make things easier. Isolate, resolve, and repeat the new behavior many times during the lesson, and be sure the student understands the importance of daily reinforcement outside the lesson. Stay focused on the issue as long as necessary, repeating the routine as needed until the new habit is established.

9. Vary your teaching approach.

Gives students an opportunity to understand a concept from many perspectives, to enhance the learning experience and reinforce understanding.

Aural: Aural learning is most basic to musicians. Play or sing a phrase, and ask students to play the same phrase, comparing similarities and differences. Teach students to listen in a variety of ways for the purpose of analysis, imitation, and inspiration. (See Chapter 2, *Listening.*)

Visual: A visual approach gives a student the opportunity to see how his teacher creates a rich tone, to watch himself making a correction, or to observe how a string vibrates. Draw the shapes that movements create, and use visual images from nature, science, architecture, sculpture, painting, and engineering for visual representation of techniques, physics of sound, instrumental mechanics, compositional structure, and musical nuance.

Kinesthetic: Kinesthetic learning has to do with the experience of body position, weight, or movement. Kinesthetic experiences directly relate to fundamental positioning issues and a variety of skills, but can also be used to explore emotions and life experiences with gestures and physical responses that can be applied in music-making.

Verbal: A verbal approach enhances learning through talking, reading, or writing about a skill or concept. Eloquently chosen words can enhance performance when they are used to explore phrase structure, clarify musical intent, and deepen expressive meaning. Despite music's "wordless" reputation, language is an indispensable tool for music teaching, and therefore the struggle to find the best words that describe technical information, expressive ideas, and even the most elusive concepts is a worthy one.

10. Give students specific instructions for practicing.

Don't just say "Practice!" Clearly define your goals for students' work until the next time they see you. Make sure they know what to watch and listen for, how many times to repeat specific passages, what the tempo goals are, and how much to have memorized by the next lesson. Be wary of practice charts and goals that are based only on time spent. Approximate time frames can be helpful if they give students a sense of expected depth and detail of work, such as "If you practice the entire piece the way we've worked on this section today, it will probably take about an hour." But saying "Practice an hour a day" can make students more aware of the clock than their work. No one approaches homework this way ("An hour is up, so that means I'm finished writing this report!"); so they shouldn't practice this way, either.

11. Give students a chance to play.

Once you have given your students the necessary feedback to be sure they are fully set to play or sing, then let them. You will see and hear issues to address, but exercise self-control, jot notes if need be, and don't interrupt. Allowing students to get into a performance flow gives you the opportunity to see and understand much more about them and their developing abilities than if they are constantly being stopped for every problem. Even when portions of the lesson involve detailed technical work, balance this type of focus with opportunities to apply the new information in the musical context.

12. Define artistic standards.

One potential source of frustration for performers who teach is the gap between their high artistic standards and the raw behaviors of a beginner. Teachers need to first define excellence for themselves and then for their students. You have learned to play with a "beautiful tone" and "fine intonation," but can you define and describe the components of these attributes? (See Chapter 1, *Musicianship*.) If so, you can begin teaching to this standard from the first lesson: how to sit or stand, the position of the instrument, the shape of the hands, or the way to breathe.

Your focus on artistry from the beginning does not mean that students will be able to reproduce high standards immediately or every time they perform, but with persistence you can foster an artistic standard as a habit. If not, students will fill in the gap by learning something else. Remember, it is not the piece that makes a student an artist; it is the artistic approach to any piece that makes an artist. How would Rampal, Heifetz, Ma, Stoltzman, Primrose, Horowitz—or you—play "Hot Cross Buns"?

Consider This

If a student performs with a bad tone or seems to be working too hard to play the instrument, don't be critical until you've tried to play on their instrument. Your students' lack of experience already makes playing challenging; combine that with a badly set up instrument, and it's sometimes a wonder they can play at all. Check their current instrument to identify any repairs and adjustments that could make playing easier for them. Recommend a good instrument shop to have it set up as professionally as possible (while mindful of potential costs) and be on the lookout for sources of affordable, good-quality instruments for your students.

---

13. Foster the full potential of every student.

Teach with the maximum potential of every student as your goal. Make no assumption that a student "isn't talented" or "doesn't have what it takes." It is up to the teacher to find pathways that help each individual learn. Don't underestimate a student's potential to be better than "just okay." Work to make every student really good—even great! Any willing student can and will progress with the guidance of a thoughtful and skilled teacher. Provide the tools and environment for each to achieve his or her highest potential while creating a positive, meaningful, and enduring connection with music.

> Our chief want is someone who will inspire us to be what we know we could be.
> RALPH WALDO EMERSON

14. Approach each student with optimism.

When a student is challenged by a certain technique or concept, stay optimistic that with perseverance—yours and your student's—there will be success. When students struggle, don't allow them to practice bad habits or inefficiently repeat passages they simply can't execute. Instead, go back to the most fundamental aspect of the technique and then move forward. This allows you to reinforce all the things your students can do well, and when you find a weak link, that spot can be targeted for clarity of understanding or skill development in a simple direct way.

15. Do no harm.

Teachers are authority figures. They are in charge of what happens in the learning environment. Lessons and classes should be positive growing experiences. Students can be challenged, and they might struggle, but at all times you should be working alongside your students, helping them to move forward. If a student isn't learning, take an honest look at your teaching before you blame the student. If a student isn't practicing enough or demonstrates a lack of discipline in any other way, explain clearly what is necessary and expected. Calmly end the lesson if you think you might lose your temper, and if problems continue unresolved end the relationship.

> I have come to a frightening conclusion.
> I am the decisive element in the classroom.
> As a teacher I possess tremendous power to make a child's life miserable or joyous.
> I can be a tool of torture or an instrument of inspiration.
> I can humiliate or humor, hurt or heal.
> In all situations, it is my response that decides whether a crisis
> will be escalated or de-escalated, and a child humanized or de-humanized.
> It is my personal approach that creates the climate.
> It is my daily mood that makes the weather.
> HAIM GINOTT

16. Keep a balance between personal involvement and objectivity.

As you come to know and care for a student, it's important to keep a balance between being a friend and being a teacher: supporting them personally while staying focused on their growth as musicians. Remember, you are not being kind to students when you ignore problems—in fact it is kinder to demonstrate your belief in their ability to make changes for the better. Shifting your perspective can enhance your level of objectivity. Try to observe your student as if another teacher (perhaps your most revered teacher) was in the room. What would he or she see, hear, and correct? Or imagine that the student in front of you studies with someone else— what do you hear and see now? You could also imagine yourself performing like your student just did—what would you correct or change?

17. Cultivate thinking, independent musicians.

Students should not be utterly dependent on their teachers to make music. They should be challenged to listen, notice, solve problems, and think for themselves. Can your students read music? Can they count rhythms, understand key signatures, and name notes? Can they tune their own instruments and recognize good intonation when they hear it? Do they understand how to play in different styles, translate terminology into meaningful sounds, shape a phrase, and create a musical performance? (See Chapter 8, *Fostering Student Independence*, for a thorough discussion on this topic.) These are all essential skills every musician must acquire. It is your job as a teacher to make yourself obsolete.

18. Foster confidence in students.

"I know you can do this" speaks volumes to students. Follow encouraging remarks with the necessary information to make a goal become a reality. Don't hold back information because you assume it's too detailed or challenging—clearly explain a concept, engage their intellect, and give students the opportunity to demonstrate their understanding. Celebrate accomplishments and bolster confidence during the process of learning, at every lesson if possible: "You reached a new level in your playing today. Well Done!"

19. Keep students motivated.

A good teacher is sensitive to the student's level of interest, engagement, and forward momentum. All students, even those who seem self-motivated, need their teachers to provide ongoing sources of inspiration. Demonstrate beautiful sounds, share a favorite recording, or take students to concerts. If you sense a student is discouraged, consider changing repertoire or exploring a new musical style. Be sure they are involved in activities with their musical peers. Continually reconnect students with their initial desire to study and play music. Encourage them to offer their talents in personally meaningful situations: playing at school events, for family and friends, or for their religious community. The most powerful motivator for anyone, however, is the satisfaction of doing something well—and knowing it.

20. Take responsibility for your students' progress.

It is always the responsibility of the teacher that students leave a lesson playing or singing better than when they came in. We fail our students if we

- Let students play through a piece without providing feedback.
- Vaguely comment "Good," turn the page, and assign the next piece.
- Stop to fix a problem, fail to make a change for the better, and then abandon it without resolution.

Moving students from piece to piece is not evidence of progress if the student plays no better than before, and giving up on a potential correction can leave both teacher and student feeling hopeless. Divide a skill to be learned into simple incremental steps that move toward a more complex goal. Guide the student in a positive direction along those steps, helping him or her to be aware of each improvement along the way by immediately repeating and reinforcing it. Even if the ultimate goal is not reached in a single lesson, the student should come away with improved skills and ideas for effective practice to ensure continued progress.

21. Make short- and long-term plans that support a vision for each student.

Beginners won't be beginners forever; a modest middle school student can become a confident section leader in high school, and a good college student can become a fine professional. Make plans with and for your students, always teaching with a bigger picture in mind. When they know you are thinking that way, it tells them that you believe in their potential, and helps them create a positive vision of themselves as well.

22. Demonstrate your integrity.

You don't have to be perfect to earn respect as a musician, person, and teacher. Your students already look up to you. By modeling how you deal with mistakes and problems, you show your students how they can do the same. Explain how you improved or overcame a challenge, or how you mastered something that was once difficult for you. Students need to know that not everything comes easily to their teacher: teachers make mistakes, they practice, and they work hard to solve problems.

Your work ethic and perseverance can inspire students to approach their work with comparable integrity.

> Setting an example is not the main means of influencing another, it is the only means.
> ALBERT EINSTEIN

Ideas for Further Exploration

1. Thinking ahead twenty years from now, write a letter to yourself from the perspective of a student who studied with you. What important principles did you instill in your student? What significant memories, large or small, stand out in your student's mind as evidence that you cared for his or her well-being?

2. What motivated you to keep working to become a musician? What, if anything, did you find discouraging? What role, positive or negative, did your teacher play in these experiences, and how will your memories influence who you will be as a teacher?

3. Choose one skill from your master list of techniques and create four different approaches to teach this skill by utilizing the aural, visual, kinesthetic, and verbal learning styles as described in principle 9, "Varying Your Teaching Approach."

4. While the principles in this chapter are numbered, they are not necessarily ranked in order of importance. If you were to prioritize them, what order would you choose? Are there any missing principles that should be added to this list?

Recommended Reading

Duke, R. A., & Simmons, A. L. (2006). The Nature of Expertise: Narrative Descriptions of 19 Common Elements Observed in the Lessons of Three Renowned Artist-Teachers. *Bulletin of the Council for Research in Music Education* (170), 7–19.

Gladwell, M. (2000). *The Tipping Point: How Little Things Can Make a Big Difference.* New York: Back Bay Books.

Goleman, D. (2006). *Emotional Intelligence.* New York: Bantam Books.

Sand, B. L. (2000). *Teaching Genius: Dorothy Delay and the Making of a Musician.* Portland, Ore.: Amadeus Press.

Schnebly-Black, J., & Moore, S. F. (1997). *The Rhythm Inside: Connecting Body, Mind, and Spirit through Music.* Portland, Ore.: Rudra Press.

Suzuki, S. (1983). *Nurtured by Love: The Classic Approach to Talent Education.* Trans. W. Suzuki Smithtown, N.Y.: Exposition Press.

Suzuki, S. (1982). *Where Love Is Deep: The Writings of Shinichi Suzuki.* Trans. K. Selden. Van Nuys, Calif.: Summy-Birchard.

Thompson, W. F. (2009). *Music, Thought, and Feeling: Understanding the Psychology of Music.* New York: Oxford University Press.

Whitehead, A. N. (1957). *The Aims of Education and Other Essays.* New York: Free Press.

7　Sequencing

> **Personal Inventory:** Remembering that there is only limited time to convey information and build technique and musicianship, refer to the list of skills and experiences you compiled in the introduction and expanded in Chapter 3, *Technique*. Sort this list of skills and experiences into categories of beginner, intermediate, and advanced stages of study.

The Significance of Sequencing

A logical sequence of instruction and materials is central to efficiency and effectiveness. While it is important to develop a process to teach each essential technique, your ability to sequence those techniques in a logical developmental order will facilitate your students' ability to progress from the beginning stages to a high level of musicianship and skill. The plethora of literature that exists most certainly provides enough materials to teach. However, the subject of sequencing runs much deeper than the *what* part of teaching—it's the *when* part that can get really tricky.

Musicians with experience teaching students at all levels of development—beginners through artist-level players—probably have the greatest understanding of the importance of intelligent learning sequences. Having seen the results of both thoughtful and not-so-thoughtful instruction, they are aware of the direct correlation between fundamental skill and virtuosity, and they consider artistry as an ongoing guide to all choices concerning teaching and learning. Effective teachers have developed the ability to see an overlay of repertoire, skill development, and experiences that work together toward musical maturity and independence. These individuals discuss short- and long-term goals with their students, identifying the most efficient methods and the most valuable experiences that allow students to reach their full potential in a finite amount of time.

Students who work with this type of teacher most often experience a consistent sense of accomplishment. They are also like a gift to their next teacher: no remedial teaching, well-developed intonation and rhythmic sense, good tone, and excellent fundamental position. What could be better? And of course, the best-case scenario for the student is to repeat this experience with each subsequent teacher.

Unfortunately, not every student is so lucky as to have such guidance. Poorly taught skills and illogical leaps in repertoire or technique create students with underdeveloped proficiency and gaps in understanding. Later, with their next teacher, they will have to spend time backtracking and relearning in order to become competent musicians. Such a scenario can be frustrating and disheartening to students, and challenging for a teacher who has much to fix while trying to keep students encouraged and motivated.

Of course, no one deliberately teaches badly. Sometimes students are taught by approximation (for example, the rhythm is *almost* right, or the intonation is *pretty* close) because refining specifics just seems to take too much time. Some teachers overlook fundamental problems because they aren't sure how to correct them and take refuge in the hope that their students will eventually correct the problem. Often teachers simply recreate their own learning experience without considering ways to reorder and improve the approach and materials. Using repertoire in their cabinet as a grab bag of possibilities, they assign piece after piece and assume that after learning enough literature their students will be "good enough."

While a certain amount of insight into the teaching/learning process might emerge with time and experience, nothing will ever substitute for thoughtful sequential planning. Even if you were taught by a teacher who was skilled at arranging your development as a musician, it is important for you to understand the process now from a pedagogical perspective—why it worked and even how you can improve it.

> **Personal Inventory:** Reflect on your own learning experiences. Did neglect, inattention, or poor sequencing of a skill or concept affect your development? Are you aware of how thoughtful sequencing of a specific skill allowed you to develop that skill without problems? If you learned more than one instrument in your "instrumental family" (in particular, winds, keyboards, and percussion), when were these introduced, and how effective was the timing and process?

Sequencing Considerations for Early Levels of Instruction

> We begin with the hypothesis that any subject can be taught effectively in some intellectually honest form to any child at any stage of development.
>
> JEROME BRUNER

When a particular instrument has caught the eyes and ears of students—or their parents—they are often in an excited rush to start lessons. In some circumstances, however, it is impractical or unwise to start formal one-on-one instruction, for instance, with the six-year-old who is desperate to play French horn, or with the string bassist wannabe who just turned four. When you are approached about instrument lessons for a young person, especially one who has had no other experiences with music, point the family toward movement- and singing-oriented music classes for a year or two. Children's music classes, in particular those based on Dalcroze Eurhythmics, Kodaly, and Orff Schulwerk methodologies, are designed to nurture important music fundamentals. Such classes are considered by many to be an essential step *before* channeling students' musical enjoyment into the narrower and more disciplined study of an instrument.

FUNDAMENTAL POSITION

Once you have accepted a beginner, it is you who can set students on a positive trajectory of learning. Good habits will not develop automatically. Teachers need to be obsessed with their students' best technique and constantly direct their students' attention to the same. Retraining a desired approach to the instrument can take more time than learning it well at the beginning. As the revised adage expresses, "Practice does not make perfect—practice makes permanent."

One of the most fundamental skills you are responsible for is physical setup and positioning the instrument. As experienced musicians, the gestures we so naturally use to get into "performance position" are in fact a series of many steps combined into a seamless motion that transitions us from a relaxed conversation with a colleague to physical and mental readiness at the tap of a conductor's baton. Yet telling students to get into a singing or playing position will mean nothing until they have been taught a logical sequence of steps to create it.

> ### Consider This
> Young children in general have a relatively short attention span and have a more difficult time understanding logic and following directions. Using more imitation than explanation is advisable, and shorter, more frequent lessons are better than longer weekly ones.

With this in mind, it is important to be sure your instructions to beginners are well-sequenced and clear. Younger students are exceptionally vulnerable to less skillful teaching techniques, as they do not make inferences that may correct vague directives and connect disjointed pieces of information. Consider this scenario:

A young teacher faces a group of eight-year-old violinists and instructs them "Place the violin on your shoulder," only to find that nearly half of them place the violins on the wrong shoulder. "Oh, no, no, the left shoulder!" he says. Confusion ensues, and the students look around to see what the others are doing. Some who had been correct switch to the wrong side. "Okay, wait, stop, watch: this is what I meant." Now the teacher faces the same way as the children and, in a clear, deliberate way, grasps the violin in the left hand and lifts it to his left shoulder.

The teacher's first directive in this situation was based on presumption. What became very apparent is that many more steps and more explicit instructions were necessary in order to ensure student success. This is just a small example of a technique approached without thoughtful sequencing. While we all work to avoid teaching moments like this, any similar situation in your work should alert you to the complexity involved in your own habituated behaviors, and cause you to rethink your sequence of instruction.

> **Personal Inventory:** Refer to your notes from "Physical Components of Technical Stability" in Chapter 3, *Technique*. Choose one component that seems most fundamental to your performance area. In the third column of the table, make notes regarding the technical steps toward establishing this essential component, and then organize those ideas into a learning sequence. Continue this process with each of the physical components listed.

EAR TRAINING

Ear training is a vital part of complete musicianship. Singing and matching pitches, while they are essential skills for instrumentalists who must generate their own intonation, are vital to the musical development of *all* instrumentalists. Producing vocal and instrumental "sirens," identifying high and low pitches, comparing similar pitches (e.g., the higher of two notes in the upper register), matching voice to voice (teacher to student, student to teacher), voice to instrument, and instrument to instrument are all exercises that develop the essential ability to recognize and manipulate pitches. These exercises are easily turned into fun games for younger students and can be introduced at the earliest stages of learning.

Once students are ready to begin playing familiar melodies on their instruments, singing a melody—in tune—can lead them toward creating the same pitches on the instrument, so that the instrument can "sing in tune" as well. Improvisation can also be included as a part of the development of pitch and rhythm. For example, an improvisation exercise within the first weeks of study might involve simple question-and-answer games using clapping, tapping, the voice, or the instrument to allow a student the opportunity to experiment with "cause and effect" in music.

DEVELOPING MUSICALITY FROM THE BEGINNING

Expressive musicianship is fundamental to all students' development and should not be delayed until technique is in place. Technique exists so that it is possible to make music—therefore it is important to remember that making music is the reason for technique, and not the reverse. This is an inseparable partnership. Many of the ideas below can be explored on an instrument during the first lessons, weeks before students play their first pieces.

- Dynamics and tone qualities can be explored with simple concepts: size (large, medium, and small), distance (far away or close), weight (heavy or light), touch (rough or smooth, soft or hard), emotions, and characters. All can be expressed through both the voice and the instrument.
- Articulations are easily accessed through verbal expression: vowel and consonant sounds, or sounds associated with moods, characters, or movement, such as rocking or jumping.
- Stylistic differences can be addressed by simply asking students what they think the piece "sounds like": a march, a dance, a song, and so on. Gestures and movements appropriate to each style can be used to "translate" the style into an approach to the piece.

- Phrasing and timings can be compared to hills, roller coasters, winding roads, or waves on a beach and explored through familiar children's playthings like balls, swings, or bikes. Reading out loud and finishing one sentence before the next begins captures the essence of completing a phrase.
- Simple forms such as ABA and rondo can be created with visuals, stories, or improvised sounds; the concept can then be transferred to the music.

Of course, creating these sounds will require technical guidance and development, but when music-making is linked to life, the student now has a reason to acquire the necessary skills. Teaching musical playing by demonstrating two possibilities—one musical and the other not—is one way to teach the importance of expression, but teachers should be careful not to imply that there is one right way and one wrong way to create musical expression. Presenting a variety of options and meaningful choices is an honest approach to fostering real musicianship at the foundational level. As students progress, musicianship becomes more sophisticated. Teach them about harmony and historical performance practice while building on their more mature and nuanced understanding of the world around them.

> **Personal Inventory:** Choose one aspect of musicianship, such as phrasing or dynamics, from Chapter 1, *Musicianship*. Create a teaching sequence consisting of at least five steps designed to cultivate that aspect from fundamental expression to artistic sophistication, taking into account a student's developing technique and emotional maturity.

ARTISTIC STANDARDS FROM THE BEGINNING

The formative stage of development is the best time to consider the highest levels of artistic, technical, and musical accomplishment possible. It seems paradoxical to think about the end at the beginning, but that is exactly how skilled teachers design their sequences of study. The fundamental position of any student should allow consistent growth in every aspect of playing the instrument. For example, an embouchure should be formed so that the student can steadily progress toward a consistent, professional tone, advanced technique, and extended range. A beginning flute student should feel balanced on both feet and feel freedom of movement that can accommodate the facility needed for any virtuosic concerto. Or as you watch a young violinist play *Twinkle, Twinkle Little Star* ask yourself "Will that bow hand be able to play spiccato?" and "Will that left hand be able to shift and vibrate?" If the answer is no, the time to address the problem is now. You won't be directly teaching advanced technique during this stage of study, but you will be creating the foundation on which all advanced technique is built. So when you are teaching *Hot Cross Buns*, you are in essence teaching the Tchaikovsky Concerto—or at the very least, teaching a preview of what is about to unfold.

At the beginning stages of study and all along the way, assign music that allows the student to demonstrate the highest standard of mastery for his or her level of development. Keep the big concepts in full view: excellent tone, correct intonation, sense of pulse and rhythmic understanding, and aural awareness. This will not be possible if you ask students to play music that is too difficult or if you give them too much to learn. You can consistently uphold your artistic standards by choosing music that the student can play well.

MUSICAL LITERACY

Once beginning students establish the basics, musical literacy is the next stepping-stone on the path toward the intermediate stage of development. All teachers have different criteria for when music reading is introduced. Be aware, however, that the beginning stage of playing any instrument requires a tremendous amount of attention to basic posture and relaxation. Don't divide your students' attention between playing the instrument and deciphering notation until you see them demonstrate a relaxed and balanced approach to the instrument.

Note reading can be compared to language learning: the word is used and understood before you see what it looks like on the page. Students can learn to sing, clap, and play notes before you show them how they look. Students can play simple folk tunes by ear, and later discover how the music they already know looks on the page. In this way, the expression of the symbol has been previously experienced by the student.

Pedagogue Winifred Crock describes three skill levels involved in reading music. The first is *note and symbol recognition*, where a student recognizes notes and rhythms much as a beginning reader sounds out simple words. C-A-T spells CAT. This is a good time to begin developing an awareness for melodic contour, as students learn that notes that look higher on the page will also sound higher, and vice versa, whether by skips or steps.

The second skill level is *note translation*, where a student can read pitch and rhythm independently of one another at a slow or inconsistent tempo. Because notation gives us two kinds of information, pitch and rhythm, students may not be able to decipher both at the same time. This is an ideal time to combine the understanding of melodic contour with students' inner listening skills. Young students can exercise the ability to use melodic contour as a visual cue by identifying "mystery songs." These are familiar pieces that are notated, but with the title removed. *Old MacDonald* or *Frere Jacques* will be identified by most students, and if they can do so without the use of an instrument, you will know they are using their inner listening. Another aural exercise involves supplying the first note of a familiar tune, then directing the student to use his ear to find his way to the end of the piece by the next lesson, at which time the teacher or student can notate the tune. Tunes such as *Happy Birthday* or *Jingle Bells* will surely be requested by family and friends at some point, so this is one way to make them part of your students' repertoire while developing an important skill.

Ultimately, students will be able to sight-read notes and rhythms while observing dynamics, articulations, instrument-specific notations like pedalings or bowings, and interpreting terminology with relative fluency. Once able to sight-read, students can continue to cultivate their "inner listening" as a way of monitoring their own accuracy. Just like reading language, the final stage of music reading—speed and fluency—will improve consistently with practice.

Students (and occasionally parents) need to be reminded that sight-reading skills and technique skills are often at very different levels. Students may be successfully navigating intermediate student concerti but sight-reading at a beginner level. At times even the most advanced players rely on a note translation approach to decipher complex music. However, with repeated music reading experience, the gap between what musicians can sight-read and their level of technique narrows.

> **Consider This**
> Sight-reading practice as part of group lessons can make beginning readers feel safe: notes lost by some will be saved by others. Standard class method books, early-level graded anthologies, and folksong collections work well for group sight-reading experiences. You can create your own sight-reading notebooks arranged by key or meter or centered on a specific rhythm pattern or technique.

SEQUENCING CONCEPTS AND INFORMATION

Part of sequenced instruction involves recognizing the progressive nature of the things that students need to understand, not just do, as they develop, such as music theory, historical information, acoustics, and performance practice.

For example, in the beginning stages of understanding how a stringed instrument works you might explain the pitch difference between the highest and lowest strings using thicker and thinner rubber bands held at different tensions. Harmonics can be introduced by simply, saying "Look what your string will do if you touch it here," and asking if they know why that happens. Students can then learn about the overtone series and other harmonic divisions. Sympathetic vibrations—why they exist, what "sympathy" has to do with strings, and how to use them for tuning—can follow.

Awareness of and familiarity with composers and their stylistic periods is another example of important information that can be sequenced according to student's maturity. No matter how young or old, the only way students learn the significance of this information is by the teacher making a point of referencing the composer and the era when introducing each new piece. With younger students, talk about how people lived then, the kind of music they wrote and listened to, and offer some memorable pieces of information about the specific composer and how that relates to the piece. You can continue to build on that familiarity by adding more details each time the student learns additional works by the same composer. Anecdotal information can be developed into a more sophisticated understanding of compositional trends and personal influences, culminating in interpretive skill as the student matures. In sequencing other components, the same logic applies: dynamic variations can be developed as loud and soft in echo passages, after which more subtle variations in dynamics, crescendos, and more sophisticated markings like *morendo* can be explored.

COUNTERINTUITIVE SEQUENCING

Many sequences we have addressed so far are approached with a slow-to-fast, small-to-large, or simple-to-complex logic, but some of the best teaching defies that logic. Is it always smart to start from a small movement and gradually make it larger, or start with a slow gesture and make it faster? What many of us experienced as "difficult" or "advanced" skills were so because they were labeled that way. Such so-called advanced skills can be introduced as part of early learning experiences as long as they are not harmful to fundamental position or your students' physical health. Certain skills do not require sequential development—they can be introduced as simply part of what we do: another technique on the instrument. For example, there may be harmless and fun ways to extend range immediately: beginning pianists can move their hands up and down the range of the keyboard, finding a given note in all the octaves; young cellists can learn *Twinkle, Twinkle Little Star* in thumb position at the same time they learn it in first position; a saxophone teacher can capitalize on a student's tendency to overblow in the lower register by introducing the use of overblowing to achieve the pitches in the altissimo register.

Consider This

As you read the list of typical learning sequences below, consider a different approach that might work on your instrument, perhaps even creating a higher level of experience without causing harm to a student's development.

- Small intervals become large and move from steps to skips to leaps.

A different approach might be _____

- Naturally slower movements become faster, and naturally faster movements become more controlled.

A different approach might be _____

- Sound production moves from tone awareness toward style, expressive quality, and differences in articulation.

A different approach might be _____

Continue to question conventional approaches, and explore alternative, effective strategies that could allow students to experience components of advanced skills at an earlier stage in their development.

Repertoire, Etudes, Exercises, and Excerpts

Personal Inventory: Write down as many pieces and studies as you remember playing in the order that you learned them. Does the sequence seem logical? Do you know why certain pieces were assigned? Are there thin spots, where you may have skipped steps or have very few pieces or etudes for a particular stage of development? These might indicate an underdeveloped area in your own training, and you will want to find additional repertoire at that level to enhance your students' technical and musical needs.

CHOOSING AND SORTING REPERTOIRE

A thoughtful sequence of repertoire creates a musical context in which technique and musicianship can be developed. A teacher's core repertoire usually consists of standard literature for the instrument: pieces that regularly appear in instrument-specific, graded syllabi and anthologies. In addition, you will want to become familiar with supplementary literature that replicates and reinforces the skills needed at each stage of development. These pieces allow students more opportunities to practice parallel technique and musical skills in a different context, and can be assigned concurrently or consecutively. Additionally, look for miniature pieces (one or two pages in length) that are easily memorized and appropriate as encore pieces, recitals, or informal family gatherings.

Consider your list of music again, paying attention to the quality of the literature. Some of these may be pieces you really love; others you might hope to never hear again in your life. If you really don't like certain pieces, you won't have the energy to teach them well, and your student isn't likely to enjoy them either. Pruning your repertoire list will likely make it necessary to find new pieces. Music shops, catalogues, and the internet can be great resources for new repertoire; however, you will want to avoid spending money on music that you haven't heard and may ultimately never use. Below are some effective and less costly ways to identify suitable repertoire for your students.

- Discuss repertoire choices with teaching colleagues.
- Judge solo and ensemble contests as a way to gain insight into what repertoire other teachers are assigning at your students' levels.
- Check summer festival, college, and conservatory audition requirement lists for important and often-requested pieces you might have missed.

Learn the music well yourself before you try to teach the pieces to your students. Be on the lookout for hidden challenges, and consider how you will approach the more difficult aspects of these works. The last thing you want to do is start a piece with a student only to realize that the piece is really too difficult.

TOO EASY OR TOO DIFFICULT?

Choosing appropriate repertoire for your students is an important responsibility. Intelligent, logical, and thoughtful choices will help ensure student success. Assuming your priority is to have high artistic standards as a student progresses, starting a new piece that introduces one or two skills or concepts is usually plenty. You never want to overload a student with four or five new techniques to acquire before a piece can be mastered. Better that he or she learn the piece quickly than spend months trying to bring it to performance level, growing tired of it before it's polished. The teacher should be able to say "This is the perfect piece for Mary right now because . . ." rather than "I wonder if Mary can manage this piece?"

When a student becomes disinterested in a piece, it is usually unhelpful to keep that student on it for weeks or months until the technique is fully developed. Make a decision about what the student can do to bring the piece to completion. You might even want to let go of an unresolved technical problem for the time being, choose a new piece that focuses on a different area of technique, and come back to the unresolved aspect at a more opportune time. No matter what you choose, a new piece will likely be a breath of fresh air and revive the student's motivation.

You might also need to consider that "music to learn" and "music to perform" might fall into two different categories. If you have a student who has memory lapses or issues with performance anxiety, a melodic work would be appropriate for a recital, whereas a more contemporary, unaccompanied, multimeter work might be excellent for lesson material only.

Asking students "What do you want to play next?" rarely contributes to a logical sequence of skill development. As the teacher, only you can see the bigger picture. Your familiarity with

> ### Consider This
> If you have purposefully chosen a piece for a student as a way to target a particular technique and the student complains "This piece is too easy," you will need to point out that any piece played beautifully is not too easy and that the components of excellent musicianship should be apparent in every performance. Great artists have been known to follow major concertos with an encore of a simple melody. After hearing an artistic performance of a melody like *Londonderry Air* or a hymn tune like *Shall We Gather at the River*, you never hear anyone say "Why did Perlman or Galway play that 'easy' piece?"

both the repertoire and your student's current level of development allows you to choose the piece that is the perfect fit. Very young students currently playing folk tunes might hear an exciting performance of a major concerto and appear at the next lesson wanting to play the piece. In a case like this, assigning the piece would be inappropriate, but since you don't want to dampen the student's enthusiasm, you might want to write out one of the main themes in solo or duet form and then show them the real piece of music. Ultimately, students will independently choose repertoire that fits their technical level, but until they are able to objectively assess their own development (which could be a very long time) you need to make those choices for them.

INTELLIGENT USE OF ETUDES AND SCALE BOOKS

Throughout the course of your experience as both a student and a teacher, you have no doubt accumulated many different etude and scale study books. Just like repertoire, it's easy to assign only the etudes you learned yourself. That might be fine if your teacher had a logical, intelligent sequence for etude study. However, even the most well-organized sequence of etudes deserves examination from a different perspective—to reveal its pedagogical and (ideally) musical value in the bigger picture of your students' development.

Some etudes are universally considered standards for particular instruments, for example Kreutzer 40 Studies for the violin or Klose for the clarinet. These are often assigned cover-to-cover for overall technical development. Such an approach can be used as part of your "curriculum," or you can assign selected etudes or technical studies for particular areas of development, either to address a weakness in a student's technique or to preview and develop a skill needed for an upcoming piece. As with any repertoire, be sure to learn any unfamiliar etudes yourself before deciding how they will enhance your students' overall development, and assign them in a thoughtful sequential order.

Decide whether it is better for the student to invest their time learning an entire etude or mastering a particular skill in specific sections. For example, a three- or four-page etude might have been written to develop stamina or the ability to maintain stability through a variety of challenging keys. If this is an important goal for your student, then it might warrant assigning the entire etude. If the skill is well addressed in the first four lines, and the rest of the etude consists of repeated material, then perhaps skim the cream off the top and move on. However, as a third consideration, repertoire itself can frequently be offered in lieu of etudes. Students can master skills through pieces that feature a desired technique. Difficult passages can also be excerpted from concertos and other virtuosic repertoire, converted into an etude, and learned by the student in advance of undertaking the entire work. Either way, technique and repertoire essentially become one in the same, disencumbering the learning process while simplifying sequencing issues. (See Chapter 9, *Comprehensive Teaching*, for more about etudes.)

Sequencing Considerations for Different Lengths of Study
EXTENDED STUDY

If you are fortunate enough to nurture your own student right from the start, you have the satisfaction of shared momentum as you proceed through the process of learning together. In cases like this, you might be lucky enough to work with a student for ten years or more, developing not only his or her skill on an instrument, but attitude toward learning, music-making, competition, even other people. In a sense you become like a surrogate parent and play an important role in preparing the student for the next stage of life, one that hopefully includes continued music-making.

This experience is especially comfortable and gratifying for teachers who have established a core repertoire and developed a sequence for teaching technique that produces consistent, positive results.

THE TRANSFER STUDENT

Many students will come to us from another teacher. Students who have had previous experience with the instrument will have strengths that should be validated as well as challenges that need to be addressed. It is important to assess what they can do, especially in regard to fundamental technique, and what skills are yet to be developed. Rather than asking for a difficult piece of repertoire at the initial lesson, request long tones, scales, or a piece that allows the student to relax and perform with his or her most beautiful sound. Performance of a simple folk tune or familiar melody will supply enough information to get you started and should help reveal the hierarchy of skills that need attention. It is very important in the initial stages of your relationship with the student to acknowledge his or her strengths as a musician and demonstrate a sincere interest in continued musical growth.

REMEDIAL TEACHING

Some students will come to you with major technical issues that must be corrected in order for them to be able to move forward. Some are aware they have a problem; others are not. Students in the first group are often more ready to face the necessary changes; those in the second group can be more challenging to teach because the way they play feels familiar and seems okay to them. Invariably, however, the best approach is to create a situation where students can immediately see, hear, or feel how a new position or behavior will improve their singing or playing.

When making a change seems unnecessary to a student, or the new behavior feels too foreign, students will sometimes react defensively and resist change. While it can be difficult for teachers to recall their own experiences making significant changes to their technique, remember that students can easily be overwhelmed with the corrections that are needed, since establishing a new habit takes so much more effort than chronically using the old one. Keep the remediation process as simple as possible, starting with the most basic aspects of the technique and moving forward incrementally, in the same manner as teaching that skill from the beginning. Give the student clear, specific instructions for practice that directly address the correction, then assign an exercise or limited portion of a piece or etude that employs the new behavior and demonstrates its value.

At least initially, the student is operating from a limited viewpoint, and is often only aware of what he cannot yet do. As the teacher, however, you have the advantage of seeing the big picture. Be sure to share what you can see with your student: where he is now, how long the adjustment might take, and what the future holds. Explain that, while you understand the challenges, his ongoing daily efforts will start to produce gratifying results within days or weeks; and that while this modification is a necessary obsession now, there is a time in the near future that it will simply be a part of his new level of technical excellence. Increase motivation by connecting the desired new habit to something the student himself covets (even if you see rewards of more lasting value) such as learning more sophisticated repertoire, performing with a better ensemble, or improving chair test results. Be sure your student understands that the change he is making is truly for his benefit, not simply to please you—although you will indeed be very pleased when he reaps those benefits and more.

> ### Consider This
> Resistance to change is sometimes exacerbated when a new behavior feels *wrong*, even if it is simply different. A good way to demonstrate this distinction is to have students fold their hands, intertwining the fingers. Have them notice whether the right or left thumb sits on top. Whichever way the hands came together, next have your students unfurl their fingers and refold them with the other thumb on top and fingers intertwined in the reverse order. The unexpected "wrong" feeling caused by this simple position change can deflate some of the initial resistance and bring you and your students to a closer understanding about change.

If the repertoire a student has been playing is out of sync with his or her skills and understanding, this can pose another problem. For example, a student who comes to you playing a Mozart concerto (albeit badly) would be embarrassed and discouraged if asked to practice *Go Tell Aunt Rhody* for her next lesson, even if from your vantage point that seems a more appropriate repertoire choice. If a much easier piece is appropriate for a student, you can of course assign one, but you might want to avoid labeling the music as "easy" or using discouraging phrases like "We need to go back." Remember that fundamental posture and technique can be developed with scales and basic technical exercises, and that more challenging music can also be made "simpler" by slowing down the speed or breaking the challenges into reasonable incremental skills. (See upcoming section, "Out-of-Sequence Sequencing".)

Even though it can be tempting to let a new student continue with his or her current piece, it is almost always easier to establish new routines and new behaviors with new music. While poor habits are not specific to one piece, old habits tend to be integrated and associated with a piece itself. Rather than continuing with the same music, have an arsenal of repertoire at each level, and be ready to assign a different but appropriate piece that will give the student a fresh start with his or her new and improved techniques.

TEMPORARY TEACHING SITUATIONS

Sometimes students appear in front of us for a very brief amount of time. Perhaps they come for a week to take some lessons while their teacher is away, or they take five or six lessons with us during a summer festival or music camp. In these short-term situations, you want the student to leave with information that is valuable in the long-term.

Whenever possible, a conversation with the primary teacher can be extremely helpful before the lessons begin. Inquire about what goals the teacher has for his or her students and adhere to those goals to the best of your ability: to focus on a particular technique, to learn particular etudes or scales, or to keep preparation on a piece moving forward. Since you won't fully know these students' needs until their first lesson, be ready with a few possibilities, including warm-ups and other technique-building routines and a variety of your favorite short pieces. After the first lesson, you'll be able to plan a sequence of study that is suited for the length of time you'll have with each student.

If you see the need to change something about a student's technique, be aware that your suggestion may be at cross-purposes with the home teacher. Ask a simple question like "Has your teacher ever asked you to stand up taller?" (". . . breathe more deeply?" ". . . fix your bow hand?"). If the answer is yes, offering your own set of solutions might be just the intervention needed to fix the problem. If the answer is no, your input might not be so welcome, and you'll have to decide whether it might be better to find another focus, such as introducing a series of technical studies, or selecting a short piece that is feasible to learn in a short amount of time. (Additional information on teaching at music camps is in Chapter 12, *More Teaching Situations*.)

Keep in mind that not only have these students come from another teacher, they are returning to that teacher. No matter what you think about the instruction they have been receiving and the technique or approach being used, never criticize the home teacher in front of the student. Focus directly on making a positive impact on the student with the time that you have.

SEQUENCING FOR IMMEDIATE SKILL DEVELOPMENT

"Did you notice that the leading tone was flat each time?" "Yes," the student answers. "Be sure to practice that," the teacher says, and turns the page.

Consider This

Never assume that students are fully aware of a problem just because they answer yes to a question that already gives them the answer. Students almost always answer yes because they want to be right and please their teachers. Better questions are ones that get the student to think and observe independently, like "What did you notice?" (More ideas on nurturing independence are in Chapter 8, *Fostering Student Independence*.)

In the scenario above, the issue that prompted the teacher's comment is addressed but never remedied: the cause of the problem is not made clear (was it physical, aural, or something else?) and any instruction toward a permanent solution was absent. So has the problem been corrected? Not likely. Let's consider a more effective approach to such a problem:

"Did you hear an intonation problem in the last few measures?" the teacher asks. "Yes," the student answers. "Which note was out of tune?" the teacher asks. "I don't know." The teacher then directs the student to play it again and listen more carefully. After this second attempt the teacher asks, "Did you hear the problem that time?" "I'm not sure." At this point the teacher plays the passage with the desired intonation, and asks, "What is the difference between the way I played the passage and the way you played the passage?" "Your F-sharp sounds higher than mine." Now the teacher and student consider why the higher F-sharp sounds more appropriate. The student now hears the difference and plays the section five more times with the improved intonation. "Be sure to practice that," the teacher says.

Although a younger student might need a more specific assignment, the words "be sure to practice that" in this scenario are more meaningful than in the first. The second lesson segment takes longer, of course, but real learning has taken place: now the student understands the concept, has made progress in the lesson, and has been shown a way to continue practicing. If a technical or musical issue arises at a lesson that causes you to stop the student, it is probably a big enough issue to warrant immediate and focused attention. After all, it is the teacher's job to help students develop skill, not just point out problems without giving solutions.

Let's consider another scenario:

A student has problems with a sixteenth-note passage, missing notes and unable to maintain tempo while struggling from one end to the other. The teacher says, "Try again," and the student does, with the same results. Now the teacher says, "Try again, but keep the tempo steady," and raps the pencil on the music stand as the student plays. Now the passage sounds even worse. "Try a little slower." Tap . . . tap . . . stumble . . . stumble. Now both teacher and student are frustrated. "Didn't you practice this?" The teacher is annoyed, the student feels bad, and the rest of us have knots in our stomachs just envisioning this.

> **Personal Inventory:** Stop reading for a moment now and consider what went wrong in this dead-end lesson, and how it could have been handled differently to make it a positive learning experience.

All of your "wiser teacher" solutions probably have to do with making the directions specific as well as limiting or modify the goal. The teacher in the scenario should have realized that a *slower* tempo, not a *stricter* one, would have made it possible for the student to play more of the notes. Or if the teacher's priority was truly even notes, asking the student to play fewer notes would likely have yielded far more rhythmic accuracy. The teacher did eventually decrease tempo, but too little and too late. At the point where the story ended, the student's increasing mistakes and the teacher's escalating agitation left little hope that this lesson could be redeemed.

Should the student have practiced more? Probably, but that isn't the point. An important teaching moment was lost at this lesson. Not only did the teacher's insistence on repeating the poorly prepared passage reinforce the unwanted behavior, but the too-gradual reduction of parameters led to more mistakes and contributed to decreasing momentum, frustration, and discouragement. A far more productive approach is to reduce a requirement to a single fundamental, such as correct notes or steady rhythm. Even if that immediate reduction feels like a big step backwards at first, the student now has an opportunity to fix the fundamental problem, giving the teacher a reason to be positive again. Once the correction is repeated, reinforced, and encouraged, more notes or a faster tempo can follow. This approach not only allows the lesson to have forward momentum, it reinforces the desired skills, gives the student a tangible sense of progress, and teaches an important lesson about effective practicing.

Out-of-Sequence Sequencing

A young cellist needs to learn an etude that is technically a little out of reach. He can play it in tune when he plays slowly and carefully, but as soon as he tries to play it up to the requested audition tempo the intonation goes out the window. The teacher has to choose which is more important, his playing the piece at the "required" tempo or his learning to play in tune.

In a best-case scenario, the studio teacher always has the opportunity to sequence literature, technical exercises, and etudes for students. However, there are situations in which you are expected to teach music that is currently too difficult for a student.

For example, a less advanced student might be required by the school band director to participate in highly competitive regional or state auditions, or a school or youth orchestra conductor might chose overly ambitious music for the next concert. While the difficulty level of the music might be entirely appropriate for a few advanced students, many more students will find it overwhelming.

This kind of situation can be uncomfortable for both teachers and students. No teacher wants to force students to overextend their range, facility, or stamina, causing posture or tension problems that are not easily repaired; nor does a teacher want to see any student set up for a potentially bad experience. So what do you do when students *must* learn excerpts or pieces that are too difficult for them right now?

Wise teachers will never push their students past their physical or psychological breaking point for the sake of an audition or a grade. The teacher is realistic enough to know that the student is not capable of mastering the music in the limited amount of preparation time, but instead of being consumed with whether a student will "measure up" to the highest standards, the teacher considers how the student could benefit from such a challenge. What aspects of learning parts of the music will help this student become a better musician? Working from this perspective, there is a much greater chance for growth and success.

With the priorities in order, students can, in spite of the odds, rise to the challenge and perform quite well. The only chance for this to happen, however, is for the teacher to show students how to break the burden down into small, attainable goals, a scenario similar to the one described in the previous section. Another possibility is to count the number of lines of music in the piece, and ask the student if he or she could learn a line a day. If there are ten lines of music, then the piece could be learned in ten days. If a line is too much, try a measure or two a day, and start the process right then and there at the lesson. While a bit simplistic, this approach gives the student a more finite sense of what is possible, rather than simply feeling overwhelmed by the undertaking as a whole.

Teach your students all the best preparation techniques that you know, starting with the practicing basics and ultimately working toward performance preparations. Be willing to share stories about yourself: challenges

> **Consider This**
> It's easy for students to lose their sense of their best playing when attempting to decipher overly difficult music. When the preparation of the challenging piece seems all-consuming, students benefit from the stability of practicing, reviewing, and performing pieces that are within their comfort levels. Suggest that they "borrow" their best tone or feeling of comfort and ease while playing portions of the more difficult music.

you have had, and your best strategies for overcoming the odds, even times that you didn't succeed. Students are relieved and even encouraged to hear that even their teachers were students, and not always able to play everything perfectly from the start.

The positives that emerge from this situation will come from the teacher who has the ability to keep things in perspective. Help students focus on the parts they can play well, and be enthusiastic about their hard work and how they have improved. The student always matters more than the music or the external requirements. If the teacher says, "It's far more important that you've worked very hard on this than whether you win or lose," the student will have a much more balanced and realistic perception of how this experience fits into his or her overall development as a musician.

Thoughtful sequencing in all aspects of teaching is vital to the success of our students. However, we do have to recognize that most students learn rather unevenly, and all exhibit a variety of strengths and deficiencies. There will never be "one place" along an idealistic timeline that can specifically pinpoint a student's technical and musical development. Nor should the students in your studio be compared as "ahead" or "behind" each other—they are where they are. Our job is to determine the appropriate sequence of learning that allows each individual student to become a more skilled and self-reliant musician.

Ideas for Further Exploration

1. List three standard pieces that are traditionally assigned to develop or showcase a specific aspect of technique on your instrument, for example extended range, speed and agility, endurance and control, or a technique that is unique to your instrument. For each piece, list the following: (1) the technique(s) used pervasively, (2) what repertoire would be appropriate prerequisites, (3) what piece you might assign after the student masters this piece, and (4) three to five pieces that demand the same requisite skills that could serve as an alternate to this piece.

2. Identify a technique that was sequentially developed in the formative years of your training, for example, vibrato. Write down as many steps in the process of learning the skill as you can remember. If you worked on this skill with different teachers, do you think one had a better approach than another, or were they simply different? Which aspects of this training have you embraced, enhanced, or changed in your own teaching?

3. List the first ten directions that will result in playing position on your instrument. Be as precise as possible in your directives. Find an individual who has

never held your instrument before. Letting that person use your instrument, teach your "student" by reading your setup instructions aloud, making note of any misunderstandings and need for clarification.

4. Identify a difficult passage from a major work. Design a learning sequence (task analysis) that will allow acquisition of the passage. In other words, state exactly how you will teach this passage: notes first without rhythm, rhythm first on a single pitch, perform as written at a slower tempo, and so on. Notate the "etude" based on the passage and/or provide a written step-by-step sequence of instructions. Maximize the value of learning the passage by designing a technique drill that will transfer to other pieces. Specify the technique(s) that can be acquired, metronome gradations, and an approximate level of study during which the "etude" would be introduced. Demonstrate your sequence of instruction to a colleague.

Recommended Reading

Bruner, J. (1960). *The Process of Education*. Cambridge, Mass: Harvard University Press.

Duke, R. A. (2005). *Intelligent Music Teaching: Essays on the Core Principles of Effective Instruction*. Austin, Tex: Learning and Behavior Resources.

8 Fostering Student Independence

GREAT PROGRESS WAS made at the last lesson, and you are really looking forward to hearing your student this week to continue building on that momentum. You can't believe your eyes and ears when he plays for you as if that last lesson never happened. "Did you practice?" you ask. "Yes, every day," he replies, and by the earnest response you have to believe it. If it's really true that this student practiced every day, you wonder, what on earth is the problem? How is it possible that nothing improved between lessons?

The answer could be complex, but it's probably not. Lessons go well because the teacher directs every move the student makes and masterminds solutions to every problem. Because this is the teaching path of least resistance, students often become entirely dependent on their teachers to work productively. Progress away from the lesson setting won't happen if students didn't notice what the teacher noticed, or if they don't know why the teacher made a correction. Even if students can remember how to recreate a correction, they'll still be at a loss if they can't remember what the newly improved way is supposed to sound like, feel like, or look like.

On a practical level, students need their teachers to give them information and guidance to learn to play well. However, teachers can't simply supply their students with all the answers and expect that they'll take care of the rest. The key to nurturing independence is to use the lesson time not just to offer information, but to show the student why the information is important and how to use it effectively.

In other words, the "do this" part of teaching is only the first step. To be certain that students are aware of how an improvement is made, a teacher can create approaches to teaching that fully engage the student. Here are some examples:

- Demonstrate first, pointing out and describing what you're doing, hearing, feeling, and seeing—or have the student describe what they hear and see. Prompt with questions like "Do you think I'm tight or relaxed?" You can verify or adjust the answers accordingly.
- Ask your student to copy your sound or movement and describe what he sees, hears, and feels as he imitates. Give feedback and help him make adjustments.
- Continue the process until he has arrived at the desired position, sound, or movement. Be sure this is a "big deal" moment—lots of praise and excitement—followed by focused attention and repetitions.
- Have your student explain what he did in his own words, and how he'll be able to rediscover the desired result again during practice.
- Turn the tables by acting as a student with a similar problem and have your student "teach" you.

This kind of teaching routine greatly increases students' awareness of their technique: not just fixing a problem but knowing what they will see, feel, and hear when it's working. It's still not a guarantee that such an approach will always bring clarity to their independent practice, but certainly the possibility is greatly increased from the "Do-it-this-way" approach.

The "Path of Least Resistance" Problem

If this kind of teaching is the best way to increase awareness and get students thinking for themselves, then why don't teachers naturally gravitate to it? Let's look at the typical reasons:

- *It takes so much time.* The "do this" approach can lead to a quick fix which initially seems more efficient. However, if you consider the number of hours of heedless practicing that would probably follow, the ten minutes it might take to raise awareness and reinforce understanding is time well spent.

- *It's too easy to tell them what to do because we know and they don't.* When a multilayered answer to "Why didn't that sound good?" is painfully obvious to us, watching our students struggle to identify just one reason sometimes takes more patience than we think we have.
- *Students are often resistant to making observations.* "I don't know" is an easy way to get out of responding when teachers jump in with the answer immediately. Students might also be afraid they'll be "wrong" or believe that being a good student means being quiet and doing what the teacher says.
- *It's too easy to assume our students understand more than they do.* After all, when we say "Do you understand?" or "Does that make sense?" students usually say yes. Yet ask them to explain a concept or technique back to us and, more often than not, the reality is an entirely different matter.

So the answer to all these problems is this: it is never a waste of time to ask students to observe themselves, critique themselves, and demonstrate understanding of technique, musical concepts, and effective practice. Teachers are wise to ask more questions, and not rush in when their students struggle to answer. Let's look at some fundamental areas in which student independence is essential to our students' development.

> ### Consider This
>
> Students who care about improving their skills and musicianship will eventually assimilate some critiquing and practicing skills, but many years often go by before this happens. Compare this to the fact that before they learn to drive, many students (even teenagers) are challenged to give someone good directions to their house. Why? Because someone else has always been responsible for getting them there: so many trips to and from—so many observations and corrections—with no real need to pay attention. So the sooner we can put them in the driver's seat, the better . . . with musicianship, that is.

Essential Skills of Independent Musicians

PHYSICAL BASIS FOR TONE PRODUCTION

The posture and physical freedom of any young musician is a strong predictor of future advanced technique. A free, comfortable setup forms the foundation for growth and musical independence. Depending solely on one half-hour lesson per week to establish a student's fundamental technique is a painfully slow method if the student doesn't understand what to observe in her own playing.

For instance, consider this scenario, when a cello teacher recognizes tension in a student's shoulders that is affecting the tone on the C string.

"Relax your shoulders and just use your arm weight to get into the string—great, that's perfect. How does that feel? 'Weird,' you say? That's okay, you're not used to that feeling yet. Let's just say that this week it might feel 'weird.' As long as your shoulders are down and relaxed and your arm feels heavy, just consider right now that 'weird' is good. Look in the mirror. What do you see when your shoulders are up? Now put them down. What's the difference? Right . . . When your shoulders were up, I couldn't see your neck either! Keep watching to be sure you can see it when you are practicing."

The student plays again on the C string. "Can you hear a change in your sound when your shoulders are down? What is the difference? Close your eyes . . . can you hear it? Can you feel the difference when your eyes are closed? You can feel the cello vibrating more? Great! This week I want you to play open C strings every day for two or three minutes—play in front of the mirror and watch—what will you see? Your neck! Good!—then close your eyes and listen for the sound and feeling of relaxed shoulders and arm, and feel your cello vibrating as much as possible."

> **Personal Inventory:** Choose one aspect of fundamental setup from your list of techniques in Chapter 3, *Technique*. Create a scenario similar to the one you just read, including ideas for guiding a student's awareness with visual, aural, verbal, and kinesthetic learning approaches, and offering practice suggestions.

INDEPENDENT PRACTICE

You can safely assume that students don't know how to practice unless they have been taught. Like any technique important to your instrument, it is a skill that must be learned. Lessons are the only opportunity teachers have to influence the practicing students do at home. While teaching students how practice takes time, and likely means you won't cover as much other material that day, in the big picture, it is one of the most high-return investments a teacher can make.

Observation and Critiquing

The first step in an effective practice routine is to notice what needs work. Yet for most students the default setting is to give little or no thought to what to improve, with the exception of "learning the notes" or "getting through the piece." While teachers are often quick to blame students for this inept approach to practicing, we must realize it is primarily our own fault if in lessons we endlessly repeat the cycle of "problem happens; teacher makes suggestions." If students never have the opportunity to self-critique and problem-solve, it's no surprise that they don't understand the process.

The most direct way to teach students how to observe and critique themselves is quite simple: after your students play, but before you say anything, ask them what *they* noticed. Be forewarned, however, that if you've never taught this way before, you can't expect your students to be enthusiastic about this turn of the tables. Comfortable with their passive role in lessons, students aren't always happy about this added responsibility and the effort it takes. Some sincerely believe that it is the job of a good teacher to make all the observations, and that it is the job of a good student to follow directions, period. Students might also be concerned that their observations might be "wrong" and they don't want to take that risk.

Pressed for an observation, students might respond with vague or evasive answers.

"It sounded bad" is a catch-all answer based on the assumption that something had to be bad or the teacher wouldn't be asking. *"What* sounded bad?" is the follow-up to the first answer—make sure the observation includes both *what* went wrong and *where* it went wrong.

"It was okay" leaves things open-ended: some things good, some not. Ask the "okay" responders to tell you something they liked and something they didn't, again with appropriate specifics, such as "I liked my vibrato at the beginning, but the legato section didn't sound smooth."

> ## Consider This
> Note to teachers: remember there is no wrong answer to the question "What did you notice?" Whatever the answer, it is what the student noticed, whether astute or misguided. "OK, let's go back and check that" is an appropriate response to any observation, since the problem is less that they made a bad choice, and more that they really don't know what they were hearing, good or bad. Let students "fix" what they consider to be the problem: once an already-even run is consciously made even—or an already-tuned note is clarified as in tune—students' awareness is greatly increased, and their attention (with your encouragement, when needed) will turn toward resolving more significant issues.

"I don't know" usually means they really want the teacher to return to the old default setting of supplying all the answers (and hopefully to never attempt this again).

To help jump-start their thinking, you might want to offer a checklist of components—"How was your rhythm? Tone? Phrasing? Pedaling? Bowing? Intonation?" and so forth. But if a more specific critique isn't forthcoming, don't consider for a moment telling students what you heard—simply have them play again (a few times, if necessary) until they can make a real observation.

If asked often enough, students' resistance to this routine wears down, and they begin to expect it, which at minimum makes them more attentive—an excellent step in the right direction. Over time, their responses will gradually need less prompting and assistance from you. As that happens, you can encourage them to be more analytical about discovering the source of the problem. Draw your student's attention to fine details of technique, looking "under the microscope" for subtle adjustments that can make significant differences in overall performance ability.

Consider This

Encourage all your students to start their observations with something positive, since being aware of what was good reinforces the ultimate desired outcome: "My tone was good in the second section" or "I exaggerated the dynamics"—and allow them the chance to reinforce their best playing: let them do it again, describe what they hear and why it's working, and perhaps consider how to make it better still. The goal is for students to become observant of *everything* they do—and in fact focusing on their best playing or singing helps them access it more readily in every situation.

Teaching Students to Practice Effectively

> It's scary to realize I was teaching lessons in such a haphazard manner: randomly assigning repertoire, and simply expecting my young students to know how to practice. When I finally started working with a teacher who not only described how to practice, but went through practice routines in my lesson, my practicing became well organized, my progress was evident, and I was much more self-motivated. My success prompted me to help my own students who were struggling to see evidence of change from week to week.
> RECENT GRADUATE

Once your student has identified a problematic area, give him a few minutes to resolve the problem independently. You will likely observe several weaknesses in the practice routine: practicing hurriedly and making many mistakes, not repeating a correction often enough, being distracted by other problems and forgetting the original goal, and so on. After you've seen which issues are most problematic, guide him through a more productive process, pointing out which areas need the most attention.

It's important to note that students, especially younger ones, do not understand the value of repetition—in fact, to many of them, repeating a correction twenty times is punishment. (Remember, they aren't required to solve the same math problem twenty times to show they understand it.) A conversation about the brain—how synapses are created and how automaticity is developed—can be critical information in persuading students the repetition is a necessary part of their work. Be sure to discuss the importance of correct repetitions, since the brain will remember anything it is taught. Compare performing to test-taking: while they might get several tries at a math problem, and can even skip it and return to solve it later, in a performance there is only one time to do it, and one chance to get it right. (See Chapter 4, *Practicing*, for more discussion on this topic.)

Practicing in lessons need not be a spontaneous event. If practicing notes were made at the previous lesson, a student can demonstrate how that plan was implemented, so you can see how effective the notes were, and how well the student was able to follow directions. (See the next section for more about practice plans.) More mature students can explain how they practiced if it is warranted. Nevertheless, their improved performance will be the evidence of successful practicing, and the remaining problematic areas will be the focus of further review and modified plans.

Once the student knows how to fix a problem, however, don't allow yourself to slip back into "business as usual" by making the corrections yourself. Begin to place some responsibility on the student: "You just did a great job fixing a very similar problem five minutes ago, so I know you can take care of this without my help." While nothing can guarantee that students will work with clarity and focus when they go home, such lessons in independence, especially when incorporated into the weekly routine, significantly increases the likelihood of productive independent practice.

Notes, Goals, and Practice Plans

Students do not always make the connection between what the teacher does with them at a lesson and how they will practice at home. Solving a problem during a lesson can be considered a one-time fix in a student's mind, unless the teacher deliberately points out that this same work needs to continue throughout the week. Therefore, at least initially, teachers need to show students how to translate a lesson into a practice plan for the week.

Be very wary of charts or assignments that seem to suggest that the number of hours or minutes practiced is the primary goal. The best practice plans are goal-directed; therefore goals accomplished, not time spent, should be established as the focus. Younger students usually need some kind of practice checklist, as well as a notebook to record specific directions on how to practice each assignment. You or a parent can write about specific sections to be practiced, what the student must watch or listen for, how many repetitions are required, specified tempo variations, exercises, and so forth. Mature students can be encouraged to write their own notes, either during or just before the end of the lesson. These lesson notes can be coupled with more general handouts like a glossary of practice techniques, basic checklists, or a "practicing pitfalls" sheet to support their independent work.

No matter the age of your students, end-of-the-lesson questions work well to reinforce what was covered in the lesson and ensure understanding and focus for the coming week: "What did we do today?" or "What will you practice this week?" Don't let students answer "I'm going to practice my scale, my etude, and my piece." Students should be able to mention specific goals that require attention, including what they remember from their "in-lesson practice session." Verbalizing goals in their own words help to create a direct connection between students and their work. This recall time also offers an opportunity to reassert—and clarify if necessary—the most important elements covered in the lesson.

Foster an independent streak in your most mature students by encouraging them to develop specific techniques on their own. Start by defining a skill and determining their current level of accomplishment. Establish a final standard of mastery, and then suggest a practice process for development

---

Consider This

To some students, there is nothing more important than getting to the end of the piece without stopping, and "learning the next piece in the book" is the primary goal of lessons. In these cases, students (and sometimes their parents) need to hear that simply being able to get through a piece does not demonstrate real progress—and that instead this should be regarded the very beginning stage of learning a piece of music. Clearly defined performance goals for each piece helps keep the focus on the student's developmental priorities and the needs of the music. When a student is asked "What are you working on?" the name of a piece needn't always be the default response. Keep the focus on their fundamental skills by encouraging them to answer more specifically "Intonation!" or "Tone!"

toward that goal. It can then be your students' responsibility to chart their own improvement, keeping you informed of each week's progress.

Consider This

Create a "Glossary of Practice Techniques" as a part of your standard teaching materials, using the ideas, processes, and practice techniques you listed from the "Personal Inventory" sections in Chapter 4, *Practicing*. If you teach a class of students, you could highlight one each week as a "Practice Technique of the Week": demonstrate how it is used, include it on their practice chart, and at the end of the week have them discuss in class how it helped their work.

I was actually in graduate school before I clearly understood how to practice. Teachers would tell me to practice for three or four hours a day but I never had a systematic way to break down passages, a scale routine, or repertoire goals. My time in the practice room was often spent inefficiently—not because I didn't want to practice, but because I didn't know what to do for three hours other than repeat passages. If my earlier teachers had included practice skill as a teaching goal, I would have been much better prepared for my life-after-teachers.

DOCTORAL CANDIDATE

MUSIC LITERACY

Music literacy is one of the most important pathways to musical independence. To become capable, independent musicians, students must learn to read notes, decode meters and rhythms, understand key signatures, translate terminology, and decipher symbols that appear on the page. (See Chapter 7, *Sequencing*, to understand more about the best time and approach to introduce reading.) When students are entirely capable of learning and applying this information, continuing to say "It goes like this" is detrimental to your students' growth. So at the next lesson, when faced with the choice of teaching a student to count

Consider This

Just as a parent runs alongside a child learning to ride a bike, so can the music teacher help a student gain confidence in reading music. Sight-read music together, and then gradually play softer and softer until the student is playing alone. Keep the pulse moving by jumping in when there are hesitations, acting as the "training wheels" for music reading, gradually allowing your student to develop momentum and balance toward independence.

and read notes, or falling back on rote learning to save time, remember that no short-cut to music reading will ever save time in the big picture, nor will it ever cultivate a thinking, independent musician.

Musical Decisions

> Having a teacher who asked me to repeat passages, listen for differences from one repetition to the next, and describe what I was experiencing made me realize that I was not only capable of fixing intonation and technical issues, but I was also competent to make musical decisions on my own.
>
> COLLEGE JUNIOR

Coaching students through the principles of musical choice can foster a sense of ownership of the music and inspire expressive musical performances. Letting students choose aspects of their musicianship creates a personal connection that is absolutely necessary for real musicality and expression to unfold.

Sometimes it is helpful for the teacher to demonstrate only two ways to play a phrase—a "musical way" as opposed to an "unmusical way"—since it's almost inevitable that the former will be selected as the "better" performance. When students can describe the differences between the two, and explain why one was preferable over the others, you will know they can recognize the rudimentary qualities of a musical performance.

However, making music is never quite as black and white as "the good way" and "the bad way," as the previous approach implies. Another drawback to this teaching method is that young musicians often feel compelled to copy the musical performance to be "correct" while not necessarily understanding or "feeling" it from the inside. Unless students understand the underlying concepts and expressive meaning that fostered the musical rendition, it is likely that they will continue to be dependent on demonstration and teacher directives to make their performances sound musical.

Fortunately, there are a variety of ways to invoke musical expression from students. Very young children are capable of highly expressive speech and inflection. If you listen to a five-year-old child describe something that is exciting, sad, or scary, you will begin to understand the range of their emotional understanding. Directing verbal expression toward musical possibilities is often a simple matter of expressing an emotion with the voice or with a gesture, identifying the characteristics, and then exploring ways to create that on the instrument. Allowing students to choose a mood for a folk tune gives them ownership of their own expressive sensibilities, and even the most unusual choice will not matter, like a despondent *Baa Baa Black Sheep*. It is real music-making from inside the student, and the first step toward making important, independent musical choices.

The discussion in Chapter 1, *Musicianship*, guided you to define and explain many facets of musicianship from the music itself, including form, genre, composer and compositional period, and descriptive terminology. Virtually any of these concepts can be explored in an age-appropriate manner to offer insights into compositionally based interpretations. Introducing these musical concepts as early as possible teaches students that there is more to music-making than getting the notes right. When students are consistently encouraged to interpret clues in the music and combine them with personal expressiveness, they can perform with genuine musicianship. (A further discussion on this topic can be found in the next chapter, *Comprehensive Teaching*.)

> ### Consider This
> There is always more than one way to musically play a piece or a phrase. Try demonstrating three or more possibilities for your student. Have a conversation about the differences, and whether one version seemed more appropriate than the others. You could also listen to recordings of great artists playing the same piece, comparing the interpretations, noting differences in tempo, dynamics, and phrasing. How does this approach contrast with the "musical/unmusical" method? What are the advantages and disadvantages of each?

Student-Centered Learning Activities

Students come to lessons to gain information from their teachers—that's the way it should be. However, this doesn't mean that the teacher should be an endless supply of definitions and answers to all questions. Teachers can guide students toward discovering answers for themselves. When a student doesn't know the meaning of a word in his music, is unfamiliar with a composer, or wants to learn more about his instrument, ask him to do a bit of research and tell you about it the next week. Students can also find works of art, architecture, literature—or better still, create their own—that represents to them the style, form, or meaning of the music they are working on. Simple score analysis, such as circling every occurrence of a repeated motif, or figuring out the major tonal centers, can be an easy way to introduce approaches to dig deeper into a piece and understand more about music composition. Group lessons or studio classes can be a great time for your students to share the results of their independent work, take pride in some newfound expertise, and further reinforce learning.

Teachers tend to habitually make decisions about fingering, bowing, or breathing, leaving students out of the process, and perpetuating their need for "help" every time they get a new piece of music. Restrain your automatic impulse to do it all for them. Share your decision-making process out loud while you mark one section, and then allow the student to do the next section independently, either there at the lesson or as a home assignment. Follow up with a discussion about the choices the student made, where you agree, and why you might have chosen something else. As an extension of this assignment, consider sending a student home with a few lines of music to learn to the best of his or her ability. At the next lesson you can observe how well the student applies not just appropriate fingerings, bowings, or breathing, but overall accuracy with rhythms and notes, as well as dynamics, phrasing, stylistic choices, and so forth. This kind of assessment will give you an overview of how dependent your students might still be, and what areas should be targeted for more development.

Understanding Intonation

Individuality is often encouraged in areas such as musical interpretation, tempo, or phrasing—these are accepted and welcome as part of each musician's unique qualities. Intonation, however, is a component of music that has little room for variation and individuality. Faulty intonation can keep even the most expressive performance from ever being considered artistic. In other words, if the performance is out of tune, it doesn't matter whether it was fast and clean or the tone was beautiful—it won't be good until the intonation is fixed. In fact playing or singing in tune is so important that it trumps virtually all other aspects of technique. Therefore, when you think toward your students' musical life after they leave your studio, you will recognize that the time to teach the concept of "in tune" is right now and always.

In the beginning stages of instruction, the mechanics of just making sound on the instrument is all-consuming. At this stage, intonation problems are usually the result of students being overwhelmed with many other issues. Yet the teacher who optimistically thinks intonation will eventually get better on its own is probably mistaken. The key is making good intonation both understandable and important to students from the start.

Teachers cannot assume that all students start lessons with a clear concept of what is meant by "good intonation." (In fact, many students think the term *intonation* is another word for tone—so be sure to find out before spending a lot of time on it in a lesson.) While some students have little difficulty matching pitches, those who are challenged to play in tune on their instruments are likely to find singing in tune challenging as well. Instrumentalists produce pitch through a secondary source, but if their perception of pitch is external only, it is nearly impossible for them to recognize good intonation. Pitch must first be heard inside and then generated through the voice. Therefore it is necessary that all students be taught listening skills and basic vocal control.

Instrumental students are of the reluctant to sing in lessons (they didn't sign up for voice lessons, after all), so to ease the way forward, the teacher should sing first. Start by singing two different pitches, and have student tell you which is higher and which is lower. Then reverse roles and ask him to sing high and low pitches for you to identify. If the student's voice seems stuck on one note, "siren" your voices together to expand his vocal range and develop the flexibility needed to change pitches. Singing simple songs together is a fun way to encourage younger students to use their voices: give them a starting pitch that is in an easy range for them, and encourage them to correct pitches if they stray.

Actual intonation work can begin by asking a student to sing any pitch and then matching her pitch with your voice. Bend your intonation in different directions and then return to the unison pitch. Change roles and ask her to try to adjust her voice to yours. Next, ask her to play a pitch on her instrument; again you match your pitch to hers, both with your voice and with your instrument; then reverse roles again. Insist on the student matching with exactly the same note—don't settle for a close approximation. Anything less than an exact match is problematic because (1) you won't be able to assess whether the student understands the concept of intonation, and (2) you've taught the student that close is good enough.

It might take weeks to establish the ability to match pitches, but your persistence will pay off. Once students can

> **Consider This**
> When developing your students' independent sense of intonation, be careful not to respond too quickly to a well-tuned pitch. You might recognize the good intonation first, but you don't want to train students to wait for a positive reaction from you to know they are in tune. Wait patiently for that important moment when they recognize for themselves that a note is indeed in tune—then you can enthusiastically agree.

match unison pitches and adjust with relative ease, you can begin tuning intervals, starting with unisons, octaves, fifths, and fourths. Teach them to recognize the characteristic sound of a perfect interval: even a rough sketch will give them a picture of how sine waves can align and vibrate together. Nonperfect intervals and more dissonant intervals can follow, but at this point you will have established the fundamentals necessary for students to understand and make good choices about their intonation.

Unfortunately, knowing how to play in tune does not always mean that students will. They often need to be taught how to keep an ongoing connection between their inner voice and the pitches they produce. To check for that connection, ask a student to perform a short passage very slowly (without tempo), playing only the pitches the inner voice is singing. If every note is in tune (or adjusted to the correct pitch) you know that the student understands the concept and simply needs to make intonation more of a priority. Teach students a variety of ways to practice intonation, and give them assignments that focus specifically on intonation practice: playing against a drone, recording themselves, reinforcing muscle memory for accurate measurements between notes, testing pitches to harmonics, and so forth.

> ### Consider This
> When increasing younger students' awareness of intonation, you might want to use a strobe tuner to show students how pitch adjustment "works." With the goal of moving the strobe, students very naturally make adjustments such as finger movement or embouchure change without detailed instructions. Once they have had the experience of moving the strobe, you can explain what they did to bend the pitch. Emphasize that placing a certain finger on a fingerboard, depressing the correct valve, or finding a position for the trombone slide creates the possibility for good intonation, but is only the first step toward playing in tune.

> ### Consider This
> Students need to know how to tune their instruments, so don't always do it for them in lessons. Show students several approaches to tuning that are appropriate for their instrument: using an electronic tuner or strobe; referencing a tuning fork, piano, or other instrument; comparing harmonics and overtones. Teach them to listen for "beats" and how to make them disappear while drawing their attention to the resonance of good intonation.

Performance Preparation

Performing is the ultimate independent experience. Whether anyone likes it or not, students are completely on their own during performance, and teachers are powerless to help them. Everything we've done to foster their independence as musicians will be evident in their ability to perform well: from their confident walk out on stage, to the well-executed and expressive performance, to their graceful bow and exit. While it is the teacher's job to be sure all these performance skills are fully prepared in advance, they will be most reliable and meaningful when students have a sense of ownership about each and every aspect.

SUCCESS TAKES PRACTICE

Performing, just like every other skill, takes practice. Yet students who study classical music typically do not perform more than a few times a year, due to the fact that preparation of a new piece often takes months. This is not usually enough to increase students' sense of comfort in front of an audience. Remember, however, that the music to be performed needn't always be the latest addition to their repertoire. Have younger students "recycle" previously prepared pieces in frequent, low-profile situations, such as group lessons and in-house concerts for friends and family. A similar strategy can be used for music majors as well, since the infrequency of formal recitals does not necessarily promote a relaxed, comfortable approach to performance. Scheduling more performances than required allows students to experience success and ease, especially when performing the same repertoire in multiple recitals, in multiple venues, for multiple audiences. Similar to the way concert artists schedule several recitals of the same program, this performance approach can be a pathway to developing confidence and reliability.

MINDSET AND FOCUS

Even with the most thorough preparation, high-profile performances can create anxiety. You can help students direct their focus away from the fearful aspects and toward their musical and technical plan. During a lesson, encourage them to "talk" themselves through a performance as if they were a coach watching from the sidelines: "Relax shoulders before the forte." "Light, free sixteenth notes." "Vibrate before the shift." By verbalizing their thought processes, they cultivate the habit of directing themselves toward their best playing, while giving you a window on how they are mentally preparing for each technical and musical moment. (See Chapter 5, *Performing*, for a discussion about performance plans.) To reinforce these self-directed thoughts, place sticky-notes on their music and give them an assignment to make notes of those performance goals and directives that help them the most during the week's practice. With some trial and error, a list of the primary technical goals and musical qualities will evolve. The final version of this list can be left on the music for the rest of the preparation, and reread just before a performance to help students keep their focus under pressure.

Consider This
A student's self-evaluation immediately after a run-through or performance is extremely valuable, maybe even more valuable than the teacher's feedback. Review a recording of the performance with the student and help her form constructive critiques rather than making comments like "That part was bad." Encourage a more objective assessment of why a section didn't work, and how it could be improved.

Relying on inspiration during a performance to deliver a potentially special or powerful moment leaves room for disappointment. To increase the odds that your students' thoughts and technique will reliably deliver their musical message, help them decide in advance what effect they want to convey, for example, suspense, longing, or despair, and translate that into the technical requirements to make it happen. While focusing on the "how-to" aspects of musical effects might seem overly calculated to some students, such a well-planned approach readily emerges as a spontaneous musical gesture in performance.

OTHER PERFORMANCE-RELATED ISSUES

Stopping due to a technical or memory issue is a common fear associated with performance. When practicing, students get in the habit of stopping during certain passages or slowing down an entire section because of a technical challenge. Teachers can help by insisting that they "play through" many times before the actual performance. Show them how to use pre-performance mistakes as opportunities to learn how to recover quickly. If the student is tempted to stop anyway, use the metronome as a tool for the technique of grabbing the next beat rather than lingering to try to fix a problem. Introductions, extended tutti sections, and even a few bars of rests cause a flow problem when the student is not in the habit of counting through these sections. Play the piano accompaniment or orchestral introductions and interludes for your students often, either on a keyboard or on your own instrument. Ask students to sing interludes or other parts that fit with their passages until they are fully aware of the bigger picture.

Less experienced students should be encouraged to verbalize any concerns and expectations about a performance, which could potentially cause problems if left unaddressed. General anxiety about "messing up" can be answered by reminding students about how well-prepared they are and how their performance plan will carry them through. Discussing a worst case scenario and how to deal with it if did happen can dissipate distracting fears. In addition, "I want to play better than . . ." comparisons are unhelpful, and students must recognize that they have no control over how someone else might play. They do, however, have full control of their own best playing, and this of course is where their focus needs to be. These conversations can help center students and remind them that they have the power to do what needs to be done; in other words, to take independent responsibility for their performance.

> **Consider This**
> When students' auditions require concertos and orchestral excerpts, the importance of inner hearing is particularly important. Be sure students listen to recordings of the full orchestration to be intimately acquainted with how their part fits with the full score. Just like any professional audition, the performance should be nuanced so as to make it obvious to the audition panel that the musician hears and understands his or her part in the bigger picture.

PERFORMANCE TIMELINES

Advanced high school and college students need to learn the importance of advanced preparation before a major event like an audition or recital. Marking the date on a calendar and creating a practice plan leading up to it helps students to see what their responsibility is in the process. Create a plan that reflects an intelligent timeline in preparing major performances, and include scheduled recording sessions and informal performances for self-review. This increases the intensity well ahead of the actual performance, and helps unseasoned performers adjust to the experience. Put the responsibility of preparation in their hands by offering books that support their efforts. Once students have had success with such thorough preparation—perhaps in contrast with an unfortunate experience of an ill-prepared performance—they learn to take more responsibility in the future.

> **Consider This**
> What would be the benefits of a student performing the same piece on every required jury and degree recital throughout his or her academic career? Even as a hypothetical construct, what evidence of growth and independence could be revealed through this process?

Independent Repertoire Development

One of the major benefits to your students in becoming musically literate is the ability to choose and learn music independently. As students mature, they should be encouraged to choose and prepare some music on their own. While similar to an assignment suggested earlier, this is yet another step in the direction of full independence. If you want to set some reasonable limits, you might want to offer an anthology of pieces that are at their skill level, knowing that any choice is a safe one. Beyond that, however, set them free to learn as much of the piece as possible. These independent learning assignments encourage students to apply what they have learned rather than "waiting to be told," which, to be fair to students, has most probably been the primary experience imposed on them by many teachers. Here you are asking them to apply everything they know—so give them credit for what they can do initially, and perhaps send them home with a checklist of other elements you know they can figure out for themselves.

As students advance, they will be faced with learning more difficult music, such as orchestral excerpts or major concerti. To develop their independent efforts, students need to learn how to approach music at this level step by step. A checklist like this one can help guide a student's week-to-week development of a piece with minimal input from you.

- Listen to multiple recordings of the piece.
- Consider stylistic and interpretive ideas from different artists' interpretations.
- Identify the most challenging technical requirements of the piece; identify passages that might need to be learned one component at a time.
- Identify aspects of the piece that transfer previously learned skills, or if a new skill is needed, begin creating an etude to develop that technique.

Using your ideas as prompts, encourage your students to think of their own ways to break down difficult passages, increase speed, shape phrases, and present musical ideas. Not all the strategies mentioned above will apply to every piece, but by offering a toolbox of ideas you can encourage the student's ability to independently decipher a score, design a practice plan, and establish his own artistic performance standard.

Independence through Experience

Sequencing repertoire and developing technique are much more obvious teaching responsibilities than considering experiences that help prepare student for the day when he or she will no longer be a student. It would be just as impossible to write a "one size fits all" prescription for raising an independent and responsible musician as for raising a child to become an independent and responsible adult. However, if you are a teacher of a more mature student, it is important to consider which experiences could effect a positive transition from your studio to an independent life in music.

MUSICAL FLEXIBILITY

An important aspect of becoming an independent musician is developing the ability to be flexible in a myriad of performing situations. Playing or singing in different styles, reading different clefs, transposing into different octaves and keys, being able to follow or lead, improvising a simple cadence—all add to students' confidence about performing in any situation, and go a long way toward a sense of being "comfortable in one's musical skin."

Independent musicians must have command of their own performing while staying aware of the music around them. When listening skills and musical understanding merge, performers develop a musical intelligence that allows them to automatically adjust in unpredictable situations. For example, when a soloist skips a measure and a ninety-member orchestra makes the adjustment in two beats, that's musical intelligence in action. Flexible performers can make decisions that allow them to collaborate successfully with other musicians at all ability levels. They know when to play and when not to play, where to play, and when to take things down an octave, create an obbligato line, or improvise a cadence. You can test your students' knowledge and decision-making ability by simulating group situations in which they will have to make quick adjustments in order to make musical sense in the moment.

Most working musicians today must also be able to function in many different musical styles and situations. To expand your students' musical experiences, you might need to expand your own knowledge of other types of music, including world music, improvisation, and contemporary styles. Being open-minded for the purpose of increasing your student's musical flexibility doesn't mean you are not committed to developing fine classical musicians or are negligent in regard to standards. On the contrary, it means that you are committed to your students' ability to bring excellence to any style or situation in which they perform.

IDENTIFYING ARTISTRY

To become independent artists, students need to identify and understand components of artistry. There are identifiable behaviors and characteristics that cause us to be inspired by some performances and not others. A performance your students may describe as "awesome" is so for many reasons, but identifying and describing the components of artistry might be an ability they have not yet cultivated.

Virtually any artistic component can be analyzed and taught. You might want to consider organizing your class around listening to a wonderful recording of a piece (or perhaps two or three of the same piece). Create a discussion related to what students hear by posing intriguing questions. (See Chapter 1, *Musicianship*, for ideas.) Interject your own comments as little as possible while you let your students wrestle with what makes a performance artistic and meaningful.

Developing Professionalism

With skill development and confidence come special opportunities and professional prospects for your students. As their teacher; it is your responsibility to instill a level of professionalism that will earn them respect and acceptance in the world of working musicians.

> **Personal Inventory:** How did you learn professional standards of behavior? How did you learn the importance of being responsible, respectful, and disciplined? Do you wish you had been given more guidance on these matters? If so, what information would have been most helpful?

MASTER CLASS PERFORMANCES

A master class performance is different from a concert performance in that it includes both a performance and a lesson component. Even if a student is comfortable in a performance situation, it is another skill altogether to be in a public setting making changes to the requests of an unfamiliar teacher. Preparing your students for this experience goes beyond helping them to learn the music. A studio class that mimics a master class situation can be a useful part of this process. Whether you are arranging a mock master class or helping a student prepare for the real thing, here are some points you may want to share:

- The master class teacher might respond to a student's performance with suggestions that conflict with your instruction or that are difficult to incorporate in the moment. The most important role of the student is to be receptive and respectfully "give it his all."

- The guest teacher may have a very different personality or unfamiliar teaching style. Again, teach your students to be accepting, be adaptable, and do their best to follow directions.
- Students should never challenge or refute the opinion of the teacher in this setting unless they are asked to state their own opinions.
- Students should feel confident to ask for clarification of verbal instructions or demonstrations.
- Students should memorize the repertoire if expected, and bring a copy of the music in case the master class teacher wants to reference the score.
- Students should be reminded that besides their musical performance, others also notice their receptivity, flexibility, poise, and politeness.

RESPONSIBILITY OF ENSEMBLE MEMBERSHIP

Many of your students will participate in ensemble situations outside their school and studio settings. By assisting students with their music preparation and attending these events whenever possible, you demonstrate to your students that you value their participation in ensembles. Students about to embark on independent careers in music need to understand their viability as working musicians will be based as much on their dependability and professionalism as their performing skills. If possible, take them with you to a rehearsal, recording session, or performance so they can see how you work in a professional situation beyond the teaching studio. This gives students the opportunity to ask you questions about the professional world and gives you the opportunity to share insights and advice that might not otherwise be discussed, such as how important it is to

- Respond to job invitations in a timely manner.
- Learn parts well before the first rehearsal.
- Arrive early, and warm up appropriately for all rehearsals and performances.
- Bring what you need to the job: music, pencils, mutes, endpin stops, extra reeds, strings, drumsticks, and so forth—in other words, be prepared.
- Respect time limits on breaks.
- Observe requirements or requests related to dress.
- Demonstrate respect for conductors, contractors, and other musicians.
- Remember that as a professional your attitude and actions speak louder than your words.

As students mature, the line between "words of wisdom" and "parental nagging" becomes obscured but remind students that you are giving them sage advice because you know they are ready for bigger things, and even one important tip could save them a job or their reputation some day.

The best teaching creates a balance between offering information and encouraging self-reliance in students. Ultimately, all artistry and career decisions will be entirely their own, but if along the way we have offered as many opportunities as possible for them to think for themselves, solve problems, and make connections, they should be fully ready for independence. When we teach well, our students become successful and we become obsolete—a most honorable way to lose a very fulfilling job.

Ideas for Further Exploration

1. Refer to your notes from Chapter 5, *Performing*. Create a short list of approaches that would help a middle school student prepare for a performance. Turn this list into practice assignments that could be utilized over the course of a few weeks.
2. Review the list below and make notes related to each of your students' strengths and deficits. Use this information to pinpoint aspects of student independence that you may need to address in your teaching.

THE TEACHER'S INDEPENDENT MUSICIAN TRAINING CHECKLIST

My students typically . . .

_____ tune their own instrument
_____ learn and perform music independently on some level
_____ recognize incorrect notes or rhythms during performance
_____ maintain a relaxed postural relationship with the instrument in practice and performance
_____ demonstrate the mechanics of beautiful tone production
_____ adjust tone quality during performance
_____ sight-read music appropriate to their level of development
_____ sing accompaniment interludes in solos and excerpts
_____ control and vary dynamics
_____ readily adjust to changes of fingerings, bowings, breath markings, and articulations
_____ discuss music in an intelligent manner, using appropriate descriptions and correct terminology
_____ translate lesson directives into a logical practice plan

_____ demonstrate flexibility by performing the same piece of music in different styles

_____ break down difficult passages of music into manageable practice increments

_____ perform memorized repertoire on a regular basis

_____ demonstrate appropriate stage presence

_____ accept critique and direction related to their performance

Recommended Reading

Beeching, A. M. (2005). *Beyond Talent: Creating a Successful Career in Music.* New York: Oxford University Press.

Gladwell, M. (2009). *Outliers: The Story of Success.* New York: Little, Brown.

Green, E. A. H. (1987). *The Dynamic Orchestra: Principles of Orchestral Performance for Instrumentalists, Conductors, and Audiences.* Englewood Cliffs, N.J.: Prentice-Hall.

Greene, D. (2001). *Audition Success: An Olympic Sports Psychologist Teaches Performing Artists How to Win.* New York: Routledge.

Kaplan, B. (2004). *Practicing for Artistic Success: The Musician's Guide to Self-Empowerment.* Morris, N.Y.: Perception Development Techniques.

Kreitman, E. (1998). *Teaching from the Balance Point: A Guide for Suzuki Parents, Teachers, and Students.* Western Springs, Ill.: Western Springs School of Talent Education.

Nathan, A. (2000). *The Young Musician's Survival Guide: Tips from Teens and Pros.* New York: Oxford University Press.

Sand, B. L. (2000). *Teaching Genius: Dorothy Delay and the Making of a Musician.* Portland, Ore.: Amadeus Press.

Ueland, B. (1987). *If You Want to Write: A Book about Art, Independence and Spirit.* Minneapolis: Graywolf Press.

Watkins, C. (2008). *Rosindust: Teaching, Learning and a Life from a Cellist's Perspective.* Houston: Rosindust.

9 Comprehensive Teaching

EARLIER IN THIS BOOK, we thoroughly examined the interwoven aspects of skill, understanding, and expression that are essential to becoming a fine performer. Our firsthand experience with developing and integrating these elements in ourselves makes us aware that teaching another to do the same is no small task; and given the very limited time of the teacher-student relationship, the challenge seems to become even more formidable.

Many music teachers complain that with so many technical issues to address there is simply no time to teach anything else. An entire one-hour lesson or rehearsal can easily be spent adjusting positions, drilling rhythms, and fixing notes, leaving no opportunity to teach musical concepts or explore real music-making. Every teacher can relate—we've all experienced this at one time or another. However, teachers who feel hopelessly caught in a skills-only teaching trap are probably more in charge of their situations than they realize.

The cause of such frustration is often the result of neglecting one or more of the concepts covered in the past three chapters. These are so essential to good teaching that it is virtually impossible to overstate their importance. Let's review the significance of each, and examine how the integration of these concepts can create a highly productive learning environment.

- A thoughtful, sequential approach establishes a solid foundation upon which new skills are readily developed, minimizing remedial work and maximizing forward momentum.
- A working partnership is established when students apply learned skills and knowledge independently, which frees more time for teachers to introduce new concepts, skills, and expressive ideas.
- Enriching encounters with a trusted and caring teacher inspires students to work harder towards higher artistic standards, which in turn increases their appreciation of music, their instrument, and their own capabilities.

While the sum of these statements conjures a scenario that perhaps seems overly idyllic, such a result is actually attainable—in fact you might have once been on the student side of such a situation, or perhaps are still now. When teachers intentionally incorporate these concepts into their approach, rather than feeling hopeless, they are eagerly engaged in ways to effectively draw students into the rich world of meaningful music-making. In fact, a skills-only approach is a compromise no fine musician would ever make in performance, and no great teacher would ever consider for his or her students.

Integrated Musicianship

Musicianship is comprised of three inseparable components: technique, knowledge, and expression. Like a twisted rope of three strands, technique, knowledge, and

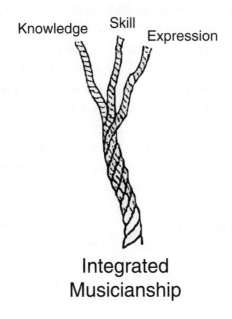

Knowledge   Skill   Expression

Integrated
Musicianship

expression work together to create supple yet durable musicianship. While it is possible to pull these fibers apart, their strength is reduced if simply placed side by side, so they must be entwined again to act as one; and, like the rope, musicianship is weakened when one strand is removed, and is severely compromised when two are missing. Whether on the stage or in the studio, our musical life needs to demonstrate the interrelationship of all three, and the decision to teach comprehensively is inevitable.

Consider This

Describe a musician who has developed only one or two of these elements—skill, knowledge, or expression—for example, an instrumentalist who has "chops" but no sense of music expression or understanding, or someone who sings with great passion but has little technique or knowledge to support it, or a conductor who knows the score, but has terrible baton technique and little emotional range. What would it be like to work with these musicians? If they asked for your guidance, what suggestions would you make to help balance their musicianship?

The Significance of Great Repertoire

Even under ideal conditions with skillful teachers, lessons go by quickly, and in the big picture there just aren't that many hours to develop a fine musician. In order to fit it all in, comprehensive teaching must be embedded in the work teachers already do in lessons. Fortunately, great repertoire is the answer to many of our needs. As all performers know from experience, the better the repertoire we play, the more gratifying our music-making experience will be. If we choose only the best pieces for our students, we have the ultimate resource for teaching technique, expression, theory, composition, and the importance of societal influences and historical context. Therefore, excellent repertoire can be a self-contained offering of a powerful teaching and learning experience.

GREAT MUSIC AT EVERY DIFFICULTY LEVEL

What is great music? If our definition includes only the standards in our repertoire, this means that our beginner students, and perhaps even the intermediate ones, will have to wait "until they are good enough" to begin learning truly great music. However our most advanced students should not be the only ones to receive our best teaching simply because they are able to play more difficult pieces. We must make it a priority to choose excellent music for all our students.

Every piece a student plays should be a valuable addition to his repertoire, no matter the difficulty level. Repertoire should be chosen on the basis of its quality and representation of a style or form. Folk tunes that have endured many decades, even centuries, include simple but high-quality pieces like *Ah! vous dirai-je, Maman* (*Twinkle, Twinkle Little Star*), *Simple Gifts*, and *Amazing Grace*. Classic themes, like the slow movement of Tchaikovsky's Fifth Symphony, the *Going Home* theme from Dvorak's "New World" Symphony, and *Ode to Joy* from Beethoven's Ninth, can begin a young student's lifelong relationship with great melodies. Many highly regarded composers, notably Bach, Mozart, and Schumann, wrote short pieces for children. While many of these are keyboard pieces, other instrumentalists can benefit from learning their simple yet elegant melodies, with the harmony provided by a secondary part. In addition, some teachers have composed wonderful pieces for their instruments that are delightfully idiomatic, fun to play, and provide substantial material for teaching.

However, since not all pieces have great value, how do we decide whether a simple piece is worth teaching and learning? While it's a challenge to quantify quality, a good piece will have many teachable elements, such as a recognizable form, identifiable patterns, harmonic interest, contrast, and inherent expressive qualities. A satisfying melody often utilizes a pattern in rhythm or note choices but then alters that pattern by adding or subtracting an element or changing direction to make the melody balanced and interesting. Pieces that are formulaic, predictable, or gimmicky might provide some technical or entertainment value but often wear thin in a short time. There are too many delightful pieces for any skill level and too little time to waste any of it on unsatisfying repertoire.

> ## Consider This
>
> Thoughtfully sequenced repertoire choices (see Chapter 7, *Sequencing*) are important not only to your students' technical development but also to your ability to offer depth and breadth in your teaching. There simply won't be time to teach comprehensively if most of the lesson is spent sorting out technical difficulties. Therefore, the next piece for any particular student needn't always be the next big step on the technical learning curve. Consider choosing new pieces as a means to introduce students to a composer, teach them a different form, or develop a new stylistic approach. When pieces are within reasonable technical reach, students can actually learn more repertoire while they reinforce skills and deepen their artistry.

Consider This

A series of progressive repertoire books can be convenient for sequencing, but beware of pitfalls. Students are often more aware of what book they are in rather than the actual music they are playing. In addition, teachers can start to teach a sequence as a matter of habit rather than out of thoughtful choice. The best teachers continue to keep their enthusiasm for making great music in the foreground, from which their repertoire choices and energy for teaching emerge. If you can't say "I love this piece and you're going to love it, too," perhaps it is time to find something else to teach.

KNOWING THE MUSIC

When a musician walks on stage, there is an expectation that the performer knows not just the notes but understands the music deeply, and will communicate that fully formed understanding in a well-developed and nuanced performance. We should approach teaching the same way: arriving at the studio with music we know intimately, and with a well-formed plan that will effectively communicate its significance and value to our students.

Now, here's the catch: Think of a piece you performed as a student and perhaps have taught as a professional. You have mastered the technical demands, your tone is lovely, your phrasing is impeccable, and you have enjoyed sharing that piece with many students. Good enough? Perhaps. But since great music offers so much more, learning to perform the piece can be only the beginning. No matter how many times you have played, conducted, or sung a piece, nor how many times you might have taught it, you will not fully know it until you really *study* it.

THE GREAT QUESTION: "WHY?"

Score study involves thinking like a composer. Most music theory courses have taught us to recognize compositional specifics such as genre, form, harmony, melody, instrumentation, rhythmic motifs, and compositional devices. But a performance analysis also involves speculating about why the composer made such choices and considering how each aspect informs our interpretation. "Why did the composer use a deceptive cadence rather than resolving the harmony?" "Why does the harmonic rhythm move faster in these measures?" "Why is the melody eight bars long in the exposition but ten in the recapitulation?" Questions that ask "what" and "how" work well, too: "What is the function of these sixteenth notes in the melody?" "How do the altered harmonies in the third statement change our experience of the melody?" Naturally, some choices that composers make are arbitrary; however, a well-conceived composition contains a wealth of meaningful choices. By searching for the answers to such *why* and what questions, we begin to shed light on the inspired choices that make it a masterpiece.

Digging below the surface of great music is further enhanced by getting to know more about the composer. Who was this person, and what were the strongest personal and social influences in his or her life? Was there a specific event that inspired this composition? Even if you think you know, extra research will almost invariably teach you something new. If the composer is alive, all the better: ask him or her about the inspiration and compositional process that resulted in the piece. Research is sometimes regarded as being too cerebral for a passionate performer, but the information you uncover and the new connections you make can be positively transformational to your performing and your teaching.

Translating Your Understanding into Great Teaching

Once the treasures in a piece have been revealed, you're likely to have abundant possibilities for your teaching. The next step will be to decide which of the skills, information, and expressive aspects are most essential to the piece and turn each of these into substantial goals for your student. Remember that the best goals are the ones students can transfer to other learning and performing situations: important concepts that have broad application and help to move them toward becoming strong, independent musicians.

KNOWLEDGE

After studying a piece, consider what information is the most essential to a meaningful performance. There will be a variety of concepts you will want your student to understand, but try not to teach too many concepts at once. Choose a limited number of significant teaching goals, and spend more time on depth of learning, using a variety of ways to reiterate and reinforce the information and make it a permanent part of your students' understanding.

The information you offer students should of course be suitable to their age and development level. Form is often a good starting point for beginners, since many of their pieces are in ABA (ternary) or rondo form. Another option would be show them how motifs are used; for instance, students can identify how many times the six quarters/one half note rhythm is repeated in *Twinkle, Twinkle Little Star*. You might also consider teaching them something interesting about the composer's life to make the composer memorable to a young student. Terminology, harmonies, and stylistic considerations all make excellent choices for learning; but whatever you choose to teach, make sure the information is not only relevant to the performance of this piece, but will transfer to pieces the student will play in the future. As students improve technically and perform more sophisticated music, you can offer comparably sophisticated information, building on what they have learned during the study of previous pieces.

SKILL

As a well-developed musician, you could scan any relatively short, simple piece in your repertoire and probably identify at least five essential skills needed for a successful performance. Out of those skills, one will probably stand out as being essential to the character and style of the music. This skill will be the primary focus of your technical work with your student. Undoubtably there will be other techniques addressed in lessons, but the teaching goal is to help the student achieve a new level of accomplishment on that particular skill. In other words, if beautiful legato is essential to meaningful expression of the piece, excessive work on the few staccato notes is a potential distraction. The target skill should be given the most focused attention, and you may decide to choose a piece next time that allows you to spend time on staccato. Of course, in the case of a longer and more complex work such as a concerto, the list of necessary skills is compounded in many ways; but presumably, by the time you introduce a piece at this level, your student will be well prepared to meet these challenges.

As you choose which skills need focus, remember that you needn't look outside the piece itself for technical development: the music will offer the most direct route toward developing that skill. As discussed in Chapter 7 *Sequencing*, small sections of the piece can be turned into "mini-etudes." For instance, scale and arpeggiated passages can be expanded by varying rhythms and pertinent articulations, and practiced with both ascending and descending patterns. Approaching passage work in this manner not only develops the targeted technique but teaches the student excellent practicing possibilities. If you choose to supplement your students' repertoire with separate etudes and exercises, make sure these directly support the technique needed for the current or a future piece. Scales and arpeggios are most beneficial when directly related to the tonal centers of a piece. Short exercises that get to the heart of a technical goal are often smarter choices than assigning unrelated multipage studies that take extended time to learn.

> What does this piece require? Single stroke rolls. So why can't I then do that whilst learning a
> piece of music? And that's exactly what [my first teacher] did. And interestingly . . . when I

became a full-time student at a so-called "music institution," all of that went out of the window. We had to study from study books. And constantly, the question why? Why? What is this relating to? I need to play a piece of music.

DAME EVELYN GLENNIE, TED LECTURE (2003)

Consider This

Some teachers rely heavily on etudes and studies to develop technique, and others teach only repertoire and create essential exercises and studies from passages. Do you believe there is there value in learning separate exercises and etudes outside the literature?

EXPRESSION

While teachers cannot make students feel an emotion, a meaningful experience of playing music is a teachable element when students are shown a variety of ways to connect a piece to their own real-life experiences. In other words, teaching expression goes beyond circling dynamics and telling students to take more time at the cadences. Teachers can offer students many beautiful musical ideas through demonstration and directives, but the most valuable expressive connection will be between the music and young musicians themselves. When students are taught to explore the piece more deeply, the result is a personal response from within. Show your students some of the discoveries you made in your study of the score: "Listen to this motif never stops throughout the entire piece! No wonder the music has such a relentless quality." Or "This A-sharp is so unexpected in the key of G—what kind of sound can you make that communicates this surprise?" Share with your student something you learned in your research, such as a loss in the composer's life at the time the piece was written. When students reflect on another person's sadness they will create a far more meaningful performance than if the teacher directs them to "play this piece slower and quieter."

There are as many pathways to expressive playing as there are pieces and the musicians who play them. Find out what your students love about music, singing, or playing and work with their passion. If they love the sound of the instrument, show them how to make it sound even more beautiful, and suggest they practice with the lights turned off to listen more deeply. If a young student wants to play a special piece for her grandmother, help her create a heartfelt rendition of a familiar folk tune. The truth is that a deeply felt experience of music does not happen only because of talent or a lucky accident: it emerges when there is a meaningful personal connection between the musician and the music. With students, sometimes the two might seem very far apart, but our mission as music teachers is to create pathways that can bring the two together. Like drawing a finger between two puddles of water, once the two connect they will never be separate again.

Comprehensive Teaching Strategies

Once you have chosen goals for a piece, then you must decide how you will teach these—specifically, what will happen in lessons and what the students do on their own. With some advanced planning, you can easily work with the three elements—skill, knowledge and expression—in an ongoing manner.

STUDENT-CENTERED APPROACHES TO LEARNING

In order to direct and reinforce your students' learning, your teaching goals need to be addressed in a variety of ways. While deciding on your best approaches, remember that students' learning is enhanced by the use of more than one way to present a new idea. Aural, visual, kinesthetic, and verbal pathways can all contribute to a deep understanding of a new concept or skill. Remember also that students need to be engaged in the learning process, not just have information presented to them. During lessons, ask many kinds of questions: questions that have a right or wrong answer, problem-solving ones that have more than one good answer, and ones that ask for an open-ended response. Give assignments at home that don't always involve singing or playing. Students can look up terminology or do their own research on a composer. They can draw or write about a new concept they are learning, write mood changes into their music, or even develop a story based on the many twists and turns in their piece, and then explore a variety of styles and tone qualities to make the story vivid in performance. Let them develop a way to practice a passage, or track their improvements using a rubric or self-assessment sheet. Have them listen, watch, critique, examine, analyze, count, name, and organize. The more involved students are in the process, the better they will learn, and the more meaningful the learning becomes. (See Chapter 8, *Fostering Student Independence*, for more on this topic.)

LINKING TECHNIQUE TO EXPRESSION AND KNOWLEDGE

In Chapter 4, *Practicing*, we discussed the importance of "bundling" information to increase effectiveness and efficiency in learning. This concept also applies to teaching comprehensively. Every musician knows that technical skills are essential to performance and must be developed, assessed, and refined. However, it is neither necessary nor ideal to isolate technique from the music and instrument that it serves. Teaching a skill as its own entity is not only misleading but also inefficient. When skills are shown to be inseparable from the knowledge and expression from which they are borne, students can begin to understand the connection while learning two or more concepts simultaneously. Whether the goal is correct breathing, a flexible bow hold, or clarity of articulation, teachers can offer approaches that frame the technique in a context of expression and musical understanding.

Skill Development via Expression

Even the most seemingly mundane techniques, like the ability to play steady six- teenth notes, have a musical reason to exist when connected to the meaning of the music. If a student needs work on the finger action required by a sixteenth-note pas- sage, decide from a musical standpoint why evenly played notes make the music better (beyond "just because") and emphasize that connection. Sometimes meta- phors and analogies can help establish a meaningful connection between the music and a skill. For instance: *"This passage reminds me of a hawk swooping and then soar- ing up to the sky again—show me with your hand how that swooping bird looks,—right! But if the sixteenths are lumpy it will sound like some mechanical bird with rusty gears. Let's get those five notes at the turn-around to really dive and lift, and then we'll add the others."* If more technical adjustments are needed, such as noticing that some fingers are being lifted higher than others, then those issues can be addressed—but all framed by what the music requires.

There are also many excellent skill- based approaches that directly access some components of expressive playing. Crescendos can be learned by gradually increasing arm weight, bow speed, or air column; variables of vibrato speed and width can be mastered through metronome-based exercises; tone colors

> ### Consider This
> If a student's technical flaws tend to derail your plan to teach com- prehensively, remind yourself why the music or the instrument needs the technique, rather than why the student needs it. Focusing only on what the student is lacking tends to give teachers "technical tunnel vision." Before pointing out your student's deficiencies, first intro- duce what the music demands or the instrument requires, then help the student become aware of the significant difference in the music or the tone when the technical improvement is made.

on a stringed instrument can be explored through incremental bowing changes of weight, speed, and placement (see Appendix 9.1). It is wise, however, to immediately turn the developing skill back toward the emotions, colors, and character in the music. For instance, when teaching a crescendo on the piano by adding arm weight, have the student imagine the music becoming "heavier"; the increasing arm weight is then a translation of the increasing "weight" of the music. Size (expanding or contracting) and proximity (closer or farther away) also can be useful images to connect a musical vision with the physical approach that creates a sound.

> **Personal Inventory:** Think of other images or experiences that create both a musical color and the physical experience that reveals the expression of that color on your instrument.

Skill Development via Knowledge

There are many ways that technique can be taught through a direct link with music theory, history, and instrumental acoustics. Students can learn scales and arpeggios while studying intervals, key signatures, the circle of fifths, and triads. Teach them the mechanics and acoustics of the instrument while they master the skills needed for tone production, or the scientific concept of a perfect interval as they develop refined listening and intonation skills.

> **Personal Inventory:** Now that we have explored many ways to teach skills hand-in-glove with knowledge and expression, can you think of any circumstance when one concept *cannot* be linked to the other two?

Assessment

Whether we are conscious of it or not, assessment is an essential and ongoing part of the teaching process. We constantly make decisions about what has improved and what to work on next, and notice our students' incremental improvements in specific technical and musical areas. We might share our observations of progress nonspecifically, with encouraging lesson-ending comments like "You sounded good today" or "James is doing very well"—but sometimes that is all the feedback students (and parents) get for months at a time. Even if our teaching situations allow such a casual approach to student evaluations, more frequent and formative assessments are very important to the teaching and learning process.

From their perspective, students simply cannot see the incremental improvements they make. For them, lessons can be like hiking through the woods, passing tree after tree but with no end in sight, and little sense of how much ground has been covered or how much farther they have to go. Teachers are the ones with the overview, a kind of global positioning device for musical development, watching students make their way forward. Of course we spend much of the time alongside them, showing them the way and encouraging each next step; but occasionally it is important to reveal what we can see from our perspective, helping them become aware of their progress in the bigger picture. When they understand where they have been and where they are going, the difference in our students is often quite palpable: they become more enthusiastic and more involved in the process, show more dedication and commitment, and even have increased willingness to perform for others. In turn, their responses begin to create a feedback loop—more commitment and enthusiasm makes them want to work harder, which accelerates their progress and spirals them toward even more improvement. Therefore, anything teachers can do to help students be aware of their progress, formally and informally, will increase the likelihood of fostering more cooperative and enthusiastic learners.

It is sometimes tempting to rely on culminating events like recitals and juries to provide proof of progress, but these are usually too infrequent to sustain a student throughout a year. Even though the preparation alone usually brings a student to a new level, a performance is really just a single snapshot of a students' musical and technical development. Besides, the typical anxiety associated with playing under pressure sometimes creates less than optimal results and inhibits their awareness of personal progress. Such infrequent performances might satisfy parents or administrators, but even at best, they cannot replace the kind of continuous encouragement and momentum we wish for our students.

ONGOING ASSESSMENTS

There are many ways to assess our students' progress throughout the year, both formal and informal. These don't have to feel intrusive or put extra pressure on the student; in fact, when made a regular part of the process, they can become a more natural and efficient way to track students' development. Such assessments are helpful to teachers, but much more important, they allow students to evaluate and validate their own progress.

Recording and videotaping. Record lessons or an informal run-through of a piece and provide students a rubric with which to assess their own progress. Compare the newest recording to previous ones and note improvements and maturation, and of course areas that still need attention.

Informal observations and questions. Ask questions during lessons that probe student understanding. These can be both obvious you-know-it-or-you-don't questions like "What is the meaning of *tranquillo*?" or questions that draw connections between what students understand and know about performing such as "How will the *tranquillo* marking affect the quality and length of the eighth notes in that passage?"

Formal assessments. Provide a rubric or numeric system with which students can gauge their strengths and weaknesses, either after a major performance or at the end of a term. Be sure the assessment covers a variety of technical and musical areas as well as practicing and performing. (See appendix 9.2.)

Ask your student to identify all the aspects of one concept, whether it be creating a legato sound, shaping a phrase, or creating an optimal embouchure. Have them demonstrate this to you as they discuss it. You can also act as the "student" yourself and let your students help you improve the skill. When students can successfully identify the essential components of a skill and make the necessary adjustments, remind them that if they choose to do these things on a regular basis they can be as good as their teacher—or better.

Musical creativity and expression. Ask students to assign characters or moods to various sections of their piece, and then explore the dynamics, tone qualities, and articulations that convey their choices. Before revealing their choices to you, have students play so you can speculate on the expression they are attempting to create.

Independent musical choices. Ask your student to choose three different but effective ways to pace the flow of a passage that needs rubato, or three ways to time a fermata, including the build-up, the length of a held note, its release, and the resumption of the music. Have the student explain each different way and assess which one seems most appropriate.

Program notes. Rather than copying information from the internet, ask students to write a few sentences sharing something more personal: a technique they had to master; images, characters, even a story they hear in the piece; a new favorite composer they've discovered; or an insight they had about themselves while working on the piece. It is a wonderful way for students to reinforce their own learning, and offers everyone a small but compelling glimpse into the development of a wonderful musician.

Independent practice. From time to time, have students play or sing a piece from their school ensemble that they claim is "easy," requiring no extra assistance from you. Your students' performance will demonstrate their ability to apply technical logic and musical concepts, quite possibly revealing gaps between their actual performance capabilities and the independent choices they make.

GRADING

Musicians who teach in their own private studios often consider themselves fortunate not to be required to formally assess students, especially when it comes to grading. But in a university setting or any other situation that requires letter grades, experienced teachers use a variety of methods to create a record of students' learning and growth. Easiest to evaluate are aspects of technique and musicianship that fall into the right-or-wrong, you-know-it-or-you-don't category. Music terminology, instrument parts, human anatomy, and aspects of theory, history, and style can easily be tested and graded with simple multiple choice, matching, or true-or-false exams. Grayer areas that require students to explain the relationship of what they know to what they do as they perform can be evaluated with short answer or essay questions. Performance itself can be assessed using rubrics or numerical systems. (See Appendix 12.3 for rubric suggestions.) It will be up to you to decide how to align those results with the grading system you are required to utilize.

Beyond required grades, however, nongraded contributions will be an important part of your overall approach to assessment. You might want students to write in a journal as part of their regular activities. Be sure your prompts aren't too general (like "what music means to me") but more specific and immediate, for example, "The main idea I learned in today's studio class was . . ." or "The music we listened to made me think of . . ." or "The aspect of my playing/singing that needs the most work is . . ." Not only will the students' comments be interesting, but even more important, you'll have an opportunity to gauge their involvement—while simultaneously engaging students on a deeper and more personal level than any graded assignment could or should assess. When teaching large classes where one-on-one interactions are less frequent, such feedback will help you feel more connected to each student and help you teach in more meaningful ways.

Incorporating Big-Picture Concepts

As comprehensive as we've been so far, a life devoted to music performance involves more than musical concepts and instrumental technique. You are aware that certain values—such as dedication, integrity, perseverance, and health—are essential to your life as a musician, and fall more readily into a broader "life skills" category. How does a teacher find time to convey these important concepts? If you consider each lesson as a microcosm of your students' lives, you will be able to impart values and principles that exceed the time frame of the lesson setting.

The first step toward working these concepts into lessons is prioritizing what is most important for your student to learn. With a recital date quickly approaching, is there really time to talk about time management? With so much work to do, should we really set aside time to stretch? If it is our priority that students learn to take charge of their lives while they take care of themselves, then the answer must be yes to both questions. Any big-picture goals that contribute to our students' success in music and in life are worth building into the interaction that happens in the lesson.

Our most important values are often present in lessons simply through who we are and how we teach. If students' health is significant part of our teaching approach, then we'll be sure that stretching and warm-up exercises happen first before skills and repertoire consume all the lesson time. If we value integrity in every note, we might ask a student to play a simple passage from his orchestra music that might never be practiced, and show him how to listen to what's happening around it, and how to color and shape every note accordingly. If we believe in the importance of our students' own ideas, that message is embedded in our willingness to listen with sincere interest while a student struggles to express an important thought. Caring about our students' personal well-being is often expressed before the lesson begins, when we ask our students how they are, and then really listen and respond to their answers.

Here are a few other practical approaches that demonstrate to our students—and help us remember—some of our highest priorities:

- *Continually demonstrate the relevance and interaction of music and life.* Draw on images and experiences from outside the studio. Discuss with your student how he interacts with a sibling, and how that might relate to mischievous or playful qualities in his music-making; talk about an interesting news item or interview you heard on the radio, and how the topic, although unrelated to music, seems to connect to this piece or the student's important work; demonstrate how a math or science concept sheds light on a musical or technical issue.
- *Help students discover the music before they start playing the notes.* When introducing a new piece, rather than taking the path of least resistance by using the rhythms, notes, fingerings, or bowings as your starting point, talk about the composer, the title, and the expressive markings; look for double bars, key changes, repeated motifs and sections. Guide your student through these components like a sleuth looking for clues to solve a mystery.

- *Keep the whole piece in view.* The path of least resistance for a teacher of a solo instrument is to follow the instrumental part without reference to the piano or orchestral accompaniment. Instead, make a habit of following the score while you teach. It will remind you of the bigger musical picture that includes harmonies, imitation, motifs, and interesting counterpoint—all the things you would pay attention to if you were performing the piece yourself. Go to the piano or pick up your instrument, explore the harmonies, and play the interesting lines that weave around the solo part—make real music with your students as they learn.
- *Keep the big picture in the forefront.* Constantly ask big-picture questions as you teach and be willing to draw the student into the process whenever possible. "Why?" is a great one. "*Why* is it important that we get to know this piece, develop this technique, or understand this information?" Or, "*How* can I help my student learn this best?" Or "*What* is the most important concept my student will take home with her today?"

While it helps to think ahead about ways to make lessons meaningful, some of the most important lessons you teach cannot be planned. These can happen when your openness to an immediate situation is more important than any next item on the agenda. A student who becomes agitated during a lesson might need a chance to find his center again, and a few moments of stillness between the two of you can send a message not only about the power of silence but your commitment to share in his efforts and struggles. To the student who is discouraged about poor audition results, the words "I believe in you" could be a turning point in her life. Such significant moments rarely last long, but their message can last a lifetime. There is really no way to prepare for such situations, but knowing yourself, your principles, and your priorities will give you what you need when your students need you.

Setting Priorities: A Parting Story

A professor of philosophy stood before his class with some items in front of him. When the class began, wordlessly he picked up a large empty jar and proceeded to fill it with rocks about two inches in diameter. He asked the students if the jar was full, and they agreed.

Next the professor picked up a box of pebbles and poured them into the jar, shaking it lightly so they could fill the spaces between the rocks. The professor again asked the students if the jar was full. They laughed at themselves, and agreed that now it was indeed full.

The professor then picked up a box of sand and poured it into the jar. The sand filled the remaining spaces between the rocks and pebbles. "Now," said the professor, "I want you to recognize that this jar signifies your life. The rocks are the truly important things, such as family, health, and relationships—those things that make your life whole and meaningful. The pebbles are the other things that matter in your life, such as work or school. The sand signifies the remaining 'small stuff' and material possessions. If you put sand into the jar first, there will be no room for the rocks. The same can be applied to your lives. If you spend all your time and energy on the small stuff, you will never have room for the things that are truly important."

Ideas for Further Exploration

1. The story at the end of the chapter reveals a universal truth about life, but even in our somewhat limited world of teaching music, the message is still applicable. Sand might represent necessary but unmemorable activities, like scheduling a makeup lesson, recording payments, or scheduling recital dates; pebbles might depict more significant interactions, like choosing repertoire, teaching specific techniques, or helping students select a summer program. Rocks symbolize the most important values you want to impart as you teach and interact with students. On a piece of paper, create three columns, labeling them Rocks, Pebbles, and Sand. Starting with your "Rock" column, write down your highest priorities—those items you want your students to remember about their music study (or remember about you) for the rest of their lives. Once you have those in place, consider how those priorities can influence how you work with the Pebble and Sand items. Think of learning experiences—weekly installments as well as significant events—that would introduce and reinforce these most important concepts and ideals to your students.

2. Choose a short piece from the standard repertoire for your voice or instrument, preferably one you have already studied on your instrument. Research the piece and composer fully, using multiple sources. Discover as much as you can about the composer's life, the influences on his or her life personally or professionally, the occasion or inspiration for the composition, the premiere, and anything that was written by the composer, friends, or reviewers of the time, regarding the piece or how it was publicly received. What did you discover that you didn't know before, and how does this change your approach to the piece?

3. Choose a short piece from the standard repertoire for your voice or instrument. (If you have already completed Exploration 1, continue working on

the same piece.) Make note of the stylistic period, genre, and form. Do a thorough harmonic, rhythmic, and melodic analysis of the piece. Find motifs, sequences, and other compositional devices that are significant to the composition. If there are lyrics, do your own translation if in a foreign language, and explore the connection between the words and the composition. (If your piece is an instrumental transcription, be sure to do the same.) As you explore each aspect, ask yourself why you think the composer chose that particular element for that particular piece. What did you discover that you've never noticed before? How could this newfound information influence how you will perform and/or teach the piece?

4. Using the same piece you analyzed in Exploration 1 and/or 2, choose one learning goal that focuses on knowledge or expression. Be sure the goal has broader application than just for this one piece. In other words, if the piece is in A major but the second theme is in F-sharp minor, a knowledge goal might be to understand the relationship between major and minor keys, or perhaps to learn how composers create contrast within a piece. An expressive goal might be to explore how changes in compositional elements create a variety of moods and characters, or perhaps how different speeds and widths of vibrato can change the interpretation. Students can learn about these elements not just with this piece, but also with other pieces already in the student's repertoire.

Recommended Reading

Blum, D. (1977). *Casals and the Art of Interpretation*. London: Heinemann.

Booth, Eric. (2009). *The Music Teaching Artist's Bible: Becoming a Virtuoso Educator*. New York: Oxford University Press.

Cone, E. T. (1968). *Musical Form and Musical Performance: A Lucid and Penetrating Study of the Nature of Musical Form and its Presentation in Performance*. New York: Norton.

Farkas, P. (1976). *The Art of Musicianship: A Treatise on the Skills, Knowledge, and Sensitivity Needed by the Mature Musician to Perform in an Artistic and Professional Manner*. Bloomington, Ind.: Musical Publications.

Green, B. (2003). *The Mastery of Music: Ten Pathways to True Artistry*. New York: Broadway Books.

O'Toole, P. A. (2003). *Shaping Sound Musicians: An Innovative Approach to Teaching Comprehensive Musicianship through Performance*. Chicago: GIA.

Thompson, W. F. (2009). *Music, Thought, and Feeling: Understanding the Psychology of Music*. Oxford: Oxford University Press.

Watkins, C. (2008). *Rosindust: Teaching, Learning and Life from a Cellist's Perspective*. Houston: Rosindust.

Werner, K. (1996). *Effortless Mastery: Liberating the Master Musician Within*. New Albany, Ind.: Jamey Aebersold Jazz.

10 Your Teaching Philosophy

THIS BOOK HAS GUIDED you to consider a variety of aspects of the teaching process. If you have already been teaching, you have undoubtedly encountered many of the challenges and rewards that are an ongoing part of the profession. Even if you haven't yet taught a single lesson, your experience as a student has helped you form opinions about what works and what doesn't. Now it's time to put your ideas about teaching and learning into a statement that can help you clarify your beliefs and guide your interactions with students and other professionals.

The Benefits of Creating a Philosophy Statement

As challenging as articulating a philosophy can be, this is an important step for you to take as a teacher for a variety of reasons:

- To state your values and beliefs formally is to make a binding agreement with yourself that these values will be an integral part of how you teach—your own Constitution, so to speak.

- By clarifying your highest priorities and outlining specific teaching strategies, you align your goals with what you actually do in your lessons or the classroom.
- A philosophy statement can help strengthen your resolve regarding your most significant priorities so your teaching goals are less likely to be derailed by frustrations or distractions.
- Developing a teaching philosophy will prepare you for job interviews. Grappling with these thoughts now will help you respond more readily to questions about your fundamental beliefs and your role in students' lives.

Your philosophy statement should be as strong and clear as you can make it today, yet it will not be carved in stone: it will remain a flexible document that can change over time. It is quite possible that your priorities will shift as you gain more perspective about your role as a teacher. Nevertheless, what you believe right now is as important to the lessons you teach today as your beliefs will be to you and the lessons you teach ten years from now. So don't delay—let your most deeply held convictions about teaching rise to the top, and begin to emerge as words.

> **Personal Inventory:** Make a list of the most important abilities and/or qualities students will develop through their work with you. Preface each item with the phrase "As a result of my instruction students will . . ." Prioritize your list, and begin to consider the first three or four as building blocks for your philosophy statement.

Grounding Your Philosophy in Real Teaching

Now that you have identified your goals, you must have a way to teach them. Some are explicit goals that can be learned through specific instruction and will result in unequivocal evidence of mastery. Others are more ambiguous and require a more complex definition and multilevel approach to teaching; still others are intangible and must be evoked rather than taught, like appreciation, love, trust, and joy. Such terms should be used with care in your philosophy statement, especially when describing student achievement. While noble goals certainly have a place in your work with students, they must be grounded in observable behaviors and real experiences.

The goals you put in your philosophy statement need to emerge from what you actually do in lessons. For instance, if you make the statement "Students will discover the joy of music in their lives" but you spend the majority of lesson time browbeating students over their poor intonation, it is not likely they will "discover the joy of music"—or if they do, it probably won't be through their work with you. There's nothing wrong with a mandate to strengthen weak intonation skills, but if "joy of music" really is one of your principle tenets, then you need to actively do something about it on a weekly basis.

Perhaps you really want students to be joyful about their music-making but know they will never have a joyful career if they continue to play out of tune—fair enough. Acknowledge that well-developed intonation skills are a substantial part of your approach. Because you also need to address how you teach these skills, the statement might read like this: "My students will become accomplished musicians by learning essential intonation skills through regular browbeating." It's honest, it's specific, and it's something you actually do in lessons.

Of course, no one would ever confess to such a thing in writing, but this is a good time to take a close look at what you really do when you teach. While perhaps in the past you've been known to cover your ears and bellow "I've never heard such out-of-tune playing in my life—fix it!" you now recognize that this is not a particularly effective way to help students refine their intonation skills, and have decided to include ear training and singing skills as a part of your teaching. In this case, you'll be proud to describe these specific, effective strategies and conclude the statement with the evidence of accomplishment: ". . . resulting in performances that demonstrate consistent and beautifully refined intonation."

Now let's get back to "joy." If you see a direct correlation between joy and playing in tune, then perhaps you can draw the connection: "When students have full command of their intonation skills, their musicianship will likely become a joyful part of their lives." But is there a way to actually teach joy itself?

Examine in more detail what you really mean by "joy of music." What makes music joyful for you? How much do you bring that joy into lessons? When you are passionate about a piece of music that you're teaching, do you share that with your students? What has made you glad—joyful—to be a musician? Consider recent experiences, but also memorable times as a younger student. These might include a special event, like your first major ensemble experience, when you got a near-permanent case of goose bumps, or a small but significant moment, like the day you matched your teacher's incredible sound; or the boost you got from listening to your favorite recording with the lights off, reveling in the power of the music.

While you can't actually make someone share your feelings, you can find ways to greatly increase the potential that students have their own meaningful experiences with music. You could start by turning your own experiences into opportunities for your students. Prepare them well for an audition, so that they have an excellent chance to perform with a great ensemble; have wonderful back-and-forth exchanges of beautiful sounds in lessons; give them a recording with suggestions about a powerful way to listen—or perhaps institute in-the-dark listening as a regular feature of your studio class. (Refer to Chapter 9, *Comprehensive Teaching*, for more ideas.)

With thoughtful and creative attention to this important objective, you are now much closer to a real possibility that your work with students will result in their joyful experience of music. And if this does happen, what will this look like or sound like? Will you see joy reflected in increased enthusiasm at lessons, extra time in the practice room, more expression in their performing? This is not to imply that everything you impart to your students needs to result in something overt or quantifiable in order to be valuable. But the more you work toward recognizable results, the more intentional you become, and the higher the likelihood your goals will be attained.

Personal Inventory: Drawing from your list of teaching goals, write statements that describe what your students do to demonstrate mastery of those concepts. Start with more easily quantifiable goals in areas such as technical ability and knowledge. Then write similar statements for less quantifiable goals, such as those having to do with musical expression or conceptual understanding (for example, "the role of history and theory in interpretation"). Finally, venture into the areas of "appreciation" and other intrinsic/aesthetic qualities—how do you offer them, and how do your students demonstrate growth in these areas?

A PACT WITH YOURSELF

The most effective teaching philosophy describes your attitude and actions as a teacher, and in what ways you are accountable for the teaching-learning process. For instance, you might believe that inquisitiveness is significant to your students' development; if you have ways you nurture inquisitiveness in students, this certainly belongs in your philosophy. However, a statement like "I give quality lessons to inquisitive students" puts the burden of good teaching on what *students* bring to the relationship. Of course students are in many ways responsible for learning, and teachers can and should outline their expectations and requirements; however those statements belong in your studio policy (see Chapter 11, *Establishing a Teaching Studio*), where you can spell out specifics regarding the cooperative effort between yourself and your students. The statement you're working on now has everything to do with you and the way you cultivate the best possible musician out of every student who walks through your door.

Your philosophy will focus on your sphere of influence, and the things you have the ability to control. It is not about how students should or could respond, nor is it a platform to preach to others about what they ought to be doing. Your philosophy is also not the place to make comparisons about what you know versus what others don't, whether directed to students, colleagues, or administration. This is about who you are, what you believe, and how you will act on those principles as a teacher.

> **Personal Inventory:** Look at your current statements about teaching. If necessary, remove any wording that suggests what others should be doing. If you haven't done so already, make a statement about the kind of musician, teacher, and person you will be to your students. Statements should be strong and positive, but needn't come across as arrogant or boastful—these are your truths from within, and as such they have their own innate strength.

HONING YOUR PHILOSOPHY WITH JOB INTERVIEW QUESTIONS

The questions that follow are common to many teaching interviews. Even if you have no immediate plans to apply for a teaching position, your answers to these questions can help further clarify your philosophy statement. (For a longer list of questions and more about applying for a job, see Appendix 10.1.)

1. What do you look for in a student? What makes a good student?
2. How do you motivate your students to practice well and be the best possible musicians?
3. What makes a good teacher? What would make you a better teacher?
4. Do you see your teaching role as encompassing more than specifically teaching your instrument? How do you teach those other aspects without losing sight of your primary goal?
5. How would you define your style of teaching? How has it evolved from "teaching what your teacher taught you" to a style that is your own?

> **Personal Inventory:** Your philosophy should offer not only an overview of your principles, but a glimpse of your teaching style. After considering these interview questions, feel free to add thoughts you might now want to include in your statement.

LIFE INFLUENCES

Question 5 raises an interesting point: how much are you a product of how you were taught, and how much are you your own person? Just as children's formative experiences and family traditions affect their adult lives, a similar effect occurs as you are "raised" as a musician. Perhaps certain aspects of your background have worked well for you, and others have not. The more independent you have become, the better able you are to reflect on those experiences and make mature decisions as to what is right for you, musically, technically, pedagogically, and personally.

It's possible that you've recently been awakened to a new teaching approach and are wondering "Why didn't someone ever teach me this way? It would have helped so much!" Perhaps you were subjected to experiences that you would never impose on a student because of the negative effect they had on you. Even the teachers whom you didn't like, or whose approach didn't work well for you, can give you insights about the kind of teacher you want to be. Knowing what kind of teacher you don't want to be can sometimes give you the strongest incentive to nurture the best in yourself.

> **Personal Inventory:** What have been the major influences in your musical life, both positive and negative? Can you identify the most rewarding and formative elements of your life as a student and a performer, and perhaps even now as a teacher? How have these influences shaped your development, musically, technically, philosophically, and personally?

Another consideration in your musical upbringing is your pedagogical lineage: your teachers' teachers. Knowing your heritage can help you to see yourself carrying on a tradition of fine teaching and performing. You could research your "great-grand-teacher's" development of a particular technique, or discover that a musician in your lineage worked directly with a composer to debut a composition that is now a standard in the repertoire. Not only are these fascinating historical anecdotes to pass along to your students, they offer you skills and interpretive approaches upon which to ground your teaching.

It is also possible that you have your own unique offering: perhaps you are composing a new breed of etudes for your instrument, premiering new compositions, or developing an innovative technique on your instrument, thus creating your own niche. Harmonica virtuoso Howard Levy has taken his instrument to new levels of technique and expression, and has established a web-based school from which he can offer harmonica lessons to virtually anyone in the world. In both performing and teaching he is making an indelible mark on the larger world of music performance.

INTERVIEWING YOUR TEACHERS

Personal Inventory: What is your musical heritage? What traditions, techniques, or even "pearls of wisdom" have been handed down to you? What will you pass along to your students?

Now would be a good time to have a heart-to-heart conversation with your primary teacher, especially if you don't know the answer to the questions in the last personal inventory. Also, if at all possible, try to reconnect with a favorite teacher from your earlier years, and ask about his or her choice to work with younger students. Here are more questions that should stimulate an enlightening discussion:

1. When and why did you start teaching?
2. Did you think you wanted to be a teacher when you were first offered the opportunity?
3. What challenges have you had to overcome as a person or as a musician? How has your ability to deal with these challenges influenced your teaching?
4. What has been your most unexpected teaching challenge?
5. What has been the most unexpected reward from teaching?
6. What is your highest priority when working with a student?
7. What was (am) I like as a student?
8. What did (do) you find most challenging about teaching me?
9. How did (do) you keep me motivated?
10. Did (do) you see something in me that I couldn't see for myself?
11. Who were your teachers? How did their teaching influence yours?
12. Could you share any stories about your formative experiences that I might not have heard before, either personal or musical?
13. What is your advice for me?

Personal Inventory: After interviewing your teachers, how has your perspective shifted? You might choose to reconsider your priorities or reshape your approach on the basis of what you have learned from the interviews.

ADDITIONAL INFLUENCES

Look again at question 12, about formative experiences. Consider the life experiences that have shaped who *you* are, not just as a musician but as a person. Sometimes it is one's unique life story that gives one a special perspective as a teacher and a performer, such as grappling with a learning challenge, overcoming an injury, or growing up with a sibling who is disabled. You might also be fascinated with the acoustical properties of your instrument, or are intrigued by a particular aspect of music history. Any special circumstances, relationships, or interests in your life are important to acknowledge and can shape your life's work.

PHILOSOPHY STATEMENT TOPICS

As you review your teaching philosophy in its current stage, here are some reminders about what to include:

- The passion, inspiration, joy, knowledge, and/or skills about music and your instrument, singing, or conducting that you want to pass along to your students.
- The environment you will create to support learning and growth, including your relationship to your students, both individually and as a community.
- Who you want to be to your students, as a teacher and as a person.
- The single most important thing your students will take away from having studied with you.
- Specific ways that your teaching life will reflect your philosophy.
- Specific strategies you will use to ensure that learning will happen.
- Any aspects of learning music that you believe develop the whole person, or life skills that are cultivated in students by the way you teach.
- Anything unique or special that you bring to your profession as a musician and teacher.

You don't need to include:

- Specific books or methods you will use, unless you utilize a methodology that is integral to your philosophy. If so, explain why this approach resonates with your ideals.
- What you instrument or discipline you teach, unless it is integral to your philosophy. The more musicians teach and listen to students of varying degrees of sophistication and development, the more they are aware that high standards of musicianship are the same on any instrument at any stage of development.
- Your expectations of students (these can go into your lesson policy).
- What other teachers think, or do, or should do—just include what you believe and what you will bring to your teaching.

The Final Stages of Writing

> That inner voice has both gentleness and clarity. So to get to authenticity, you really keep
> going down to the bone, to the honesty, and the inevitability of something.
> MEREDITH MONK, COMPOSER

Now it's time to condense your philosophy into a succinct, readable document. If you avoid extended explanations and elaborate language, one or two pages should be sufficient. Keep only what is strongest and truest, and leave out the rest. Because there are no hard-and-fast rules about content and form, you can organize your statement any way you like, with bullet points or paragraphs. Be sure the document communicates your most important principles while offering an honest portrayal of who you are as a teacher.

Share your statement with a friend, a teacher, or your class, and ask for feedback. You're not asking them to agree with you, only to understand more about you and how you teach from reading the document. If what they reflect back to you is the substance of what you hoped to convey, then you have succeeded. If you find yourself re-explaining important ideals, or adding information, then jot those thoughts down and create another draft that further clarifies these important points. You want your truest self to emerge from your philosophy, with no need for further explanations.

Once you are content that your statement reflects who you are and what you believe, what should you do with it? Unless your teaching philosophy is a required component of a job application, you will probably just keep it for yourself. Place it in your teaching notebook and read it from time to time for inspiration and encouragement. If you feel so inclined, you could share it with parents or administrators, but it's not something you would hand out to your students—frankly, they shouldn't need to read it because this is what you are offering on a daily basis. However, in the future this document will help you prepare a successful job interview, serve as an introduction to a well-rounded tenure portfolio, or be the basis of an acceptance speech for a teaching award.

> Take advantage of every opportunity to practice your communication skills so that when
> important occasions arise, you will have the gift, the style, the sharpness, the clarity, and the
> emotions to affect other people.
> JIM ROHN, BUSINESS CONSULTANT

By all means, make your philosophy statement a living document. Your basic premise for teaching might not change, but time and experience will shift your perspective. Priorities tend to reshuffle themselves. You'll be exposed to new ideas that will change your outlook, and some convictions that might now seem absolute will perhaps become more ambiguous the longer you teach. You'll likely become more aware of yourself in relation to an ever-widening circle of teachers, artists, colleagues, and even citizens of the world. So if you find yourself thinking differently about a priority, make a note of it; if you become aware of an important new goal, add it in; and if you think of a better way to convey a challenging concept, write it down quickly, before it slips away!

Writing a teaching philosophy is a challenging assignment, but the intrinsic rewards are, we hope, evident by now. When you clarify your core values and capture them on paper, rather than subsisting from lesson to lesson, you will begin to teach from that wider and wiser perspective. When you work to integrate your goals and principles with your wealth of skills and knowledge as a performer, teaching is elevated far above the status of "second job" to become a true vocation: an extension of who you are as a musician and a human being.

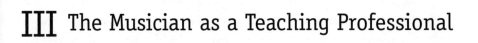

III The Musician as a Teaching Professional

11 Establishing a Teaching Studio

PERFORMERS GRAVITATE toward teaching private lessons for many reasons, some of the strongest being that it offers the most direct effect on a student's development, the most flexibility in scheduling, and good hourly pay. Private, or one-on-one, lessons can be taught in the teacher's home studio, at public or private schools, and stand-alone music schools and community centers. Each situation has its advantages and disadvantages, and all require some basic business knowledge.

Independent Studios

Many performing musicians prefer to teach individual private students at their homes. Freelance schedules often differ from week to week, so teaching schedules need to be reasonably adaptable, and this option allows the most flexibility. If you make this choice, it also means that you are completely responsible for running your own business, including creating a functional work space, setting fees, keeping track of lessons taught and money received, and establishing a refund and makeup lesson policy. For a handful of students, this is not a particularly challenging task, but the more students on your roster, the more serious you must be about establishing effective and efficient ways to manage your business.

PHYSICAL SPACE

A good studio space is at least somewhat removed from your living quarters, and even better if it is easily accessed just inside the main entry or through a side entrance to your home. Preferably you will be able to shut a door to ward off distractions. If possible, have a waiting area for students and families arriving for a lesson, and a guest bathroom for students who need to wash their hands or young siblings who just "can't wait." While students unpack their instruments, parents can read summer music camp information, studio event notices, or music-related periodicals placed on a coffee table or posted on a bulletin board.

If you teach at home, be aware that some neighborhoods have deed restrictions regarding running a business in a residential area. Since most of these rules are designed to prevent traffic problems and neon signs, it is unlikely that teaching one student at a time in your home will be cause for complaint. On the other hand, recitals and group classes might cause parking and traffic congestion in the neighborhood. A better venue for such events would be a public space with available parking, such as a church or community center. No matter the circumstances, you will want to be sure that students and parents are sensitive to the concerns of the neighbors, driving slowly on streets where children live, and not blocking neighbors' driveways and mailboxes.

GENERAL STUDIO SETUP

An efficiently set up teaching studio will probably include the following:

- A well-stocked and organized music collection, including duets and sight-reading material
- Copies of pieces marked with fingerings, bowings, pedalings, and so on, especially lengthy pieces like concertos and sonatas
- A CD player and CDs of music often taught
- A computer to access information related to pieces, composers, and so on
- A copy machine
- A video camera that is ready to be used at a moment's notice
- Suitable chairs (with extras available for groups of students)
- A piano (or extra piano) for accompaniments and theory explanations
- A date book for scheduling, recording payments received, and so on

- At least one heavy black music stand with a stand light
- A metronome (preferably with a tap function for checking students' tempos)
- A tuner (if useful)
- A music dictionary and other reference materials
- Graded repertoire lists for festivals and examinations
- Manuscript paper
- Plenty of pencils

You might also wish to create a notebook with information about your students, separate from or as an addition to your calendar. Ask students to fill out a form that includes their age and grade, the school they attend, the school music director's name, all contact information (including home and cell phone numbers, email and street addresses) and other activities in which they are involved. On the back of this sheet, ask students to list repertoire already studied, music camps attended, and any other information that might be helpful in getting to know more about their musical background. You can add to this information as you work with your students, keeping track of additional repertoire and other experiences.

Once you are organized, it is also helpful to give new students a binder-ready packet that includes important information such as:

- Your contact information
- Your lesson policy
- Accompanists' names and contact information
- Recommended businesses for repairs, supplies, and instrument insurance
- A regular lesson schedule/teaching calendar
- A studio roster with contact information
- A student/teacher assessment form (see Appendix 9.2)
- Regularly used handouts, such as scale fingerings, exercises, images, worksheets, self-assessment sheets, and so on
- Competition information and application dates
- Contact information for local youth and community ensembles
- Recommended books and recordings

Consider having separate handouts for parents, especially if they handle all the lesson schedules and purchases. Many parents might also be interested in copies of articles about parenting and practicing, information about local music events, camps and concerts, and music supply catalogues.

ATTRACTING STUDENTS

If you are new to a community, whether you have recently graduated, moved to a new area, or have just decided to start a studio after years of performing, you will need to become known as a teacher. Join a local professional teaching organization and attend meetings to learn about possible teaching or coaching opportunities, and volunteer to do a class or give a demonstration if it seems appropriate. At a minimum, introduce yourself to the other teachers and let them know you'd appreciate any referrals if they receive inquiries but can't accept more students.

To contact the public directly, it's tempting to purchase advertisements in concert programs, but these are costly and rarely yield many students. Business cards or personal computer-produced ads are far less expensive and can be placed on bulletin boards at music shops. Keep the information simple: what kinds of lessons you are offering, your name, and contact information. While including your alma mater or performance experience might help attract students, don't put too much emphasis on your credentials. Ultimately what will command the most respect is proof of your teaching ability. When your first student sitting at the back of the second violins rather quickly finds his way to the front of the section, and then wins a spot in the honors orchestra the next year, your reputation will quickly be established.

A musician's best approach to building a class of students is to get out there and teach: go to a local school and coach a sectional, or offer a clinic to help prepare students for an upcoming regional audition. Inquire about coaching positions at a local youth orchestra or community ensemble. Find out at which grade level your instrument is introduced in the local school system, and volunteer to play a short concert or teach a mini–master class. Speak to the teacher in advance about your desire to build a class of private students, and ask him or her to announce your availability at the session. Be assured that your presence in the classroom will make an impression on the students, and the teacher can pass along contact information to students and their parents who make inquiries.

You won't necessarily be paid for these services, especially if you are the one making initial contact, but when you make yourself available and accessible, and begin to establish a rapport with the students and school music teachers, students will start to flow in your direction. Even teaching just two or three classes in the schools can get the ball rolling, and if you are willing to make such sessions an annual event, you will become an invaluable resource to the teachers and a "go-to" private teacher in the minds of the students.

ESTABLISHING A SUPPORT BASE

When you establish a positive personal relationship with parents, they can be some of the best allies in your business. They can act as advertisers and business scouts.

They sit at concerts with other parents and share stories about challenges and successes in raising a musical son or daughter. They will happily recommend you to others looking for a teacher. Orchestra, band, and choir directors and private teachers with full classes will recommend someone they like and respect. Establishing positive relationships with adults—parents, public school teachers, and colleagues—is in some ways as important as your rapport with students.

SETTING LESSON FEES

If you are new to teaching, you will want to find out what other private teachers in your area are charging. Not everyone will be forthcoming with this information, but with some persistence you should be able to get a feel for the going rate. Teachers who have a consistent record of success usually command the highest fees, as they well should, and younger teachers with less experience will charge less. However, even if you haven't had much experience, if you are willing and eager to invest in improving as a teacher, don't undervalue what you can offer. You will not attract more students by charging less than the norm—in fact you might actually undercut your ability to attract good students. As odd as this seems on the surface, parents of the most serious students assume (albeit unconsciously) that a teacher who charges less money is simply not as good as one who charges more.

It's also wise to consider your "comfort zone" when it comes to setting fees. Students' ability to pay for private lessons varies from family to family. You can set fees on a sliding scale, but this is challenging to supervise. The most straightforward system is to establish one fee that you can collect in good conscience. Setting an appropriate fee will help you to be more peaceful about asking for payments, keeping your schedule, and enforcing your cancellation policies; it might also allow you to establish studio scholarships for students you want to teach but who do not have the means. Begin by charging a moderate rate if you're unsure at first. With continued success you can raise your fee with good conscience in the future. When students and parents are happy with the lessons and respect you as a person, they are not likely to drop you and move to another teacher over a few incremental increases.

When you charge an hourly rate, you might not want to divide your fee exactly in half for a half-hour session. You will find that the scheduling, book keeping, and lesson planning for a half-hour student takes as much time and energy as a full-hour student. When it comes to the personal energy needed to switch gears to a new student every half hour, teachers often find that six half-hour students is far more tiring than three students taking hour lessons. You can establish a fee scale proportionate to these considerations—in other words, if you charge $50 per hour, you might ask for $40 for a forty-five-minute lesson and $30 for the half hour. If you are offering group classes in addition to individual lessons (see the upcoming section on group classes), you need to consider whether to charge separately for these classes or bundle the cost of the group sessions into your lesson fee to cover your extra planning and teaching time.

COLLECTING FEES

On the surface, receiving payment each time a lesson is taught seems like the easiest thing to do, but while this method works for some teachers, there are considerable drawbacks. Being paid week-to-week means you will likely have to deal with bookkeeping on an almost daily basis. Commitment to the lessons also tends to be an issue. If a student or parent has paid in advance for lessons, they are apt to attend lessons more consistently than if they are paying as they go. You yourself might succumb to inconsistency, which does not bode well for your students' progress or your business. Also consider that when the parent forgets to bring cash or a checkbook, you will probably have to wait another week for your payment.

Having students pay by the month or even the semester reduces the amount of bookkeeping you will have to do. Some teachers allow students to pay for the month after they have had the lessons, but again, for commitment and consistency, requesting the month's payment in advance is a good idea. For similar reasons, some teachers also require a minimum number of lessons to be taken in one month. A simple statement in your lesson policy can clarify this: "I expect to see my students every week, but a minimum of three lessons per month is required." This way you needn't be penalized for the student who regularly finds reasons to cancel lessons. You will have to decide under what circumstances you are willing to make up any missed lessons, but at least you are guaranteed a more consistent income. It also gives you a clearer way to live within your means: after the first week you know how much teaching money has come in and how to budget for the month.

Everyone who teaches private lessons knows that income drops steeply in the summer. If you are a committed teacher who is consistent with scheduling and bookkeeping throughout the year, you might decide to have students pay a year-round, consistent monthly fee—basically like a salary. Teachers who do this must be able to guarantee a minimum number of lessons during the year. This approach to running your studio requires substantial planning—making advanced decisions about the number of lessons a student will receive in the fall, spring, and summer terms; creating a calendar; deciding how many cancellations and makeup lessons are allowed and when they will happen. Multiply your lesson fee by the total number of lessons you will teach during the year; then divide by twelve. Some months you will give more lessons than you receive payment for, but it balances out in the leaner months. You might also need to ask for one month's notice if they are quitting lessons to give you time to replace the outgoing student.

SCHEDULING

While all musicians need scheduling flexibility at times, scheduling students week-to-week can challenge your ability to be consistent. When the weekly lesson schedule is never the same twice, you will have a difficult time remembering which student to expect when, and your students will have the same problem. This often leads to the need for weekly phone calls to confirm the schedule or, worse, frustrating problems with miscommunications and misunderstandings. If lack of consistency and missed lessons become the norm, serious students will eventually find another teacher.

A smarter approach is to find a time when you and your student are most often available and make that a regular time. Once the regular time is established, make it a habit to look ahead at your performing and freelancing schedule for the upcoming month. Pencil in hand, compare your calendar with your student's, keeping the regular time whenever possible and immediately rescheduling any obvious conflicts. It won't be foolproof, since there will always be last-minute job opportunities for you, and unforeseen events for them, but at least you have established a workable schedule at the onset of the month. If you collect fees a month in advance, this is the time the student will pay for these lessons.

If you can manage regular teaching hours, you might want to consider giving everyone in the studio your teaching schedule, with shared contact information (though be sure you clear this with parents first). That way, if students need to reschedule a lesson, they can call others to see if a switch can be made, and call you only if they can't find a solution to their problem.

PARENTAL INVOLVEMENT

If you teach precollege students, parents will inevitably be a regular part of the picture: providing transportation, scheduling, and making payments. Beyond this, their expectations, commitment to, and involvement in their children's lessons can vary greatly. Some parents view music lessons as one more activity that keeps their son or daughter from being idle; some consider it a way to add to their child's sophistication and social grooming; and some see it as an important part of their child's development and personal expression. Parents in the latter group tend to be the most involved, though ideally, if we do our jobs well, all parents will come to recognize the lessons as a significant experience for their children.

Parents' level of involvement is in many ways up to you, since you can require their participation as a part of your policy on accepting students. Some teachers will not accept a student unless the parent agrees to be at every lesson and supervise home practice, and some even insist that the parent learn to play the instrument alongside the child. While outwardly this amount of involvement might seem unnecessary, the parent really is, or at least can be, your partner in making the lesson process work. Parents who attend lessons can take notes about goals and assignments while providing the structure and guidance that supports the all-important home practice process. When parents study an instrument alongside their children, they appreciate the challenges far better than if they are only observing. Even if they aren't taking lessons, you can ask them to try some of the same challenging exercises that you are teaching their children, driving home the point that it's not as easy as it seems (and at times delighting your students when they see they are actually better at something than their parents).

Probably the most important part of parents' involvement has to do with a rare opportunity to observe the child in a focused learning environment. Parents can see how their child responds to self-observation and assessment, develops skills, makes decisions, and independently solves problems. They will have a more immediate sense of your expectations of the child and are likely to be more supportive and respectful of you and your decisions as the teacher. It also gives them an opportunity to ask questions about practicing specifics or the process in general.

If a parent is in attendance at lessons, it will be important for you to be clear about how much input the parent can have. You might need a rule that protects the sanctity of the teacher-student relationship, requesting that parents save questions and comments until the end. In spite of such a requirement, you will still occasionally get a glimpse of the parent-child relationship. An interjection, passing comment, reprimand, even a nonverbal exchange between parent and child can lend some insight into the relationship and reflect the level of support the student is receiving at home. It may warrant some further discussion (preferably not in the student's presence) about your goals for the student, the challenges that might arise, and how the parent can be most helpful in supporting the teaching and learning process.

With more students will come a wide variety of parents:

They can be very supportive: *"I appreciate you clarifying the goals for the week, because I want to be sure we understand exactly how to practice at home."*

Or never seem to "get it": *"Sorry, I thought the recital started at three o'clock, not two o'clock. Could you just squeeze my three kids in at the end of the program?"*

They can stir up a competitive attitude within your studio: *"If you practice a little more I bet you could get first chair and knock Beth back to second stand."*

Or foster a supportive attitude: *"I am so proud of everyone's work this semester. The recital was amazing. Did you notice the improvement in Will's tone?"*

Parents can resent taking their children to lessons: *"Hurry up . . . I have better things to do than chauffeur you to all these events every afternoon!"*

Or be generous with their time and energy: *"If Mark's mother is busy I can pick him up and bring him to class tomorrow—that way the whole group can be together."*

In any case, do not let your personal opinions influence your primary goal: to make lessons valuable to your students. For children, this usually does mean making it meaningful to their parents as well. Include parents in as much of their children's learning process as possible, and help them see its value. Get to know the parents, allow the focus to be on what is best for their children, and foster an environment of mutual appreciation and respect.

OFFERING GROUP CLASSES

Considering the many techniques that need reinforcing and the repertoire to be covered, most teachers find that group classes are a great advantage to themselves and their students. Group technique classes allow teachers to work on universal concepts and skills with all their students, leaving more time for individualized instruction in private lessons. Performance classes provide extra opportunities for students to play in a comfortable and supportive environment. Repertoire can be both reinforced and introduced, and students are motivated by hearing others perform pieces that they look forward to learning.

Besides these positives there are also important hidden benefits. In group settings, students have the opportunity to be not only performers but listeners who learn through their vicarious engagement in another performer's experience. Students learn from the inside and outside what makes a performance work, and in a safe environment they can experiment with a variety of responses to the pressures of preparation and performance. In addition, while a group lesson might be highly structured in terms of goals and activities, the ambient music and social interactivity are a powerful part of an informal learning environment.

> Being a member of a group, in this case of the best players in the city and state, provided
> me with so much confidence. Having played every week for students and teachers I respected
> made it easier to stand up in front of my peers and perform well at auditions and
> competitions.
> YOUNG PROFESSIONAL

The group lesson can also provide students with an important social component in their development. Students get to know others with similar interests and challenges, and they encourage and motivate one another. When parents of younger students bring them to group lessons, they have the opportunity to discuss the common interests of their children and can support the abilities and efforts of every child in the group. As a teacher, you can encourage the kind of cooperative spirit that fosters civility and mutual respect within your sphere of influence.

> In addition to the numerous educational benefits, group lessons provided me with a peer group that pushed me to excel. Seeing the same people every week and watching them get better also gave me a sense of accountability in my own playing and practicing. We all wanted to get better together. Not only did I have peers to look up to, it also allowed me to be a leader to younger students. Perhaps most important, being a member of that performing group provided me with friendships that last to this day.
> ORCHESTRAL MUSICIAN AND PRIVATE INSTRUCTOR

Considering all these benefits, it should seem worthwhile to organize group sessions. A teacher with a large studio can group students at two or three different accomplishment levels, using repertoire, technique, or ensemble work as organizing factors. If you don't have enough students to make such group sessions feasible by yourself, you might want to combine forces with another teacher to assemble more students. This situation can be enriching in many ways, as it provides a sometimes rare opportunity to interact and share ideas with a colleague, and it allows your students to meet other students outside your class. If you and the other teacher work well together, you might consider pooling resources toward enrichment activities such as inviting a guest clinician or planning larger combined studio events and festivals.

You could also consider having group lessons that bring together students of varying ages and abilities. With some careful advanced planning on your part, these can also be very successful. The younger students will certainly benefit from having the more accomplished students playing with them, and the older students can demonstrate advanced techniques and perform their repertoire for the younger students to hear and aspire to.

If your life during the regular performing season is too hectic to organize regularly scheduled group classes, summer can be a great time to arrange a series of ensembles or technique sessions. In addition to weekly private lessons, you could create your own summer intensive workshop. With a well-organized teaching plan, you can accomplish a semester's worth of technique practice in a week-long intensive day camp. The focus could be on upcoming auditions or a specific technique, or you could create an ensemble festival culminating in a public recital or an informal in-house event. Besides all the previously mentioned benefits, summer group sessions give students a reason to keep practicing, and can add to your own professional schedule when your calendar is most open. (For more information on group lesson planning and teaching see Chapter 12, *More Teaching Situations*.)

RECITALS AND OTHER PERFORMANCES

In addition to group lesson activities, it is also important to organize at least one class performance a year. Recitals offer students an important opportunity to share what they've accomplished with friends and family while being inspired by hearing other students perform. Recitals are also important to the parents, giving them a chance to meet other parents and share their children's success.

Hire a good accompanist, preferably an experienced, skilled musician who can offer much more than the notes in the piano part. Music departments of universities often employ fine staff accompanists who might be available, and graduate students are also a good possibility. Be sure to find someone with a pleasant, relaxed demeanor that will set students at ease. Decide on a set fee per performer for rehearsal(s) and the performance. You can charge everyone the same amount, but if your students are playing at different levels, it's sometimes better to assess the length and difficulty of the repertoire and determine the accompanist's fee on a sliding scale. While you'll want to have more than one good accompanist to call on, it's great to have an accompanist who is able to work with your class on a regular basis so that students can develop a relationship with him or her. Your more serious students will be glad to have someone they can depend on for individual performances, auditions, and concerto competitions.

Find a performance site with access to a good piano. Sometimes a living room will do nicely, but the more students there are, the larger the venue needed to accommodate the audience (not to mention extra space for instruments and cases, when that is a consideration). Occasionally, a school will let you use their facilities, but don't take it personally if they decline: liability and insurance issues are usually the obstacle. Churches are often able to be more accommodating, and some music stores have small recital halls that you can rent for a reasonable fee.

There are limitless ways to integrate your studio into the community where you teach. Investigate prospects for short showcase performances or mini-touring experiences. Music festivals and community venues such as hospitals, art galleries, malls, schools, and libraries can provide unlimited performance opportunities for your students.

You will be responsible for most of the scheduling and logistics, and of course your students' preparation, but parents are often very willing to get involved in the logistics, so allow them to contribute. Someone might want to set up chairs for the recital, type and copy programs, bring in plants to make the stage more attractive, or provide refreshments for the reception. You can be the coordinator yourself, but with your students' preparation as your primary concern, you might be wise to let an eager parent run the show.

Running Your Business

GETTING ORGANIZED

When you create your own studio, you'll need to think ahead about how to manage it. Keep it simple if you can, especially starting out. Have one notebook, combined with your calendar if possible, where you keep all pertinent student information. The notebook can be used for scheduling as well as for keeping track of tuition due and payments received, with a pocket to hold checks until you can get to the bank. Make it a habit never to deposit a check until it has been recorded. Some teachers find it better to keep everything on their computers, but no matter what method you choose, don't make it necessary to record information in two places. This can lead to either too much work, utter confusion, or both.

Also—this is a big one—be sure you have liability insurance. It is tempting to think you don't need insurance until that dreadful moment when a parent slips on your front porch, or the dog decides to express his disdain for a student's younger sibling. Project ahead to the unthinkable, and what a lawsuit would do to your life. Find a regional or national teaching organization that provides professional liability insurance at reduced rates for their members. Join the organization, get the insurance, and then safely forget about it. (There are other benefits to joining such an organization as well—see Chapter 14, *The Cyclical and Reciprocal Nature of Teaching*, for more information.)

CREATING YOUR STUDIO POLICY

Once you have made decisions regarding your business, it will be time to establish expectations for yourself and your students. This information can be made available to your students in a concise, readable statement, known as your studio or lesson policy. At the beginning, when you anticipate having just a few students, a lesson policy might seem like an unnecessarily formal document. After a few years, a few more students, and a few problematic episodes with parents, however, the value of such a document will become evident. Conflicts and misunderstandings can be avoided when parents and students have a clear picture of your expectations in one well-conceived statement. Be sure the parents read and agree to your studio policy before their child begins lessons, and make it a practice to give a copy to every student and parent each year, highlighting any recent revisions.

Contents of a studio policy should include:

- Complete contact information
- The location where you teach, if different from your home
- Your fees, timelines, and policy regarding late payments
- Your scheduling system
- Your cancellation and makeup lesson policy
- The minimum number of lessons that students must attend per month, if this is part of your policy
- What you offer students in the way of recitals, group classes, and other events
- What you expect of students in the way of practicing and commitment
- What you expect of parents in relation to the student's musical development
- Anything else that you feel is important for students and parents to know about studying with you, from the philosophical (your belief in each student's potential) to the mundane (where to park)

While it needn't and probably shouldn't read like a legal document, make each point succinctly and immediately understandable. Say what you need to say in one to two pages. Just like good teaching, a few well-chosen words can communicate a strong message.

- "I teach at my home at the rate of $45 per hour."
- "If you must miss a lesson, notify me twenty-four hours or more in advance of the lesson, or I cannot give a refund. If the cancellation is due to a sudden illness, I cannot guarantee a makeup lesson, but will do what I can to reschedule a time."
- "Tuition is due by the 10th of each month; after the 10th, please add a $20 late fee."
- "I give my students specific practice goals weekly and expect everyone to spend a minimum of thirty minutes every day with the instrument."
- "Please do not park in front of my neighbor's mailbox."

On the other hand, be sure to sound welcoming and kind to your students and their parents, and end the document with an encouraging word about looking forward to your work together. Everything you offer to your students and their families should express who you are as an individual. While your lesson policy is an important part of your business, it needn't be void of humanity. Write a draft and ask a friend to read it, preferably someone who also teaches. He or she can help you decide on content and refine the tone that will reflect who you are as a teacher and as a person.

Other One-on-One Teaching Situations

PUBLIC OR PRIVATE SCHOOLS

Frequently, lessons offered at a school are administered by the school itself. The school program administrator sets the fees, handles the payments, and sometimes even creates the schedule for you. Although you may not be expected to hold a teaching certificate, you will likely need to interview for the job and comply with school district policies related to background checks and security protocol.

Students can sometimes take lessons during the school day, but teaching space is usually very limited, and assembly programs, standardized tests, or any other modifications to the school schedule will usually take precedence over individual lessons. After-school lessons are a little more common; they have fewer scheduling problems but other drawbacks. If convenience is a primary factor for families who choose lessons after school, the level of parental or student commitment tends not to be particularly high. Unless you go out of your way to make communication happen, you will have little contact with parents, who will pick their children up in front of the school. Students might also tend to think of after-school lessons as additional coaching sessions for their band or orchestra music, with you acting as an assistant to their school director. While such an assumption is unpalatable to some teachers, others find that the biggest advantage outweighs any problematic element, and that is the sheer number of students immediately available, eliminating the need to do much, if any, recruiting.

STAND-ALONE MUSIC SCHOOLS OR PREPARATORY DIVISIONS

Occasionally you might run across a job posting like this:

> ## POSITION AVAILABLE: STUDIO CELLO
>
> The Philharmonic Music School serves as the preparatory division of the Philharmonic Orchestra. The Music School is housed in a brand new teaching and performance facility with over fifty individual studios, six small ensemble/classrooms, and two large orchestra halls. Our curriculum includes private lessons, chamber music, orchestral training, jazz and rock groups, early childhood classes, Suzuki lessons, and community outreach. Teaching duties will include taking over an existing cello studio currently with three full days of teaching, including private lessons, group classes, and introductory parent classes, as well as participating in recitals.

Many music schools and preparatory divisions for colleges and symphonies offer special advantages: theory lessons, ensembles, prearranged recitals, accompanists, and facilities dedicated to music teaching, with pianos and music stands in most rooms.

The tuition rate is often a flat fee set by the school (although some allow teachers to negotiate their own rate) and the business of enrolling students and collecting fees is handled by the office. In either case, a portion of what your students pay will be retained by the school to cover facility maintenance and office services. This means you might have to accept less per hour than your usual fee, or your students will pay extra for the advantages of enrolling at the school—or both. Not every facility is as spacious as the one advertised here, either: many are small and at full capacity, offering little flexibility when lessons must be rescheduled. However, any disadvantages are often trumped by the prestige of being associated with an established arts organization, its ability to attract serious students, and your membership in a community of well-respected musicians and teachers.

Paying Taxes

In most countries, you are responsible for reporting your private teaching income and freelancing to the government, and should familiarize yourself with laws regarding self-employment and taxation wherever you live and work.

REPORTING SELF-EMPLOYED INCOME IN THE UNITED STATES

If you are employed by a symphony or school, your income is likely reported on a W-2 form with taxes already deducted. Nonemployee jobs—such as contracted gigs, temporary teaching situations, or your own teaching—are combined into a single amount called your "self-employed" income. A business (or individual contractor who runs a business) that pays you an amount over a certain threshold during a year is required to send a Form 1099 to both you and the Internal Revenue Service. (This threshold varies, but is currently around $700.) You alone are responsible for reporting any amounts received below that 1099 threshold and all income you receive from other sources, including private teaching. Be mindful that the IRS can check bank account deposits. If your deposits regularly total more than your declared income, or if you live much more comfortably than your tax return might suggest, you could be asking for trouble. Most self-employed musicians are insignificant in the eyes of the government, but it is not unheard-of for musicians to be audited by the IRS. On the upside, however, there are many deductions to self-employed income (reported on Schedule C) that musicians are entitled to take before their income is taxed.

TAKING DEDUCTIONS

As a self-employed person, you are allowed to take business deductions, and the more deductions you have, the more sense it makes to report your "other income" on

Schedule C. You do not need to have a special tax number or an official business name to file a Schedule C on your income tax return. Sole proprietorship with your name and social security number is all that is necessary.

The following are allowable business deductions typical for musicians:

- Instruments: you can deduct the cost of your instrument one time or amortize the amount over a number of years (many musicians are surprised to learn that they can also depreciate the value of an instrument over time)
- Instrument repairs and maintenance
- Supplies used for business purposes, such as music, strings, metronomes, tuners, music stands, and recording equipment
- Professional teaching organization membership fees and musicians union dues
- Miles driven to self-employed work (non-W-2 jobs), as well as trips to music stores and other business-related errands (with documentation—see below)
- Office supplies directly related to running your business
- Premiums for liability, instrument, and health insurance
- Your studio space and music storage closets, as long as you can prove they are used solely for business purposes (this also includes any upgrades and repairs to these areas)
- Workshops, conferences, and other continuing education programs you might attend, including travel and a percentage of meals
- Concert tickets

Business accounting computer programs are a great way to keep track of your expenses, but they require time and discipline to keep up to date. If you don't have the wherewithal to be an accountant as well as a musician, you can keep all your tax-deductible receipts for the year in a shoebox. Save utility and phone bills if you want to claim an office in the home; a percentage of those receipts can be deducted as well. When it's tax time, sort though the receipts and put them in envelopes marked for each category.

Keeping track of car mileage is a challenge. Most musicians find it impossible to remember to record their mileage when they jump in the car, running a little late for teaching or gigs. However, if you keep a calendar recording the location of each job, you can tally your mileage at the end of the year. Do a computer map search to determine round-trip miles from your home to each job and teaching location; then calculate a total for the year. Any trips you take to a job for which you are considered an employee (you receive a W-2 from this business) are considered "commuting miles." While these miles are not deductible, you still need to record them if you want to use your car as a business deduction. Because your business miles must be at least half of the total miles driven during the year, you need to remember to record your car's odometer reading as close to January 1 as possible to keep uncomfortable guesswork out of the equation.

QUARTERLY TAX PAYMENTS

If you are completely self-employed and owe taxes above a certain threshold, you will need to pay quarterly taxes or run the risk of being charged interest and penalties. You do not need to calculate your taxes every quarter, but when you sign up for quarterly taxes, the IRS will send you payment coupons. You will need to estimate the amount of tax you will owe by year's end, and pay one quarter of that amount by each date preprinted on the coupon. Some musicians who have a combination of employee and self-employed income find that by having the maximum deduction taken out of their W-2 income they can cover their taxes, making it unnecessary to file quarterly.

TAX ACCOUNTANT ASSISTANCE

If you are new to filing taxes, or unsure of the tax laws and filing procedures for self-employed individuals, you are well advised to consult a tax accountant. It is best if that person is familiar with musicians' lifestyles, routines, and expenses, because he or she can help you find the maximum legitimate deductions, offer advice about reporting income, and possibly help you set up your own tax-free retirement fund. For the first few years, you might find the services of an accountant worth the money. Many musicians do find that once they understand the process and how to keep organized records, they can manage on their own with a user-friendly (and tax-deductible!) computer tax program. This aspect of self-employment is probably the least appealing to most musicians; however, being their own boss and running their own business usually outweighs any burden of the added responsibilities.

Ideas for Further Exploration

1. Write a lesson policy. Include information about fees, scheduling, cancellation policies, what you expect of the student (practicing, preparation, outside activities, etc.) and what students and parents can expect of you.
2. Assemble a packet of pertinent information that each of your students will receive. Refer to the second bullet list in "General Studio Set-Up" for ideas,

but include anything that will be useful and interesting to your students. Be artistic and creative, if you like—make it your own.

Recommended Reading

Cutler, David. (2010). *The Savvy Musician: Building a Career, Earning a Living and Making a Difference*. Pittsburgh: Helius Press.

12 Groups, Ensembles, Classrooms, and Other Teaching Situations

IN MANY WAYS YOU are already well prepared for a diverse and stimulating career in music performing and studio teaching, but you will also want to be aware of some other potential situations that might not have been a part of your original vision. During your music career, it's likely that you will find yourself coaching sectionals and chamber music, presenting master classes and outreach concerts, adjudicating, and conducting ensembles. If you are hired to teach at the college level, there is a good chance you'll be asked to teach pedagogy, methods classes, theory, history, or music appreciation. You might even be asked to participate in research studies, serve on search committees, become a faculty sponsor for clubs and organizations, or act as a student advisor.

Besides your musical expertise, one of your most valuable assets will be your ability to articulate concepts, beliefs, and priorities. Besides the ever-present need to explain techniques and concepts at lessons, master classes, and rehearsals, you'll need well-chosen words to compose student assessments and recommendations, to apply and interview for jobs, to speak at conferences, to write articles for publication, and perhaps even to review books and recordings. Schools and university settings will require you to write course proposals, syllabi, and lesson plans; submit faculty peer reviews, prepare annual reports, and collaborate with fellow faculty members on

> ### Consider This
> Most university faculty members are required to write annual reports, which highlight your recruiting and outreach activity as well as professional activities and service on a national and international level. These are reviewed for position renewal, promotions, and tenure considerations, so outlining your well-chosen activities in a well-worded document can be highly valuable to your career. (For ideas, see Chapter 14, *The Cyclical and Reciprocal Nature of Teaching*.)

committees. It's always to your advantage to have organized thoughts and well-chosen words when meeting with administrators, board members, and benefactors. You will need to create high-impact statements for a grant proposal to launch a new program, or even defend your ideals with irrefutable arguments when budget cuts loom and the music department is regarded as nonessential. In fact, the energy and effort you devote to formulating your thoughts as a professional are likely to be second only to the energy and effort you devote to your practicing and performing.

This chapter will highlight the diversity of music teaching positions, which are introduced here with actual position postings from teaching journals and Web sites. While it's not within the scope of this book to detail each responsibility specified in the job descriptions, suggestions that follow will serve as an introduction to some possibilities that could be in your future—situations you'll want to face with eyes open and a few wheels already turning.

POSITION AVAILABLE: VIOLIN AND VIOLA

Northwell University seeks an artist/teacher of violin and viola. The candidate must demonstrate high-level skills as both performer and teacher. In addition to applied teaching, duties include recruitment and chamber music coaching. Candidate's experience must also indicate the ability to organize *weekly studio classes*, serve as division head of the string area, and coordinate *string pedagogy seminars* for performance and music education string majors. Additional responsibilities may include courses in a *secondary area such as commercial music, music theory, or music history*.

Group Instruction

Even if most of your teaching time is in the private studio, you will likely find yourself standing in front of larger groups of students as well. You have spent years of your life in rehearsals and classes of some sort or another, and are aware that the group experience provides a very powerful learning opportunity quite different from the one-on-one situation. Yet if you have never been the person leading such a gathering, you're probably not aware of the amount of planning involved, nor the social awareness, behavior management skills, and leadership needed to create an effective group learning environment. Well-defined goals and logical learning sequences are important for one-on-one teaching, but these factors become even more important when you are communicating to large numbers of students.

STUDIO AND ORCHESTRAL REPERTOIRE CLASSES

A regularly scheduled studio class provides the perfect opportunity to review or develop skills and repertoire that every member of your class needs to learn. Weekly attention to basic skills in group settings allows more time to focus on the individualized needs of students during their private lessons. With that in mind, you can choose any number of themes for the focus of the class, such as scales and arpeggios, orchestral repertoire, or sight reading. You might also choose to focus on a single technical concept such as speed and dexterity, tone, or articulations. (The tables you completed in Chapter 3, *Technique*, should be a great resource for topics.) Studio classes also provide a great opportunity to invite a colleague as a guest teacher or to arrange mock auditions.

If you decide on an open lesson (master class) format for your studio class, be sure to let all the students in your group know what others will be playing. If possible, publish a performance schedule for the semester and encourage all students to bring their own copies of the music. Following a score helps nonperforming students stay engaged, bringing them closer to experiencing the lesson themselves. Students can write in comments and suggestions, gaining insight into the literature for future study.

Even if a formal syllabus is not required for performance-oriented classes, a course packet can reflect your goals and clearly outline instructional timelines and topics. These could include excerpts from repertoire, practice guides, studies, orchestral excerpts, or scale and arpeggio routines. Besides the wealth of information such a prepared handout provides, it demonstrates to the students that you are serious about making the most of your time together, and provides structure and motivation for them to come prepared to each meeting.

> **Consider This**
> Students attending performance classes can be asked to make written suggestions for their fellow students. Teachers can collect these comment sheets and discuss them with students at the next lesson. Critiquing helps students focus their diagnostic skills while enhancing their own assessment skills and practice strategies.

Beyond the obvious learning opportunities, however, teachers use their leadership and magnanimity to create a cooperative and supportive studio environment. By validating the abilities and fostering the full potential of every student, studio classes can become safe venues for critique and performance, within a supportive community of students. Since most of the students in any university studio will eventually become teachers themselves, a studio teacher can model skill and evenhandedness while teaching students of diverse levels and strengths. An "open door" policy for lesson observations can provide even more opportunities for students to develop a deeper understanding of excellence in musicianship, instrumental technique, and teaching skills.

ACADEMIC CLASSES

It will be in your best interest to prepare thoroughly for every facet of your academic responsibilities, since you will be evaluated as a teacher not just in your applied area but in every course you teach. If you are requested to teach a class outside your area of interest or expertise, such as theory, pedagogy, or music appreciation, you may have to spend a considerable amount of time reading and learning yourself.

You'll want to begin planning well in advance of the first class. Extensive preparation is especially crucial for an extended series of classes scheduled over a semester or a year. It may even be necessary to frame the course within the bigger picture of a multiyear degree program, which involves an even more extensive and comprehensive approach. Create a list of objectives for the class that communicates aspects of the subject matter that you find most important. Develop goals and organize the pace of the learning process. To create a syllabus (helpful to both you and your students, and often required by the institution), list topics for lecture and discussion, reading and listening assignments, worksheets, and a description of your grading policy. Make sure the information you present and assignments you plan for students are both engaging and functional, by connecting history, theory, performance practice, and style to informed performance experiences.

Be prepared to spend a substantial amount of time researching, preparing lectures, and correcting papers associated with academic teaching assignments. While teaching such courses can be challenging, this is potentially an exciting and fulfilling aspect of a school or university teaching position, giving you the opportunity to interact with many more students than you would if you only taught applied lessons or conducted an ensemble. You will also gain new insights to bring to your teaching as you expand your knowledge of related areas and disciplines.

POSITION AVAILABLE: APPLIED WOODWIND

The Department of Music at Olivia College invites applications for a full-time/term-tenure track faculty position in woodwinds. Responsibilities include teaching in an area of woodwind performance, and recruiting and maintaining an active and excellent undergraduate studio. Additional courses taught will be dependent upon candidate's expertise and departmental needs, and could include undergraduate or graduate level *instrumental methods, woodwinds methods, music theory, and aural skills*. Additional opportunities may exist in the areas of *ensemble conducting and coaching*.

METHODS CLASSES

Methods classes (sometimes called techniques classes) are offered by most schools with teaching certification or degree programs. These courses are designed to prepare individuals to teach choral, instrumental, and general music classes, while familiarizing future teachers with concepts and standards needed to teach music in elementary or secondary school settings. It is not uncommon for university studio faculty to be expected to teach such a course, even if the focus is outside the instructor's primary instrumental expertise or academic area.

If you are still in school, the best way to prepare for the possibility of teaching a methods class is to enroll in a methods course yourself. If you have already secured a teaching position and have been asked to teach a methods course as part of your teaching load, there are many resources available to help you prepare for this assignment. A good starting point is to review the syllabus used to teach the course in the past. If your institution is just now adding this course to the curriculum, you can access and review syllabi from other schools as well as the *Strategies for Teaching* series published by the Music Educators National Conference; both can be helpful in designing a sequenced course of instruction.

As in the planning of any course, start with what you expect students to know at the end of the course and carefully construct learning sequences that develop skills connected to your primary objectives. For a methods course, these objectives will involve students learning basic performance skills on secondary instruments, diagnosing and remediating the most common technical problems associated with that area of performance, and demonstrating essential teaching principles. (Additional objectives and a method book review form for methods classes are in

Appendix 12.1.) Music educators in U.S. school settings use the *National Standards for Arts Education* to guide the musical experiences they design for their students. These standards can also be useful as a resource for designing a graded course of instruction in any performance area.

The National Standards address the following nine content areas:

1. Singing, alone and with others, a varied repertoire of music
2. Performing on instruments, alone and with others, a varied repertoire of music
3. Improvising melodies, variations, and accompaniments
4. Composing and arranging music within specified guidelines
5. Reading and notating music
6. Listening to, analyzing, and describing music
7. Evaluating music and music performances
8. Understanding relationships between music, the other arts, and disciplines outside the arts
9. Understanding music in relation to history and culture

Including the National Standards as part of your class activities is invaluable to students who will ultimately be responsible for writing weekly plans that must utilize these standards. For example, to demonstrate a learning sequence for standard 3, improvisation in a general music classroom, students can role-play each grade level: early elementary students improvising simple question-and-answer activities; upper elementary students improvising endings to familiar folk tunes; and middle school students exploring traditional and nontraditional sounds with their voices or instruments. Methods class students can be guided though this teaching sequence in just one class period, which can be made even more realistic by having them play on secondary instruments (creating a very immediate reminder of the awkward feeling and unrefined sounds that come with making music on an unfamiliar instrument). Students should be encouraged to design learning sequences that realize components of the other standards across grade and experience levels in school and studio settings.

While teaching a methods course might feel intimidating for a musician who specializes on a single instrument, many benefits are revealed by seeing such an assignment in a bigger picture. The knowledge and understanding you gain outside your area can have a direct impact on your teaching in the community, where, as a respected musician, you will likely be invited to lead sectionals, judge contests, or conduct local youth ensembles. Knowing how to tune a string bass, correct a squeaky tone on a clarinet, or teach a folk song to a group of third graders can fortify your confidence and compound your value as a teacher. Methods classes also provide yet another opportunity for you to analyze and strengthen what you do, how you do it, and why you do it. Remember that as a teacher of teachers, the quality and substance you bring to a methods class or any pedagogy-related course not only influences those directly in front of you, but has far-reaching effects on students you may never know.

TEACHING AND CONDUCTING LARGE ENSEMBLES

Even if you had only one semester of conducting in music school, your new university position might include directing a university ensemble. You might also find yourself working with a middle or high school level honors ensemble, conducting a pit orchestra for a community theatre production, or leading large numbers of students playing the same instrument in festival or workshop situations. No matter the circumstance or your conducting skill, your level of preparation before the rehearsal will help to determine your effectiveness with the group and, ultimately, your reputation as a group instructor.

Take time to analyze the scores to determine a logical rehearsal plan: rehearsing by instrument group, rhythmic patterns, or common voices and melodies. Make decisions regarding your expectations in such areas as pitch, phrasing, attacks and releases, and style—but also anticipate challenges. Depending on how well matched the repertoire is to your group's ability level, you may have to modify your expectations; nevertheless having a plan helps you organize your initial teaching sequence.

Rehearse with the mindset that you will lead and the group will follow. You cannot assume that all members of a group have a burning desire to learn, but you can motivate them with noticeably positive results. Work on small sections to a point of fluency and make comparisons between the ensemble's best playing and less-than-best attempts. If you do need to modify your expectations, keep it to yourself, and continue to focus on the positive. Establish an environment of disciplined but friendly productivity, and create a feeling of security that fosters courage and cooperation in the members of the group. Your attitude and demeanor will make a difference in your ability to organize the energy in front of you toward the best results.

Regardless of the level or size of your large ensemble, the following ideas can foster successful teaching experiences:

- *Start on time and end on time.* You want your ensemble members to be punctual, so model that behavior.
- *Establish quiet and focus in the room before starting instruction.* Don't allow rehearsals to start out of chaos. If possible, set up the room in advance.

Consider This

An engaging rehearsal technique appropriate for middle and high school students is to ask ten different students to each play a particular passage. Start by commenting on the strengths of each performance; then invite members of the group to suggest which performance was strongest overall. Encourage students to offer one idea to another member of the group that may make an immediate positive change: use more bow, play louder, make the phrasing more obvious, and so on. Play the passage again as a group with each member striving to make individual changes and note how the collective sound of the group is more unified and convincing.

For an ensemble member, hearing a passage played ten times by ten different students can be much more interesting than just hearing oneself, especially when invited to be part of the assessment process. When students assume some responsibility for each other's improvements, they have more investment in the positive results that are sure to follow. Be sure to set the tone for supportive language when critiquing to keep the process positive, thought-provoking, and motivating.

An orderly rehearsal space will help establish focus. You are within your rights to insist that any observers in the room are quiet: no talking or cell phones.

- *Talk less, play more.* Establish a balance between your instruction and feedback and student performance. Instruction and feedback statements should be specific and brief.
- *Use your instrument or voice for modeling.* An aural image is worth a thousand words. "Make it sound like this" can save many minutes of rehearsal time.
- *Deliver clear, direct instructions.* "It doesn't matter what you say, it matters what they understand" is a premise of all good teaching; however, having a single person confused is one thing; having an entire group confused is another.
- *Whatever you pull apart, put back together.* Give the students a sense of flow by allowing them to play or sing passages that hang together in a musically logical way. Avoid stopping and starting at arbitrary and unmusical places.

- *Establish a standard of mastery.* Raise the quality of a short passage to demonstrate the possibility for excellence, and then encourage students to transfer the newly established level of tone, precision, and musicianship to other passages.

Finally, for all directors and directors-to-be, this list:
"You're asking for trouble if you . . ."

Fail to check for misprints in the parts before the first rehearsal
Learn the music at the rehearsal
Have inadequate conducting technique and fail to seek improvement
Talk with your arms or baton in the air
Stop without a reason
Lack eye contact with the players
Talk too fast
Initiate a start without warning
Lack a system for breaking down problems
Hide your beat behind the music stand
Work too long with one section or one player
Debate with one player during a rehearsal
Rehearse extended passages when you only need to rehearse spots
Always rehearse *tutti*
Have a clock in full view of the ensemble
Negatively compare the group in front of you to another group

POSITION AVAILABLE: APPLIED TRUMPET

Central University seeks candidates for a full-time tenure track position in applied trumpet and conducting. Candidate will be expected to teach studio lessons and related courses in Brass Pedagogy and Methods for Music Education Majors, and *direct the University Wind Ensemble*. We seek candidates who are committed to work effectively with students in studio and *master class settings*. Evidence of strong artistic ability and accomplishment as a college-level performer and teacher, with professional performing experience, is required. Responsibilities also include *recruiting activities, national visibility as a performer and master class teacher*, and service to state and local band programs as a *sectional coach*.

MASTER CLASS TEACHING

> **Personal Inventory:** Think about your most valuable master class experience—consider from the teacher's perspective what he or she did that made the teaching effective. What did the teacher do to make you feel comfortable or help you focus? How did the teacher accomplish positive change?

You probably have been on the receiving end of master class teaching, whether in a studio class situation or a more public venue. Now, on the presenter side of the master class, you will have the opportunity to share your expertise with the student performer in front of you as well as an audience. Very experienced teachers, just like very experienced performers, will most likely admit to a certain amount of anxiety and excitement related to teaching a master class, at least in part because there is always some level of unpredictability involved. The title "master class teacher" implies that you have something important to share, but until you see and hear the student, you will not know what that important thing is. However, there are ways to approach a master class that will help you prepare to give your best to the situation.

The goal of a master class is to effect positive changes in a very short amount of time. The two main ingredients that lead to this end result are

1. Setting the student at ease so you can bring out the best in him or her
2. Choosing a key element in the student's performance where your teaching will effect the most significant change

Your demeanor toward the student and audience will help set the tone for the session. Being confident, yet friendly and relaxed, goes a long way toward making everyone feel at ease. Be sure to greet each performer as he or she comes forward to play, and address him or her by name. Try to assess the personality of the student—gregarious, intimidated, confident—and use this information to help make the time you have with that person comfortable and productive.

While the student is playing, be attentive to posture, physical freedom, tone production, specific technical issues, and musicianship. Is there a direct link between two or more performance components, where one might directly influence an improvement in the others? If so, this will be your best choice for focusing your work—the one that will produce the most immediate as well as far-reaching results.

When the initial performance is over, thank the student and acknowledge the positive aspects you observed. Consider whether the initial nervousness has dissipated and say something to draw out a smile—kindness and humor are both great anti-dotes for the jitters. Comment about the timing of a sneeze in the audience, or remark about the marvelously powerful entrance that ruffled their hair. Reinforcing a friendly, positive connection with the student will help him or her be more receptive to your suggestions, and you can now can roll up your sleeves and start to work.

Keep in mind that master classes are like a short guided practice session, and practicing is always most effective when you don't take on too much all at once. Even if there are many problems, trying to make every point in one session will only result in showing the student what they don't know and can't do. This is not effective teaching. Limit the focus of your work and the amount of music you cover and go straight to the fundamental issue you have chosen to address. Offer several different approaches if needed to discover the one that allows the student to grasp this concept. If possible, find a key word or phrase (or have the student come up with one) that captures your suggested change or idea—a shorthand way to trigger the concept for the student when he or she needs a reminder.

Whatever the teaching point, build on the student's understanding and confidence by asking for repetitions of short passages interspersed with your feedback. Spend as much time as possible to make this fundamental change obvious. Don't presume immediate comprehension on the part of the performer. A technical concept such as "use more weight" may not be as obvious as it seems to you. Be sure you have a way to translate any musical suggestions, such as making a tone "more ethereal" or pacing a ritard "more naturally," into clear technical directives. Follow up by asking the student to describe the new concept in his or her own words, and be sure the student is able to self-observe and critique the difference between the old pattern and the new approach.

Once basic understanding and awareness have been established, start to link the influence of the new behavior to other areas of performance, such as strength in tone, clarity of technique, or refined musicianship. Be sure the full import of the changes made is evident to the student. Draw the audience into the feedback loop as well: "Wow! Was it just me, or did anyone else hear the difference in the tone?" The audience's enthusiastic response will illuminate the effectiveness of the change and give the performer a strong incentive to continue working this way.

A few cautionary points about master class teaching:

- *Never criticize the home teacher or director.* Make suggestions for improvements without reference to what the student has or has not been taught. This may require you to filter what you are thinking, but choose your words wisely.

- *Do not criticize the student's equipment for lack of anything else to say.* Suggestions regarding types of head joints, strings, or reeds can be very appropriate when coupling this information with other suggestions. However, telling a student that she needs a new instrument, while it might be true, will not help her in the moment.
- *Do not pressure a student about memory slips, or take music away from a performer who is obviously dependent on the notation.* It will do nothing positive for the student or your reputation as a nurturing teacher. Instead, you might want to ask "How are you working on memorizing this piece?" Offer suggestions that the student can utilize later, and then let it go.
- *Do not dwell on a performer's habit that cannot be changed in the short term,* especially more personal ones like involuntary grimaces or vocalizations. While you can point out distracting or inhibiting behaviors if you feel it's important, it's better to focus your work on a technical or musical issue in which you could foster immediate improvement.

Consider This

Master Class Etiquette. While your primary job is to teach the student, speak clearly and slowly enough for the audience to hear you, since everyone is there to benefit from your ideas. Be aware of the clock when teaching multiple performers in succession. Distribute your time with each performer equally, since running overtime in a master class can set other conference or college class sessions off schedule. If at all possible, leave a small cushion of time for audience questions and an opportunity to thank the students for performing and the host for inviting you to present the class.

> Similar to a "master switch" or "master control," the term "master class" suggests that helpful comments given to the performer will also be applicable to all in the audience.
> STEPHEN CLAPP

LEADING SECTIONALS

Sectionals are regularly included as part of most student and amateur performing organizations. Whether sectional coaching is part of your university teaching load, a service provided as part of community outreach and recruiting, or the result of an invitation, you are likely to lead many sectionals during your career. Because the students have usually had at least one rehearsal on the repertoire, as well as an opportunity to practice assigned parts, the sectional coach is not typically expected to start entirely from scratch. Ideally, your role is that of a master teacher, assigned to polish and refine the section to sound as close to an artistic level as possible. Bring your instrument as well as your best analytical and problem-solving skills to the situation (along with an extra supply of pencils!) and be ready to teach, not just coach.

Prepare thoroughly for the sectional, especially if you will be rehearsing pieces unfamiliar to you. Listen to a recording and familiarize yourself with the full score, marking places where your section needs to project, blend, or dovetail with another section. Specific contrapuntal areas should be addressed as well as soli passages and unisons with other sections. Fingerings, bowings, and breathing may have already been determined by the conductor, but you should be ready with your ideas and preferences, since unity in a section is often dependent on a refined and nuanced understanding of the needs of your instrument. Your expertise and ability to make effective decisions in these areas are usually very welcomed.

If at all possible, listen to a full rehearsal before the scheduled sectional. Even if these are your very own well-taught students, you might be surprised at what needs work: weak entrances, lack of phrasing, ineffective dynamics, technically simple sections lacking substance or quality, overly heavy bass lines, and so forth. Your attention to these issues needn't take too much time but can make a huge difference in the overall sound of the group.

Once you're in the sectional, you will find there is a much to do in a short amount of time—in some cases you'll have an hour or less to make substantial improvements. Decide which passages need the most attention and set a time limit for each. Remember that quality should take precedent over quantity, so don't stretch your teaching so thin that you can barely make improvements anywhere. In fact, since your goal is to make the group sound like a unified whole, you might want to start the sectional by creating a section sound, using a warm-up, a scale, or a simple passage from their music.

Younger students often need technical instruction to learn how to listen and blend with others. A very direct route to awakening their listening and matching skills is to ask one musician to sing or play a single note with a clear, focused sound. Once you are satisfied, and everyone has heard the sound they will match, begin adding performers one by one, allowing no change in the pitch or quality. If students are playing or singing individual parts, teach them how to tune a triad, starting with the root, adding the fifth, and finally the third. With the intonation defined, you can then explore a variety of dynamic changes. Use hand gestures to help students explore increases and decreases in intensity from extreme to subtle. Besides being fun, it teaches them be more attentive and develops their ability to focus outside themselves while maintaining a high artistic level of performing.

Uniform articulations and rhythmic precision are two qualities that go hand-in-hand when creating a unified section sound. Give students detailed information about specific articulations and the use of rhythmic subdivisions for the precise length and release of notes—just what you would expect of yourself as a professional. Take as much time as necessary to rehearse the starting and ending of phrases and entrances, for tonal and rhythmic cohesiveness. The section will not recognize the potential for a truly unified sound unless they are given the opportunity to experience it.

If you were able to listen to the full ensemble, you might have heard places where the section seemed oblivious to the bigger picture—how their part duets with another section, or creates the rhythmic pulse or the foundation on which other musicians depend. Ask: "Does anyone know who has the melody at rehearsal B when you have the whole notes?" After it's determined that they really should be listening to the bassoons or the altos, be sure they write it in their part. Choose an obviously neglected "easy spot" in the music, and show them how the section's sound on those simple notes really does matter to the quality of the ensemble as a whole. Encourage students to make good choices about their sound at all times, not just during the challenging or exposed passages.

As you finish your work on each passage, especially if you won't be seeing the students again in the near future, suggest practicing ideas for individual work. Instill section pride by encouraging them to be the "best section" in the ensemble. Acknowledge everyone in the section and make sure they know that each individual's contribution truly makes a difference.

Consider This

Demonstrate how the same dynamic marking can be performed differently in different contexts. For example, find two areas in the music that are marked *piano*, and ask section members to decide whether that dynamic was chosen by the composer for the same or different reasons. Perhaps the first *piano* requires the horns to offer unobtrusive harmonic support to the clarinet solo, while the other is there to suggest a hushed but expressive quality in the beautiful chorale section. This kind of exploration engages students in the musical decisions made by the composer, and gives them a reason not just to observe the dynamic but to actively create a meaningful performance.

PERFORMANCE CLINICS

Whether recruiting for your university or working on your own, occasionally you will be asked to lead a clinic on music required for a local or regional audition.

These clinics are similar to sectionals in that everyone is learning the same music, but the performers will ultimately be playing or singing by themselves, so your approach will be more focused toward developing individual technique and musicianship rather than creating a synchronized and unified performance.

Often the required music is more challenging than the typical middle or high school repertoire, and although some students can play this music quite well with little help, many of them will face a steep learning curve. In the session you'll want to challenge those who already have a fundamental understanding of the music while showing the less advanced students how to master the basics. For instance, if half the bassists in your group are still working on finding the correct notes, have them play with all separate bows, focusing on the notes and shifts; direct the more advanced players to be attentive to left-hand precision and bow distribution across slurs.

Ideally, the clinician doesn't provide information just for the session, but offers ways for students to continue their preparation after they leave. Presenting a thoughtful handout that you've prepared in advance will support the students' progress. This could include practice suggestions, exercises that develop necessary techniques or week-by-week goals—whatever you might offer your own private student. Important performance goals are also very helpful—anything from tempo suggestions to "the judges will be listening for great dynamic contrast in this piece" or "whether or not you're able to catch every note in this fast section, the staccato notes should be as short as possible."

FESTIVALS AND CAMPS

University faculty are usually expected to recruit, and summer music camps and festivals are an excellent way to be visible to potential students outside the school setting. But, whether you are a university professor or an independent teacher, summer programs can offer fun and rewarding teaching experiences: the change of pace, new faces, and different surroundings can be refreshing, and it's a wonderful opportunity to work with students who are committed to their music studies and free of other distractions.

Besides leading chamber music coachings or sectional rehearsals, you might be asked to teach private lessons as well. Because these are not your students, don't tackle major changes in approach to the instrument that may contradict what the home teacher has prescribed. For example, if the student's approach to the instrument is functional but different from the approach you use, a major reorganization of bow hold or embouchure, for example, might be more confusing than helpful. Even if you are aware of its value for that student, making such a change might require more time than you have with the student and upset other aspects of the festival experience for him or her.

Instead, look for a way to enhance skills and musicianship that is liberating and motivating to the student, making positive change evident in the short term. Introducing a variety of scale and warm-up routines can be very beneficial in reenergizing a student's interest in fundamentals. Show the student new routines that focus on particular techniques that might facilitate a difficult technical passage. Using different repertoire or a different tactic to remedy a problem that the permanent teacher has already addressed can be satisfying for all concerned. The goal is to offer students interesting and functional information that can be experienced to a level of genuine understanding in a short amount of time—and, one hopes, have students leave with a new vision for themselves and a positive impression of you as a teacher and as a person. (See Chapter 7 *Sequencing* for more on this topic.)

POSITION AVAILABLE: PROFESSOR OF PIANO

College of the North seeks Professor of Piano, with Master's degree in music, preferred Doctorate. Applicant must have sufficient academic preparation and/or experience to teach applied and class piano, and courses in music appreciation, fundamentals of music, and ear training. Candidate is expected to participate in *student recruitment, placement, and advisement*. Position includes *curriculum and assessment development*, and collaboration with colleagues to incorporate results in degree and certificate programs. Candidate should demonstrate a *talent for working with graduate students, undergraduates, and non-majors*, and be prepared to function as a resource for *community-related music development projects, outreach concerts, and adult education courses*. Candidate may teach evenings and/or weekends utilizing nontraditional delivery methods such as interactive television or web-based classes.

Assessment

While teachers are constantly assessing student progress informally, there will be situations in your teaching life that require you to formalize that process. Entrance auditions, chair placements, performance examinations, semester grading, and competitions not only call for a systematic identification of techniques and musicianship, but will challenge you to assign a quantifiable value to each aspect of performance.

PERFORMANCE EVALUATION

Whether the musicians perform prescribed repertoire or music of their choosing, you will be listening for evidence of artistic development and technical accomplishment in specific, essential areas. Sometimes there will be instrument-specific technical considerations on your list, but no matter the performer's instrument, assessment parameters typically include

- Note accuracy and intonation
- Appropriate tempo
- Rhythmic accuracy
- Appropriate articulation
- Tone
- Dynamics
- Phrasing
- Flexible timing
- Stylistic interpretation
- Expressive interpretation
- Artistic nuance
- Delivery (stage presence, confidence, poise)

If no specific grading system is being utilized within a group of judges, you can create your own point system, starting with a maximum grade for each performance category, and taking deductions for mistakes and flaws. Another approach involves working with a rubric, in which each artistic or technical category is followed by a series of descriptions, starting with the highest level of achievement and gradually working down toward an unacceptable level. (For a universal rubric suggestion see Appendix 12.3.) Remember that students can rise to high accomplishment levels in some categories and not in others. In other words, if the rhythm was steady and secure, that assessment category might warrant a top grade even if the same player gets virtually no points for intonation or dynamics. Even so, use the categorical information combined with your best judgment to render an honest assessment of the musician's overall performance.

> ### Consider This
> When judging and grading students, remember that not every student has a wonderful instrument. While it's not always easy, try not to penalize a performer for the tone of an undersized or poor quality instrument.

ADJUDICATING COMPETITIONS

When you are charged to rank performers or choose a winner, the biggest challenge is to find a balanced, even-handed approach to be sure that the first players and the last players—and of course everyone in between—are judged by the same parameters. To maintain as much consistency as possible across a field of judges, the adjudicators are sometimes required to use prescribed grading sheets. Even so, you will probably be asked to attend a judges' meeting to discuss expectations beyond what can be written on that score sheet. A moderate amount of individuation between judges is normal and expected, but as much as possible, try to follow the specified guidelines and instructions.

It's important to be clear about your baseline expectation. If you begin judging from your sense of how well a good student might play or sing, you might be in trouble when a performer exceeds your expectations, or if your expectations shift after several performers. It is wiser to have an ideal baseline—how this piece or excerpt would sound if played by an artist. If the first player comes only halfway up to that standard, then grade the performer accordingly. Even if that performer turns out to be the best one you hear all day, at least your standard will not have changed from the beginning of the process to the end.

Time can also factor into the judging process. When a performer is playing a single excerpt that takes a minute or less to perform, or when the time between performers is short, you will need to establish a shorthand way to arrive at fair and consistent results. While you won't remember all the specifics of the audition and how each student played, your score sheet is sometimes needed afterward to appease a disgruntled student or parent who feels deserving of a better placement in the section. Take anecdotal notes if possible and do not discard them immediately after the audition process—this information could be important if there is a need to break a tie or substantiate a result.

When the competitors are performing a concerto movement, an entire piece, or even several pieces, you will have much more time to assess several performance areas and make notes about your perceptions. This is when detailed and copious notes will make a difference. You may think you will remember specifics regarding the performance of one particular performer, but after a long series of auditions, you will not. Your notes become especially important when adjudicating over the course of days, having to designate a ranking order two or three days after your initial hearing of a performance. This written feedback is also greatly appreciated by the contestants, providing objective comments that can help them continue to improve.

Finally, while technical difficulty is often a factor in competition, a piece of moderate technical difficulty played beautifully usually prevails over a more technically challenging piece played poorly. The competition organizers might have built in scoring contingencies, such as additional points for pieces of exceptional difficulty, but ultimately you must use your best judgment to decide which performance demonstrates to you the highest artistic standard of accuracy and expression.

Teaching Nonmajor and Adult Students

Many universities require their applied teachers to accept nonmajor students (such as a Bachelor of Arts candidate with a music emphasis) or to teach in their continuing education division. Even as an independent teacher, you might be surprised at the number of lesson inquiries you receive from adults. Some are complete beginners, but many have varied levels of musical sophistication and experience: opera patrons, jazz aficionados, church choir soloists, and former high school concertmasters.

Start your relationship by identifying their goals for learning. If the student is in an arts degree program, he or she might need to play a recital to demonstrate a level of competency. Adults who have made an independent choice to study might wish to become a better home practice coach for their children, to play or sing in a community ensemble, to play chamber music, to continue an education in music that was interrupted by life events, or to fulfill a lifelong dream to make music themselves. Knowing their goals will enable you to design individualized instruction that might require adjustments in your typical teaching sequence and repertoire. Those with previous experience are likely to need some remedial work, and you'll want to be sensitive to the difficulties of making significant changes to established habits. (See Chapter 7, *Sequencing*, for suggestions about remedial teaching.)

Adult students are a breed apart from your typical school-aged student: they have lived longer and had far more experiences in life, professionally and socially—perhaps even more than you. Adults are usually far more comfortable with being accomplished at skills than being novices, so the journey of learning an instrument can elicit emotions that range from exhilaration to utter frustration. Be understanding and encouraging while you apply the same level of thoughtful teaching as you would with any other student in your studio. Recognize that if the tables were turned, you would probably struggle to excel in their area of expertise, so acknowledge and respect their accomplishments outside music and draw parallels whenever possible.

Adults are in some ways easier to teach than younger students, because they often have the ability to be more self-reflective and practical. This means it's possible to converse with them and plan realistic goals on a purely adult level. For instance, if an adult student's goal is to play the viola part to his favorite Mozart quartet but he still struggles to hold the instrument comfortably, don't be dismissive or patronizing: explain exactly what is needed to achieve that level of technical and musical competency. If the student is undaunted and willing to work for several years to accomplish this goal, then write out a plan that includes the necessary skills and chart a course that will set the student on his way. If possible, avoid assigning music designed for young children—find repertoire and studies that will appeal to more sophisticated sensibilities. Be sure to set many intermediate goals, of course, so the long road will have plenty of "arrival" moments along the way. Remember to balance the desire for perfection with a sense of humor, optimism, and respect for the student's efforts. As much as high-quality musicianship is the aspiration, musical satisfaction and a sense of accomplishment are the most important objectives.

The social aspect of music is often very important to adult students, so make an effort to help them connect with other adult musicians. If you have more than one adult student, consider creating an ensemble that meets one evening a week. Many universities have continuing education colleges that offer a variety of interesting courses that were once available only to those enrolled in degree programs. Among the many subjects, music is often well represented: music-related lectures, ensembles, and workshops specifically for adult learners. If you would like to have more teaching opportunities, you might want to propose a course that could attract new students, such as *Flute 101 for Adult Beginners*. Put your students in touch with civic ensembles in your area, or if you don't know of any, certain organizations can be very helpful in locating other ensemble opportunities, workshops, and festivals. Such organizations include the New Horizons International Music Association, Associated Chamber Music Players, Music Educators National Association Adult and Community Education Special Research Interest Group, and the North American Coalition for Community Music.

OUTREACH CONCERTS

As a recruitment tool, a supplementary educational program, and a community service, outreach concerts can be a gratifying part of your career that combines your performing skills directly with your teaching ideals and creativity. Many young children discover their passion for music at these informative concerts that are conceived to introduce, instruct, intrigue, and inspire.

Creating such concerts takes substantial planning—perhaps more than any other single aspect of teaching discussed so far. The subject needs to have a clear focus: you're there not just to play and show your instrument, but to introduce an aspect of music, demonstrate why you love it, and most importantly, allow your audience to experience its relevance to their own lives. The theme of your presentation could be about your instrument and how it works, but it could also be about a composer, a style of music like a dance or a march, or an aspect of music like rhythm or melody. Selecting your topic is just a starting point—you will need to be able to articulate why it's important to you, and why it should or could be important to everyone. While saying "this is important" won't get your message across, the activities you plan, the words you choose, the questions you ask, and the music you perform all need to be an extension of those beliefs. Activities should allow a large group of children to be involved in the process of discovery and learning (but without creating utter chaos). Since every audience and situation will be different, prepare more than enough activities at different levels. This will allow you to adapt your presentation to the age and comprehension of your audience, and give you flexibility to either go deeper into a topic or move on as each situation warrants.

All of this (and more, when done well) is usually built into a thirty- to forty-five-minute concert. Occasionally you will have the opportunity to do a series of concerts, or work with students in their classrooms over an extended period. Such residency programs allow you to go into more depth and make stronger connections with the students, perhaps even give them introductory lessons or help them compose music. If you have the opportunity to present outreach concerts and programs, we recommend that you read the two excellent books by Eric Booth and David Wallace listed in this chapter's bibliography. These will give you the information you need to create a program that is meaningful and rewarding for all involved.

POSITION AVAILABLE: APPLIED VOICE

The Department of Music at Ondinnonk University invites energetic, motivated vocal artists to apply for a tenure track applied voice position at the assistant professor rank. Minimum qualifications include ABD status or a completed doctorate in music. The candidate should demonstrate potential for success as a performer, teacher, and scholar; breadth of experience in vocal performance, knowledge of vocal pedagogy, demonstrated excellence in studio teaching, functional keyboard skills. Preferred candidate should have experience teaching at a culturally diverse liberal arts institution, *demonstrate a commitment to equity and diversity, and be willing to make reasonable accommodations for students with disabilities.*

Meaningful Music Experiences for Students with Special Needs

JAMES AND MAHLER: A STORY

One day I [Laurie Scott] was visiting a seventh-grade orchestra classroom and noticed a student attending the class along with an aide. The student, James, demonstrated stereo-typical behaviors associated with autism. He sat off to one side of the classroom, rocking, flapping his hands, and repeating short verbal phrases. As the other students practiced independently, the director walked around the room assisting them in individual prep-aration for an upcoming concert. When I asked the orchestra director if James had learned to play an instrument, he responded, "He chose orchestra as an elective and really enjoys listening during class time." I recognized this as a common but unfortunate scenario: a well-meaning teacher interpreting the mere presence of a student with a dis-ability in a music classroom as a participatory experience. This student was a consumer of the music in the orchestra classroom but certainly not a participant.

I asked the teacher if it would be okay for me to try to get him to hold a string bass. "You can try," he said, "but whenever I ask him to play, he repeatedly says NO!" Standing across the room from James, I began plucking an open string, moving slowly closer to James until I was standing next to him plucking the bass. I asked him to put his hand on the bass and feel the vibrations. He complied with hesitation. I stood in front of him and asked if I could help him pluck the strings—he didn't answer. I asked his aide to lift his hand and make it hit the strings. The cause and effect was quickly evident to James, who began plucking the open strings without assistance. I asked him to hold the instrument. He refused; however, he kept plucking the open strings. I assisted him in controlling his motions enough to pluck one string at a time. Within ten minutes, he was holding his own instrument and plucking D, A, D, A with a very steady pulse.

Once he seemed steady and focused, I picked up a viola and started playing the minor "Frère Jacques" theme from the bass solo in Mahler's First Symphony. The sound of our duet made the other students in the room stop their practicing and listen. It was rhythmic, it was in tune, and it was musical. Others in the classroom started to join the ensemble. Some were imitating the melody by ear, and others joined James on the bass line. In the span of forty-five minutes, James went from a bystander to the rhythmic center of the entire orches-tra. Following that class period, I talked to the orchestra director about having James's paraprofessional learn the bass alongside him. With the two of them learning together along with the support of the director and the enthusiasm of his classmates, James was able to successfully perform with the orchestra at the following concert.

There are many students just like James who could become active participants in music activities through the collaborative efforts of teachers, parents, and para-professionals. As a music teacher in a school setting, your relationship with students often lasts three or four years. During this time, you can greatly influence a students' attitudes toward music-making by arranging thoughtfully sequenced lessons and providing opportunities that not only ensure learning, but validate each individual's contribution to the group.

ACCESS TO MUSIC

Approximately ten to twelve percent of the world's population has a disability. A person with a disability is defined as an individual with a physical or cognitive impairment that substantially limits one or more major life activities. Many disabilities, however, are characterized by symptoms that do not in any way impede an individual's ability to successfully manage music instruction and performance.

In her book *Including Everyone: Successful Music Learning for Children with Disabilities,* Judith Jellison describes five guidelines for enabling the musical development of children with disabilities in inclusive settings. These guidelines suggest that:

1. Participation in socially valued roles and socially valued activities with typical children is a significant part of the routine of daily life.
2. Collaboration and coordinated efforts among parents/guardians, professionals, other significant individuals in the child's life, and the child (when appropriate) are part of the design and implementation of the music education program.
3. Social interactions with same-age typical peers in inclusive music environments are frequent, positive, and reciprocal.
4. Self-determination is fostered in music environments where children experience autonomy, demonstrate competence, and make choices and decisions about music, music-making, and other music activities in their lives.
5. A meaningful curriculum should be designed to be flexible and accessible, where instruction is evidence-based, and adaptations of the curriculum, instruction, and assessment of progress are only as specialized as they need to be.

These guidelines, focused on meaningful musical experiences, have been chosen from research findings, social policy, and special education policy suggesting ways the musical lives of children with disabilities can be improved. While these recommendations were written with children in mind, the overarching principles regarding experience, collaboration, learning environment, and curriculum can serve as a guide in teaching any individual.

Personal Inventory: Think about a time when you were learning something difficult in a one-on-one tutoring session or a group setting. It may have been in a computer or karate class, or it may have been in an academic setting, for example a statistics class. Consider situations that challenged your physical stamina or coordination: long-distance running, dancing, or for that matter performing a difficult passage on your instrument. Can you remember someone or something that helped you achieve success and how the reactions of the instructor or your peers affected you?

STUDENTS WITH DISABILITIES IN SCHOOL AND STUDIO SETTINGS

At every educational level, a continuum of services and legislative mandates provides protection against discrimination to individuals with disabilities. As a professional educator, you need to be aware of policies and guidelines related to you, your students, and your institution. It is important at all times to be in compliance with federal regulations regarding access to education and civil rights. Those most pertinent for music teaching and learning, are described in detail in Appendix 12.3.

Teachers in public school settings are required by the Individuals with Disabilities Education Act (IDEA) to make specific arrangements for every student with a documented disability to receive education in "the least restrictive environment" meaning that every child in the school is educated in inclusive classroom settings whenever possible. Special education staff, teachers, parents, and, when appropriate, the student are part of the team that designs the Individualized Education Program (IEP). This document outlines goals, accommodations, modifications, and related special education services for the student.

Parents of children with disabilities form strong networks and share information and recommendations regarding teachers who create positive and productive learning situations and consistently help students develop skills in specific areas. These teachers become known as *the* swimming teacher, or *the* piano teacher, or *the* soccer coach for students with physical, cognitive, or behavioral challenges. While many have received training specific to working with individuals with disabilities, their success most likely emerges from understanding the way all people learn.

STUDENTS WITH DISABILITIES IN A UNIVERSITY SETTING

Students with disabilities who enroll in a university are required to meet the same standards of qualification and fulfill the same prerequisites as any other student, regardless of need for accommodations. However, students with disabilities have equal opportunity to participate in and benefit from any program for which they qualify. Students requesting accommodations must provide professors with documentation verifying needs related to their specific disability. Once documentation is acquired, classroom or studio accommodations may be necessary for students to achieve success.

Whether or not students in your studio or classroom have informed you of a disability, all university syllabi should include a statement such as the following: *State University provides upon request, appropriate academic accommodations for qualified students with disabilities. For more information, contact the Office of the Dean of Students.*

In regard to individuals with disabilities, remember the following:

- Use "people first" language when referring to your students, for example, the student with a hearing impairment, not the hearing-impaired student.
- Respect the emotional, social, and intellectual intelligence of the person you are teaching.
- Maintain confidentiality related to student disabilities as required by law.
- Create a network of support and ask for help when needed.
- Ensure access to your teaching and performing space for individuals with mobility challenges.
- Do not stereotype any individual because of a disability.
- Be inclusive in planning studio or classroom activities.
- Advocate for inclusive music performing activities.

Collaboration is one of your most valuable resources: with the student, parents if appropriate, and campus and community organizations designated specifically to enable students to benefit from educational programs and activities. Knowledge of laws, services, and accommodations will allow you to be a source of information for parents, students, and other faculty members. Most important, however, is your readiness to work with all students, taking them from exactly where they are, and teaching them with optimism and respect. (For more information on Disability Law, IEP, and accommodations, see Appendix 12.4.)

Ideas for Further Exploration
1. Create a syllabus for a semester-long (12–14 classes) technique class for your instrument. Design assessable objectives, and create lessons that progressively and sequentially work toward the specified goals.

Methods Classes

2. Review three copies of methods course syllabi either from your institution or accessed online. Compare course objectives and assignments stated in each syllabus.

3. Enroll in a methods course at your institution and visit a group class in a school setting. Make a list of the challenges and benefits of teaching in group settings. Does the class you're taking address the most pertinent issues related to teaching technique and musicianship in groups?

Master Classes

4. Describe a typical posture or technique-related problem in your area of study and prescribe at least three different ways to approach solutions.

5. Observe three master classes and consider the substance and approach of each: what was effective, and what, if anything, would have made it better.

6. Gather a small group and assign one person as performer and one as master class teacher; have the rest observe. Operate as a master class with observers taking notes on what fundamental issue they would choose to work on, and offer feedback to the "teacher" on his or her approach. Over several sessions, rotate roles until everyone has both performed and acted as the master class teacher.

Assessment

7. Create an assessment rubric for judging a concerto competition that reflects your beliefs about artistic excellence. Refer to the rubric in Appendix 12.3 for organizational structure and gradation ideas.

Job Application Preparation

8. Update your curriculum vitae and create a resume. Write a cover letter highlighting your strengths and philosophy as they relate to the job for which you are applying (or your ideal job). Share the resume and letter with a colleague and get feedback on clarity and organization.

Recommended Reading

MUSIC METHODS BOOKS

Bailey, W., Miles, P., Siebert, A., & Stanley, W. (1991). *Teaching Brass: A Resource Manual.* Columbus, Ohio: McGraw Hill.

Bluestein, E. (1995). *The Ways Children Learn Music: An Introduction and Practical Guide to Music Learning Theory.* Chicago: GIA.

Campbell, P. C., & Scott-Kassner, C. (2006). *Music in Childhood: From Preschool through the Elementary Grades.* 3rd ed. Belmont, Calif.: Wadsworth Group.

Cook, Gary. (2005). *Teaching Percussion.* New York: Schirmer Books.

Dick, W. J., & Scott, L. P. (2004). *Mastery for Strings: A Longitudinal Sequence of Instruction for School Orchestras, Studio Lessons and College Method Classes.* Austin, Tex.: Mastery for String Press.

Green, E. A. H. (1966). *Teaching Stringed Instruments in Classes.* Englewood Cliffs, N.J.: Prentice-Hall.

Hamann, D. L., & Gillespie, R. (2004). *Strategies for Teaching Strings.* New York: Oxford University Press.

Haritun, R. (1994). *Music Teacher's Survival Guide: Practical Techniques and Materials for the Elementary Music Classroom.* West Nyack, N.Y.: Parker.

McPherson, Gary. (2008). *The Child as Musician: A Handbook of Musical Development.* New York: Oxford University Press.

MENC, the National Association for Music Education (U.S.). (2007). *National standards for arts education: What every young American should know and be able to do in the arts.* Lanham, MD: Rowman & Littlefield Education.

Valerio, W. H., Reynolds, A. M., Bolton, B. M., Taggart, C. C., & Gordon, E. E. (1998). *Music Play: The Early Childhood Music Curriculum Guide for Parents, Teachers and Caregivers.* Chicago: GIA.

SPECIAL NEEDS

Adamek, M. S., & Darrow, A. A. (2010). *Music in Special Education.* Silver Spring, Md.: American Music Therapy Association.

Hammel, A. M., & Hourigan, R. M. (2011). *Teaching Music to Students with Special Needs: A Label-Free Approach.* New York: Oxford University Press.

Jellison, J. (2011). *Including Everyone: Successful Music Learning for Children with Disabilities.* Austin, Tex.: Learning and Behavior Resources.

Levine, Mel. (2002). *A Mind at a Time.* New York: Simon and Schuster.

ADULT LEARNERS

Knowles, M. S., Holton, E. F., & Swanson, R. A. (1998). *The Adult Learner: The Definitive Classic in Adult Education and Human Resource Development.* Houston: GULF.

GROUP INSTRUCTION AND PLANNING

Svinicki, M., & McKeachie, W. (2010). *McKeachie's Teaching Tips: Strategies, Research, and Theory for College and University Teachers.* 13th ed. Florence, Ky.: Wadsworth.

Trimble, J. R. (1975). *Writing with Style: Conversations on the Art of Writing.* Englewood Cliffs, N.J.: Prentice-Hall.

OUTREACH CONCERTS

Booth, E. (2009). *The Music Teaching Artist's Bible: Becoming a Virtuoso Educator*. New York: Oxford University Press.

Wallace, D. (2008). *Reaching Out: A Musician's Guide to Interactive Performance*. New York: McGraw-Hill.

13 Daily Considerations and Challenges

Teaching Relationships

It's the first lesson for a transfer student, who has taken lessons for two years with another teacher. She arrives with a stack of method books you've never used, and lots of problems: bad posture, no sense of rhythm, and terrible intonation. Addressing all these issues will take weeks, not a half hour. Besides which, she seems resistant to your suggestions, and you feel like a fish out of water trying to work with the unfamiliar studies and repertoire. How do you deal with it?

First lessons can be a challenge: for the student because everything is different—the teacher, the expectations, even the place; for the teacher because there are invariably more things to talk about than there are minutes in the lesson. Even an experienced teacher has to work to make the best of the situation, starting with setting the student at ease and getting to know her a bit. At the first meeting, let the student perform music that is familiar to her and perhaps make an initial assignment using those books, but don't feel obligated to continue using that material—doing so often makes the transition feel longer and more awkward. Feel free to make requests for new materials to be purchased and brought in by the following week.

If remedial work is needed, address the issues with care so as not to overwhelm the student. It's always a balancing act to keep the student feeling comfortable and capable when there are major problems, so unless the person in front of you is very mature, don't put her back at square one with her repertoire (see "Remedial Teaching" in Chapter 7, *Sequencing*). Utilize warm-ups and scales and create an etude from sections of a new piece at her current level if at all possible. Remember, this is just the first of many lessons. Over time you will gain the student's trust, and eventually you will have time to get to it all, so don't overload the first lesson by trying to cover too much all at once.

Your student has been working with you for quite a while, yet an issue that you addressed at the first lesson—and every subsequent one—continues to be a substantial limitation to his technique. He's a nice kid, and seems to love playing, so you hate to be hard on him, but it's beginning to be a real sticking point. What do you do?

One approach is to try the question "What do you love about [singing/playing]?" Whatever the answer, acknowledge him by concurring with his statement: "That's wonderful—I love that, too." Then say, "I know one thing you don't like, and that's my reminding you about your _____. Am I right?" Draw a connection from what he loves about playing to the solution of the problem—how much better his tone will be, or how many more great fast pieces he'll be able to play when he makes the correction. Tell him that it really is possible to have a lesson without hearing you talk about this issue, and that solving the problem doesn't have to take forever, either. Give him some kind of projected time frame: for instance, if he spends the next three weeks working on it every day, there's a good chance he can fix it once and for all. Remind him that he really is the teacher of his own brain, and that if he can be a good teacher to that "student" and patiently offers daily reminders, the "student" will establish a new habit. Then give the issue a name, such as project "Stand Up Straight." Write this on a piece of paper, and have him tell you the specifics of all directives he'll give himself, and everything that he will watch for, listen for, and feel. Put it in the front of his notebook as a reminder to address the issue every day. Ask about it by name in subsequent lessons. "How's project Stand Up Straight going this week?" Or create a code to use is as a reminder: "SUS" It's not a magic wand, but you're more likely to get this behind you sooner than grinding away at the same correction week after week.

You really enjoy most of the students on your roster, but there is one kid whom you just dread teaching. Before he shows up, you talk yourself into being positive and upbeat, but within five minutes the same problems that have bogged down every lesson for the past six months are right back in your face. His lessons, and frankly the kid himself, are really getting on your nerves, and you wonder how much more of this you can take.

Remember that your relationship is primarily a working one, so you don't really have to "like" a student to have productive lessons together. If you haven't done so already, define your criteria for an effective teacher-student relationship. You may already have determined some specifics like minimum practice requirements, but most teachers find they can even put up with intermittent lack of practice when the teacher–student relationship is working during the lesson itself. Fundamentally, teachers need a student who

- Wants to learn
- Is respectful
- Is willing to make an effort

At the beginning of a teaching relationship, the student may not be bringing all these attributes to the lessons. Be patient with building your relationship, and remember that much of the burden of fostering a positive relationship does fall on the teacher. (Refer to Chapter 6, *Teaching Principles.*) Yet some way or another, sooner or later, the student needs to be accountable to all three, since the lack of any one of them could be the deal-ender for the relationship. Let's unpack why these three criteria might not be met and, even though they are your student's issues, what you can do to help the student fulfill his part of the working relationship.

THE STUDENT DOESN'T WANT TO LEARN

A student might be resistant to learning because he was told "You are going to take music lessons whether you want to or not." He doesn't yet know how gratifying the experience can be, but that's something you can fix. Do something to engage the student. Try a game: play a note, and ask the student to play louder than you play; then play a soft note, and see if the student can play softer—or try this using low notes and high notes, long ones and short ones, crisp ones and spongy ones. Once you have the student's attention (and already he's learned something), steer the lesson toward a piece of music or a scale, and apply the technique "I want you to see if you can make every note as [loud, soft, long, short, etc.] as you just did." Learning to make new, special sounds really *is* fun, and once a student experiences that kind of control over his own sound, he'll be more intrigued about the next piece of information you are about to unleash. You might need to do this more than once, but turn on your creativity, find out what the student enjoys, and make lessons something he will really look forward to. There really are few things in life more gratifying than learning something new, and it feels great to partner with someone who can help you be good at it.

THE STUDENT IS DISRESPECTFUL

Disrespect comes in a variety of forms—playing while you're talking, interrupting you, not looking at you, not answering questions, or talking back. While this kind of behavior is not common in private lessons, it can occur. Disrespectful students have not likely been shown much respect themselves—but the teacher–student relationship can be different once you show the student that you care about her as a person. Ask about her school, family, friends, pets, and outside interests. Find out what kind of music she listens to, and be accepting and open toward her responses. Listen with interest to your student's thoughts and ideas—she will be more ready to reciprocate when it's your turn to share.

If after several weeks of showing respect and interest toward the student you're still not getting a reasonable response in return, explain what you see as the problem. Let the student tell you what lessons are like from her perspective. Talk it over, reach some kind of an agreement, and shake on it, literally. If the problems return, remind her of the deal you made. Remember, however, that you should never tolerate disrespectful behavior from a student. The teaching relationship is built on respect and trust. Make it your bottom line—if need be, calmly end the lesson to show her how serious you are about this. It's not likely to happen again.

Very young students may demonstrate disrespect by pulling away when you are trying to physically position them or the instrument. In this case, the lesson of "accepting help" is the teaching point for the day. Explain to them that you are there to help them learn. You plan on being their teacher for a long time and want them to know how important it is to work together. You should also tell students that it hurts your feelings to be treated that way. Let the parent be the student for a while, allowing the child to see what a gracious and cooperative relationship between a student and a teacher looks like; then allow the student several opportunities to practice the same.

Ask the parent to assist the child with posture or positioning as you watch. You may learn right then and there why the student is resistant to manual assistance. Because anyone's reaction to being pushed in one direction is to push back, you may have to coach the parent in how to use a gentle touch or different verbal directives to achieve the goal. This can be a very valuable lesson for everyone.

Once the issue is addressed in this manner, these behaviors typically subside. If disrespect in any form continues, however, make it clear that you will not tolerate such behavior directed either at you or the parent in your presence. When the student feels secure enough to maintain a respectful demeanor during lessons, you will continue the relationship. You do not want to give students of any age the opportunity to exercise unhealthy attitudes toward you, peers, or parents.

Consider This

A student's behavior might seem disrespectful on the surface, but it could mean other things. The student who plays while you talk at a lesson could simply be very excited about making music and wants to keep playing—or you might be talking too much. You can teach him a certain amount of self-control, but be careful not to put a damper on the enthusiasm. A student who can't look at you when you talk to him might have other personal issues, so be tolerant of the possible hidden challenges. Rather than demanding a certain behavior, work first to establish a trusting relationship, and it's quite possible the issue will be resolved in a non-confrontational way.

THE STUDENT DOESN'T MAKE AN EFFORT

Low Energy

You can sometimes use the foregoing ideas about engaging the student to jumpstart an apparent lack of effort, but low energy at a lesson might simply mean the student is tired, hungry, or thirsty. Mid-afternoon lessons right after school are often the most challenging in this way. Suggest to the parent that the student eat a piece of fruit or granola bar on the way to the lesson. If this doesn't help, but you notice that the student seems much more energetic and focused at a rescheduled lesson over a weekend, you might offer a different lesson time on a regular basis.

Lack of Confidence

Sometimes a student who does not try is dealing with a confidence issue, perhaps avoiding failure by simply not making an effort. Be sure the student knows it is okay to not be perfect, and that the lesson is a safe place to make mistakes. Show her that you aren't embarrassed by mistakes and weird sounds from time to time—then deliberately make a crazy mistake yourself. Even if you both know it's just for show, sharing a laugh together reinforces the feeling that you're in it together. Of course, you'll want to follow up with plenty of no-fail ways to work: make all your requests completely manageable and easy to achieve, and give instruction on how to build on those successes. Choose one aspect to focus on at a time, and offer immediate praise for success in that area; be sure to avoid making corrections on a problem outside that focus—save that correction for later, especially while you work to build her confidence.

Avoidance of Responsibility

An inquisitive student who asks honest questions so as to better understand something should have every question answered as clearly and honestly as possible. But students sometimes use questions to distract you from the task at hand, and to avoid making an effort. If this seems to be the case, a simple response will do: "I promise I will tell you about that when it's important for you to know, but right now we have some work to do."

Eventually, the relationship requires students to accept responsibility for their part in the learning process. Some seem to have an excuse for everything, and perhaps may even try to blame you for their lack of trying. Here are some classic examples (followed by your mature and productive response):

- "I didn't know I was supposed to practice that." (Be sure it's written down next time.)
- "This is different from the way you showed me last week." (Probably not, but again, be sure the directions are completely clear—have the student repeat them back to you, and write them down so there is no question as to what directions were given.)
- "Wasn't it *any* better that time?" (It's true that we teachers can be hard to please at times, so be sure to tell students what you like about what they did before you focus on the problems. Don't fabricate the truth, but do find something to reinforce with a compliment.)
- "I had too much homework this week to practice." (This is not always a feeble excuse, especially coming from high school students. You can, however, give them some lessons in time management, and show them how much they can get done even on challenging days when they only have ten or fifteen minutes.)

Many problems like these can often be resolved between you and the student. In fact, teaching students of all personalities from a variety of life situations can give you a real appreciation for challenges you might never have dealt with yourself. At the first sign of a problem, don't jump to the conclusion that you won't be able to work with a particular student. In fact, students who seem most difficult initially can become some of your most beloved ones, if you're willing to work through the challenges and establish a solid working relationship. But if the problems continue in spite of your best efforts, you'll need to step up the problem-solving to the next level.

ENLISTING PARENTAL SUPPORT

Parents can be very helpful in resolving challenges with your school-aged students, so don't wait too long before enlisting their support. First, make parents aware of the issues, stating them as objectively as possible from your point of view without making accusations. Frame your concerns by stating why the problem is detrimental to the learning process, rather than why it really annoys you. Remember, the parents are paying for lessons so their child will learn, not so that you can be happy. In other words, rather than saying "He doesn't listen, and I get so tired of having to repeat myself," try something like "Johnny's lack of focus is causing us to go over the same material too many times, so his progress has been very slow." Ask the parent whether the student has mentioned any issues concerning his lessons, and be open to the possibility that the student might see things differently, and that you might indeed share the responsibility for resolving the problem. Create a plan that should effect a change, and continue engaging the parents on a week-to-week basis at minimum until the problem is solved.

VIDEOTAPING

Another way to avoid many of these issues in the first place is to have the parent present. Some teachers make it a policy not to accept a new student unless the parent commits to attend every lesson. Even having a parent in the next room is better than having them go to the grocery store or sit out in the car. It's not always possible, though: parents with other children or irregular work schedules might find it almost impossible to be there; and it is not always financially feasible for a teacher to turn away students for this reason. A good alternative is to videotape every lesson. Besides being a great teaching tool, recording the lesson gives you and the student an outside perspective and, if needed, gives you verification that you were acting in a professional manner and doing everything in your power to make the lesson a positive and productive experience.

WHEN IT'S NOT GOING TO WORK

Not every student who studies with you is going to be the perfect fit. Sometimes teachers wonder what to do with a student they "don't like," but in a teaching relationship, personalities and "liking" or "disliking" a student are really nonissues. When students offer the three criteria mentioned in the previous section, and you have provided your best professional approach, you will have a healthy working relationship that creates a real partnership—which can in fact lead to friendship. But if you have done everything you know how to do to correct the situation and the relationship still isn't working, then it might be time to suggest that the student find another teacher.

This is difficult for teachers who have a "never say die" attitude toward students—that if they can just find the right approach, teacher and student will work happily ever after. But after doing everything you know to do to rectify the situation—including honest conversations with both the student and the parent—the problems persist, give the relationship a time limit: perhaps one or two more lessons, or to the end of the month or the term if necessary. With certain exceptions, it's usually best not to announce this to the student in advance—it just makes lessons very uncomfortable and won't help the situation. But when the time is up, and things aren't quantifiably better, let the student know that was his or her last lesson with you. By now you will have had enough conversations about this that it won't come as a big surprise to the student or the parents. End the relationship and don't look back.

The most painful separations are ones that culminate in some negative episode, where everyone feels bad. These can blindside you from time to time, but try to learn from them so that you can avoid a similar situation in the future. Be sensitive to your student, but in particular watch yourself for warning signs: being uncharacteristically grouchy or impatient, having to freeze a smile on your face to get through the lesson, or squelching even the most minimal expectations for practice, cooperation, or respect. No one student is worth twisting yourself so far out of shape that you don't feel good about yourself or you can't even do your job. Simply state that you apparently aren't the right teacher at the right time for this student, wish them well, and send them on their way.

> A student's departure from your studio will be less painful if you acknowledge to the whole class, in a group setting, at the beginning of the year, that you want to know about a student's desire to change teachers as soon as possible, and that you will work with the student to find another teacher. The student's success and progress toward goals is your greatest desire in working with each student.
>
> When a student expresses such an intention at a lesson, probe beneath superficial clichés to learn if you could have done things differently, or if different vocabulary would have made expectations clearer. Don't "penalize" the student in remaining lessons or subsequent jury grades.
>
> STEPHEN CLAPP

COLLEGIATE SITUATIONS

At the college level, issues between teachers and students often occur when students arrive unprepared to manage their new independence and work expectations. Conflicts often have to do with areas in students' lives that are out of balance: social or personal life, sleep, nutrition, exercise, or academics—too much of one thing and not enough of something else. Students' old study habits, including completing assignments at the eleventh hour, are often not conducive to the needs of music school. Students who have become very good at last minute test preparation and paper writing might try a similar approach for their applied performance area: study-ing happens before the exam, practicing happens before the jury. What they have not learned yet is that music achievement doesn't work that way.

Teachers may interpret their students' lack of consistency and discipline in a very negative way: that the student is exhibiting immature, disrespectful, lazy, or other-wise nonproductive behaviors. The student might on the other hand believe that the teacher has set unreasonable expectations or, worse, is demonstrating favoritism, egotism, manipulation, cruelty, or other behaviors associated with having the upper hand in the power differential.

There are two approaches the teacher can take to avoid such problems. First, an *a priori* plan clarifies the justification for and nature of your relationship. For exam-ple: "You have come to this school to prepare for a career in music, and I am here to teach you what you need to know. To that end, I will do everything I can to guide you, but this endeavor does require a consistent and concerted effort on your part." At the same time, have your students tell you what they want to get out of their work with you, and what their goals are during and after college. When you and the stu-dent are on the same page regarding goals and expectations, your time together can certainly be positive and productive.

Second, create a syllabus that you give to everyone in your studio. This document can act as an agreement or contract; it outlines your expectations and policies regard-ing all aspects of attendance at lessons and studio class, practice, performances, and grading. The syllabus can also include elements of your philosophical approach toward fostering a cooperative and supportive atmosphere in your studio commu-nity. You can state your intention to treat each individual with equal interest while fostering a strong, high-quality class of students overall. You might also want to include a statement encouraging students to discuss concerns as they arise, not wait-ing until right before a jury week or audition date. Make it easy for your students to talk to you by setting regular office hours during which you will be available to have unpressured and, if necessary, confidential conversations.

If you haven't already done so, create a long-term plan by designing a technique, etude, and repertoire proposal for each student's degree program that includes benchmark events such as required recitals and juries, divisional exams, treatise pre-sentations, and so forth. Once established, each semester can begin with a review of the plan, making any necessary adjustments, and marking the calendar with specific goals and target dates for the upcoming semester. Together with your student, you can make decisions regarding repertoire, practicing, and performing goals for the term, and consider master class opportunities, audition dates, and summer festivals. Refer to your plan throughout the semester so that you are able to provide frequent and specific feedback regarding the student's progress in the short term as well as in the continuum of learning.

Consider This

Conflicts can arise when students and teachers have different expectations of the studio situation. Respond to the questions that follow from a student's point of view, and then as the studio teacher. (If you are currently in the role of one or the other, recall or project your other set of responses accordingly.) Notice any shift in attitude or perspective when you change your role. Consider the potential differences in the teacher–student relationship when such expectations are made clear from the beginning, versus answers being revealed as the semester proceeds.

- How shall the student address the teacher? (Dr., Mr., Mrs., Ms., Miss, Professor, John, etc.)
- How many private lessons and master classes are given per semester? Are these guaranteed? Is an "hour" lesson a full sixty minutes, or less than that?
- What is the expectation when a student arrives for a lesson (instrument assembled, warmed up, waiting at the door, etc.)?
- What is the contingency for not being adequately prepared for a lesson?
- What is the contingency for the student missing a lesson? Does this change whether or not the teacher was given advance notice?
- Is a grade given for each lesson, or just an overall impression at the end of the semester?
- What is the meaning of the grades A, B, C, D, and F in a one-on-one lesson situation?
- How is "progress toward a goal but still not polished" graded?
- How should the student and teacher handle disagreements of interpretation, style, or technique?
- What are the procedures for airing a grievance of any type?
- What are the procedures for requesting a studio change, if that is an option?

Professional Ethics

There's a student you've coached at the youth orchestra sectionals who is a talented kid, and you like her very much. It's easy to see that guidance from her current teacher isn't great, and you'd love to have her as a private student. Should you suggest that?

As tempting as this situation is, the answer is an emphatic *no*. Recruiting students away from another teacher's studio—as innocent as the foregoing scenario seems— is a breach of ethics. You can give her guidance and make suggestions at the sectionals, remaining deferential to her private teacher's preferences, but you cannot suggest that she'd be better off with you, or even that you'd be willing to spend extra practice time with her. Such an inquiry about private study needs to be made by her (and her family), and even then, you are obliged to say, "I cannot accept you as a student until you have talked with your current teacher."

There is a gray area that separates one teacher's class from another. No student "belongs" to a teacher, of course—students are free to do what they want. But the first time you lose a student to another teacher and experience the sting that comes with it, you'll know why it isn't okay for a teacher to be complicit in the situation. In fact, you really don't want to ever leave an impression that you have intruded on the relationship of a student with his or her teacher. Most teaching organizations have a code of ethics, and this messy gray area is invariably addressed:

> "The teacher shall respect the integrity of other teachers' studios and shall not actively recruit students from another studio."
> "The teacher shall participate in the student's change of teachers with as much communication as possible between parties, while being sensitive to the privacy rights of the student and families."

But also this:

> "The teacher shall respect the student's right to obtain instruction from the teacher of his/her choice."

That means when your student decides to leave, even if you believe he or she has been lured away by another teacher, you cannot and should not try to block it; even more important, do not express your understandably fervent opinion about it to the student. The unfortunate result of doing so will be that you as the "former" teacher will appear desperate and somewhat pitiful. This is a swallow-your-pride-and-smile-though-your-pain moment where you must be as gracious as you can to the student who is leaving. Say you're sorry to see him go, and wish him well. If you have good reason to believe that a teacher has unethically lured your student away, you could call or write the teacher and express your displeasure, or you can file a formal complaint with the teaching organization of which you are both members. Unfortunately, no matter what you do, it is virtually impossible to have any grievance like this satisfactorily resolved. Do your best to rise above it, and don't allow one teacher's unethical maneuver to get the best of your integrity or your dignity.

MAKING THE BEST OF THE TRANSITION

Even when it's handled as ethically as possible, when students move from one studio to another, it's an inherently uncomfortable situation for everyone involved. The student or parent has had to make the typically difficult decision to seek another teacher because the one he's with isn't working out; the current teacher, despite his or her best efforts, has been found to be inadequate in some way; and the new teacher, while at an advantage to be on the positive side of the equation, is surely empathetic to the chagrin on the other side, and obliged to treat the colleague with as much dignity and honor as possible.

So when a student comes to you asking for lessons, as inwardly pleased as you might be, your first question should be "Are you currently studying with another teacher?" If so, then you need to say, "Have you discussed this with your teacher yet?" Explain that you do not accept another teacher's student into your studio. Do realize that this puts the student in a bind: you have not yet accepted her, but still you are asking her to raise this difficult issue with her teacher, putting their current working relationship in jeopardy. If it seems right, you can offer to meet with the student with the understanding that this is not a lesson, only a brief "audition" where you can see if you and the student are compatible to work together. Once that has been determined, then let the student know that this new arrangement must come with the blessing of her current teacher before you can accept her.

Be sure to ask pointedly about this when she calls to schedule her first lesson. If there is any hesitation in the response, you can almost be certain that this important conversation hasn't happened yet. Insist that the student holds up her end of the deal. The first time a student shows up in your studio with marks in her music that you know are not yours, once again you'll see why this unspoken agreement between teachers is so important.

YOUR STUDENTS' OTHER TEACHERS

Most of your secondary-level students will be involved in their school music programs, and some are also members of local youth performing organizations. More often than not, this is a very compatible situation: students get great individual guidance from you, and the band, orchestra, or choir situations give them important large ensemble experiences that you cannot provide. Ensemble directors are invariably glad to have students who study privately and are usually very respectful of the private teachers' work with those students. From time to time, however, you will run into a problem with another teacher over differences in opinion about a technique or programming.

Private teachers don't want their best students to languish in underachieving music programs; on the other hand there are limits to what can be considered "healthy" challenges. Directors will sometimes assume that as long as a private teacher is involved, they can program repertoire of virtually any difficulty. Yet when the technical and musical challenges far exceed the developmental level of the student, the private teacher feels cornered into spending valuable lesson time force-feeding repertoire or techniques that are completely out of sequence with their progressive plan for that student.

Other problems can arise when a school director recommends a technique that is not compatible with the private teacher's approach. Occasionally, a student will report at his lesson that the ensemble director told him that what you've taught him is "wrong." The arrogance of that comment can easily send a private teacher into a tailspin. (Of course, to be fair and objective, the shoe fits the private teacher, too, because there will be times when you believe the director is "wrong.") Before you express your complete, unedited opinion of that teacher in front of the student, realize that he is stuck between you and his school teacher. Who has the authority, after all? Remember that school teachers give students grades and private teachers do not. In the minds of many parents and students that tips the scales heavily on the other side.

So when your student says "My teacher (translation: school music director—let it pass) said this is a better way to do it," start by taking a deep breath. If you like, let the student show you the "better way." After you've seen the alternative, you can decide on your course of action. If it really doesn't matter, or it's basically the same either way, you might let the student choose which feels better to him. If the new idea is truly better than yours, just say so: "Hey, that works really well—sure, let's mark it in your music." More often than not, however, you'll like your idea better, so you will need to show your student the reason for your choice. Let your student know that there are many ways to play or sing, and it's okay for teachers to differ about these things—but for the reasons you've shown your student, it is important that he do it your way. A more mature student can even be shown how to be flexible with what they do, empowering them to make the best of a variety of situations—a good musical and life lesson to be learned.

If problems persist, call the music director to discuss the unresolved issues. Calmly explain how her corrections, expectations, and/or choice of repertoire affects your ability to teach well, and even more importantly, how it affects the student's learning experience. Listen to what she has to say, and then try to find a mutually beneficial approach to resolving the issue at hand. You might even want to offer to run a sectional that the director could observe, which might lead to her making better choices for students in the future. When you run into a truly uncooperative director, as you might from time to time, rise above it to the best of your ability, keep your teaching as separate as possible from that situation, and carry on with what you do best.

In any situation where you disagree with any other authority figure in your student's life, it's wise to model professionalism. Teachers can take the high road by not making negative statements about the music, the teachers, a judge, or an audition panel. Verbalizing things like "These people don't know what they're doing" might make the student who doesn't make the cut feel better, but gives the student an unhelpful excuse to not take full responsibility for his or her best playing. Challenging the credibility of the people who chose the music and the judges who made the decisions invalidates the success of a student who just won her first audition. Instead of complaining, get involved in the teaching organizations where you can offer your insights and influence decisions regarding audition music and procedures. Sometimes a new voice on audition panels can make a huge difference, especially when it's coming from a teacher with many quality students involved in the process.

Fostering a Positive Partnership with Parents

Parent 1 complains that despite her daughter's three private lessons, all of her friends are being moved up to the honor band, and she is still in concert band—where are the results they were expecting?

Parent 2 announces that since they missed five lessons during the past school year, they will take those five lessons in the summer and call it even.

Parent 3 arrives fifteen minutes late for a half-hour lesson and expects you to teach the full thirty minutes anyway. "So what if it's 4:15 and you have another student at 4:30. I didn't drive across town in rush hour traffic for a fifteen-minute lesson."

Parent 4 sits in on the lesson but is not content to simply observe and take notes. She scoffs at her child's mistakes, and interjects comments like "I told you that you were practicing that the wrong way."

The most vital step toward fostering a positive partnership with parents is communication. Provide studio policies and handbooks that define and clarify your objectives and expectations. Most of the time, when all parties understand the goals from the outset, most challenges can be resolved quickly.

Undoubtedly, however, there will be times when conflicts arise over scheduling, parental involvement that borders on interference, competition between students, or differences over learning goals. If you are aware of tensions or concerns, either on your part or on the part of the parents, you should initiate conversation sooner rather than later so that misunderstandings and disagreements don't build into resentments.

Whenever possible, you should meet face-to-face. Email is convenient for many things, but with disagreements, it's too easy to push "send" and have regrets. Phone conversations can be better, since both sides of the issue can be discussed with immediate feedback, but a face-to-face meeting allows the best opportunity for clear and open communication. Arrange the meeting at a time that doesn't interfere with the lesson, and preferably without the student present so that you are free to speak openly.

If you have the opportunity, try to organize your thoughts before the conversation, but it's best to allow the parent to air his or her grievances first. As the parent speaks, keep calm, and don't react to anything. Always assume that the parent has the child's best interest in mind; give the parents uninterrupted time to state their concerns, and make a real effort to understand their point of view. When it's your turn to respond, here are some important considerations that will help the conversation go as smoothly as possible.

- Gently remind them about any aspects that might be in your lesson policy or had already been discussed and agreed to in previous conversations.
- If you have a grievance about a parent, especially when it involves the parent–child relationship, be sure to first acknowledge that parent's love and concern for the child, his or her contributions as the primary educator, and his or her desire to look out for the child's best interests.
- If a parent is interfering during the lesson, explain your need to work with the student as an individual, addressing needs as you see fit. Empower the student to speak on his or her behalf—an important life skill.
- Sometimes well-intentioned parents put undue pressure on a child at home, so be sure that your expectations for practice are made very clear to both student and parent. Because children have a developmental need to move toward independence, it is much more complicated to guide learning as a parent than as a teacher. Suggest books and articles that will support the child-teacher-parent relationship and help to keep any challenges from being construed as personal issues.

When seeking a resolution to any problem, try to keep things simple, and be willing to meet parents halfway, especially when it comes to makeup lessons, rescheduled lessons, or payments. Be willing to concede if you are in error about any aspect of the conflict. On the other hand, don't promise something just to get the parents off your back—ultimately that alone may be a source of even greater frustration and resentment. Whenever possible, try to request (rather than demand) a resolution. If you have a bottom line, then state it in as clear and matter-of-fact fashion as you can. As frustrated as you might be, you do not want to say or do anything unprofessional that you will regret later.

When rational conversation doesn't seem to be working, realize that some people enjoy complaining and are not really interested in solving a problem. If you are verbally attacked or feel abused, it may be necessary to simply end the meeting and continue communication in writing. If necessary, take notes about the meeting, and write a letter starting with the facts, stating the problem from your point of view as well as what you understand is the parent's perspective. In the meantime, don't let a disagreement affect the quality of your work with your student. Stay focused on the student, maintain dignity, and teach professionally. Many smaller problems will fade, and skeptical parents, when given time, gradually begin to understand how your approach to teaching really does support everyone's best interest and goals for learning.

> ### Consider This
> Many teachers of young students sense that they are in the business of teaching parents and helping families. Can you see how your role as a teacher could positively influence a family?

MONEY ISSUES

Because it's fair and easy, you have parents pay you cash for the lesson just taught. Last week, one parent didn't have cash or a checkbook with them and promised to pay the next week. At the last minute, they canceled this week's lesson. You were counting on the $80 from those two lessons to pay your electric bill.

Usually, delayed payment is an honest mistake: parents forgot that they spent the last of their cash at the grocery store, or left the checkbook at home, and they will come through for you the next week with apologies for a late payment. But it does happen that occasionally someone "forgets" so as to avoid paying. At worst, if you tend to give people the benefit of the doubt, such a nonpayment problem can drag on for weeks until finally the next lesson is cancelled and you never see or hear from the student again. But even if it is just a single last-minute cancellation, not only are you out the money, you can't use that time to schedule another lesson or rehearse with your quartet after all.

The best way to ensure that students will show up for scheduled lessons—and that you will be paid—is to request advance payment for scheduled lessons.

Combine this requirement with a clear cancellation clause, such as "I offer rescheduled lessons when given a minimum of twenty-four hours notice, but I cannot give refunds." If asking for advance payment makes you uncomfortable, consider all the lessons you've had at any school or college—not one place will let you attend until tuition has been paid. You sign up for lessons, you pay in advance; if you don't show up, you forfeit the tuition. It's not unusual or unreasonable. When you set clear parameters for students and parents, they know you're serious about consistency with lessons, and such a policy allows for a little more predictability with both your schedule and your income.

You've been in town only a couple months, and one of your new students is looking for a new viola. You told her to check the local shops and bring the best instruments to her lesson tomorrow so you could help her choose. The phone rings, and it's the proprietor of one of the violin shops, welcoming you to town, inviting you to stop by soon, and offering a commission on any sale that comes from your recommendation. You're trying to get your feet on the ground, and a little extra cash could help. Should you consider it?

Be very careful of conflict-of-interest situations, whether it involves money or any other advantages. Imagine how you'd feel if you knew a teacher was recommending one instrument over another and getting a commission from it. Even if it was the best instrument, you now are very aware that you didn't just pay what the instrument was actually worth, and it suggests to you that your teacher does not have your best interests in mind. You might wonder what else this teacher might be thinking or doing that's controlled by ulterior motives. Students do find out about these exchanges, even if it's years later. Such a situation erodes trust immediately. Exchanging your integrity for the money or advantages is not a worthy trade. If anything, ask the merchant to offer the equivalent commission as a discount in the price of the instrument. The merchant will immediately recognize your unwillingness to be lured by monetary temptations, and your student will benefit and appreciate the reduction in the cost of the instrument.

Looking in the Mirror: Resolving Our Own Issues

We've looked at many common problems that arise with students, parents, and other teachers, and have considered several resolutions. But we do have to recognize that problems are not always someone else's. We are human, too, with personalities, backgrounds, and life situations that can complicate our relationships or our ability to teach as well as we would like. It is important to reflect on ourselves from time to time, making honest assessments about who we are, our strengths and our weaknesses, our abilities, and our limitations. We don't have to be perfect, but there are things we can do to recognize and validate our own strengths, as well as to create a plan to make improvements in areas that are challenging for us. Being peaceful with who we are makes it possible to work from an honest vision of ourselves as people.

Personal Inventory: Teachers teach best when they work from a solid place in themselves. If you know you love music and want to nurture the best in every student who comes to you, many other aspects of teaching fall into place quite naturally. Without that center from which to operate, teaching—and anything else—will be a challenge. Establish your own comfortable role as a musician and a teacher by answering the following questions.

1. Why did you choose music instead of another career?
2. Of all the teachers you had (of any subject), which ones left the most positive impression on you? Now that you understand more from a teacher's perspective, how did he or she bring out the best in you and help you learn?
3. How will you combine your love of music with that positive teacher–student experience (in other words, your answers to questions 1 and 2) in teaching your own students?

You will be most comfortable if your teaching environment, your degree of organization, and your students (how many you teach and their accomplishment level) are in balance with the rest of your life. Lack of a decent teaching space, inconsistent bookkeeping, and unorganized stacks of music can be an ongoing source of frustration for you and your students. Feeling that your students, rather than you, control your schedule can be a huge frustration, and you might consider consolidating your schedule, or keeping certain days of the week "off limits" to lessons. Unresolved issues, tensions, and imbalances between competing elements in your life can detract from your ability to be at your best at any given time. Ask yourself these questions:

1. Do my physical surroundings support my ability to teach well? Does my appearance project a high standard of professionalism? What could I improve that would allow me to be more effective?
2. Is my schedule and teaching load comfortable and in balance with my performing schedule? Would I like to have more or fewer students? What other changes could I make for the better?

3. What level of student do I teach best (beginner, intermediate, advanced)? Does my current roster of students reflect that strength? (For example, "I wish I had more young students because I know how to connect with them better than my high school students.")

4. Do I consciously or unconsciously avoid teaching certain types of music, aspects of playing, or areas of understanding? Could I make a plan to develop myself more in this area, or add one or two challenging pieces a year to my teaching repertoire?

5. Are there any other aspects that I would change in order to feel more settled and happy in my role as a teacher? (For example, have students come to my home for lessons, adjust my hourly rates, learn more repertoire, never teach past six in the evening, get more teacher training, etc.)

Once you have a better sense of what your needs are, you can start to shape your teaching life to fit those needs. Not every one of your ideas will be easy to change immediately, but if you know what you want, you can make a plan to modify your teaching life in the next year or two. For instance, if you know you'd rather be teaching high school students, realize that the younger ones on your roster won't stay that way for long, refer new inquiries to a colleague who loves teaching little kids, and then offer sectionals at the local high schools to attract more students at that level.

If you dread the trip out to a different school every afternoon to teach a handful of lessons for inadequate pay, you're probably not teaching your best when you get there. Decide what you would charge at home and how many students you'd need to make that work. Not everyone will follow you to your home studio, but your most dedicated students likely will. If it's a feasible plan, take the plunge and announce that you'll be teaching at your home starting next year. Offer group classes and emphasize other advantages so students are more willing to make the change with you. Even if you lose a few students in the move, as you continue to develop a reputation as a good teacher, your schedule will fill up.

Give yourself the advantage of being the best at what you do—no one else can or will do that for you. Ideas for continuing to learn, grow, and teach from your strengths are covered in the final chapter, *The Cyclical and Reciprocal Nature of Teaching*.

Recommended Reading

Kempter, S. (1991). *Between Parent and Teacher: A Teacher's Guide to Parent Education*. Ann Arbor, Mich.: SHAR.

Kreitman, E. (1998). *Teaching from the Balance Point: A Guide for Suzuki Parents, Teachers, and Students*. Western Springs, Ill.: Western Springs School of Talent Education.

Nathan, A. (2000). *The Young Musician's Survival Guide: Tips from Teens and Pros*. New York: Oxford University Press.

Sprunger, E. (2005). *Helping Parents Practice: Ideas for Making it Easier*. St. Louis, Mo.: Yes Publishing.

14 The Cyclical and Reciprocal Nature of Teaching and Learning

Personal Inventory: Think about your first music teachers, and which of them were particularly influential in leading you toward a career as a professional. Also reflect on which events, including lessons, workshops, performing ensembles, and contests, were most significant to you.

Music education is a cyclical process. Music teachers and performers were once students, and some of their students will become musicians and teachers themselves, working with students who will continue this succession. Consider the ways you have participated in the cycle so far. In elementary school, you likely had a general music class. Perhaps a professional performing group came to your school and inspired you to sing or play an instrument. From there you got involved in band, orchestra, or choir in middle and high schools, and probably took private music lessons. You also may have participated in a youth orchestra, played in "adjudication festivals," attended summer music camps, and even participated in competitive region and state auditions.

Now think of the people who guided you: a teacher who transformed your playing or singing in a single lesson, or the judge who wrote an encouraging comment on a jury sheet. It might have been a parent who took you to hear a world-class musician, a choir director who planned wonderful rehearsals, or a professional musician who brought her passion for making beautiful music right to your classroom—even the trumpet-player-turned-string-teacher who was willing to give up his lunch hour to play viola duets with you.

In every instance, someone cared enough about your musical education to spark your enthusiasm, facilitate your participation in a performing group, make supportive comments about your progress, and of course, encourage you to make great music. What you might not have considered before is that *these positive experiences were not happenstance*—they occurred because there were people who had your best interests in mind, and extended themselves to give you a meaningful musical experience.

Obviously, you found at least some of these experiences and teachers inspiring enough to choose music as a career. Whether you're still in school working toward a degree in music or already making a living as a professional musician, you can further the teaching/learning cycle by offering high-quality experiences to every student with whom you interact.

QUALITY MATTERS

The future of music now needs your involvement. Teachers in school music programs probably have the most direct impact, since they work with students on an almost daily basis. As a private teacher or a professional performer, you can play a substantial role in pre-college music education not only by offering first-rate private lessons at the preparatory level, but participating in the larger music teaching community. Visit schools to offer performances, master classes, and coaching sessions that will inspire both students and their teachers. Conduct a youth orchestra, band, or choir; coach sectionals; teach at workshops and summer music programs; and adjudicate contests and competitions.

University faculty members are in a position to powerfully influence teaching and learning at many levels. Many colleges and universities require faculty to reserve spaces in their applied studios for students majoring in music education, but unfortunately some studio teachers do not embrace this opportunity. These teachers fail to see a significant connection: that the education majors will soon be conducting school ensembles, and they are the teachers who will have the greatest impact on the number and *quality* of students referred back to university teachers' own studios. Remember that as a university professor, the high standards of musicianship and inclusive community you foster in your studio can and will be passed on to the enthusiastic and well-trained musicians of tomorrow; conversely, undervaluing your work with music education majors negatively impacts the experience of the students, their potential as musicians and teachers, and their enthusiasm for recommending you to their graduating students. Your energy toward developing the highest standard of technical and musical skills of every student in your studio is in everyone's best interests.

OUTREACH

Your willingness to actively extend yourself as a steward of goodwill to local school programs can have a positive effect on the extended community as well as your reputation and visibility, and enhances your ability to attract and recruit students. As a highly valued and respected member of the music community, and you will be invited to serve as a clinician, judge, master class teacher, or conductor for music festivals, or as a guest speaker for a music class.

Acting on the suggestions that follow will demonstrate your support of music programs in the community. If you are a university faculty member, these activities can be recorded as an impressive part of your annual report. This kind of outreach is an excellent way for any teacher to realize a broader, more inclusive philosophical understanding of the music education cycle.

- Offer to lead sectionals, master classes, and clinics for local youth music ensembles and music programs.
- Serve as a soloist or guest speaker for high school performing ensembles.
- Assist high school students in preparation for upcoming auditions.
- Secure complimentary seating for high school students at university performances and make arrangements for them to meet the performers backstage.
- Sponsor and organize activities that include school-aged participants, for example Viola Day or Double Reed Day.
- Make arrangements for interested high school juniors and seniors to observe university studio lessons for a day.
- Become a visible member of local, state, and national music education organizations, and volunteer to hold leadership positions.
- Volunteer to judge auditions or adjudicate competitions.
- Contribute to scholarship funds through your state music educator's organization.
- Host side-by-side events that feature performers from both high school and university student bodies.

- University faculty can send personal invitations to school music directors to attend post-performance receptions on campus.
- Dispatch university students to assist with instrument demonstrations to recruit new music students in primary and secondary school programs.
- Organize "honor" ensemble festivals on the university campus.

Continuing to Learn

> Who dares to teach must never cease to learn.
> JOHN C. DANA

There are many ways for us to deepen our understanding, broaden our perspective, and stimulate new ideas, from simple possibilities in our studios to those that draw us out farther into the world of music and teaching.

OBSERVATION

A powerful way to gain new insight into the teaching-learning process is by watching teaching in action. Arrange to observe other teachers at their studios, at a rehearsal, or in a classroom setting. Be sure not to limit your observations to studios that only teach your instrument, and take advantage of any opportunities to observe visiting artists. If they give a master class and a performance, attend both to notice how the two roles of artist-as-teacher and artist-as-performer are aligned. You will naturally be interested in another teacher's style and approach to instruction: attention to fundamental issues; clear and precise directions; amount and quality of feedback; and persistence toward a goal. The most important people to watch, however, are the students. Effective instruction should result in observable improvements in the students during that lesson or rehearsal.

Observing yourself via video recording is extremely valuable to your growth as a teacher. You see yourself as your students see you, get a clearer picture of the interaction between yourself and your students, and become aware of any unhelpful patterns in your teaching that need to be addressed. First try watching the videotaped lesson without taking notes; then watch again as if observing another teacher, and make notes related to your body language, interaction with the student, and degree of student improvement.

Arranging master classes with colleagues gives you another opportunity to observe your student and your teaching from a different perspective. Other teachers may notice issues that have been overlooked, or have a different approach to resolving a student's lingering problem. Your student will have gained from the experience, and you will have likely learned a new, effective approach to a teaching challenge.

When life slows down during summer months, take time to observe coaching sessions at summer festivals, camps, and institutes in your area. Sometimes there are observation fees involved, but often classes are open to the public. Depending on the size of the program, this can be a great way to see teachers from all over the country. If you are seeking potential teachers for your music-school bound students, this could allow you to preview a teacher's personality and effectiveness before making any recommendations.

READING BOOKS AND PERIODICALS

Books and treatises about chamber music, symphonic literature, operas, wind ensembles, and pedagogy for every instrument and discipline, exist somewhere in print. Many have become known as standards for specific instruments, conducting, and composing, and new books are being written every day. Membership in professional organizations aligned with your performance area usually includes a subscription to their journal or periodical, comprised of pertinent articles on technical, musical, and pedagogical issues. Read as much as you can, and build a lending library of information for your students and parents to help them learn more about practice, the instrument, performing artists, and all aspects of what we do as musicians and teachers. You can also expand your knowledge of teaching and learning by reading outside your immediate performing area, as well as outside the subject of music.

MUSIC-RELATED RESEARCH

A self-assured approach to teaching is wisely balanced with an open-minded sense of inquiry that will help you continue to develop your teaching skills. Music research provides evidence-based information that can be directly applicable to the next lesson you teach. Research covers a wide variety of topics, including effective practice, aural perception, teaching effectiveness, and intonation, as well as historical studies on performance and pedagogical lineage. Interdisciplinary research connecting music learning and performance to sciences such as kinesiology, psychology, and neuroscience provides a better understanding of the interconnectedness of physical, mental and emotional lives as musicians.

Professional journals publish the results of these studies, and conferences sponsored by music organizations also typically schedule a block of time for presenting research findings. These "poster sessions" allow conference attendees the opportunity to have the results of specific studies explained by the researchers themselves. Rather than assume that a research poster session is not applicable to you, attend one with an open mind. Professionals involved in music-related research are trying to address issues that studio and classroom teachers face every day. Remember, good research starts with a good question, and you might even have one that is waiting to be answered by your own research project.

INTERNET AND WEB RESOURCES

Countless web sites provide information and support related to all aspects of performing and teaching in any discipline. Many of these sites also offer demonstrations of various methodologies, techniques, and styles with video recordings, and some extended versions can be purchased as downloads or DVDs. Even if you don't agree with every approach or sequence of instruction you see, gaining other perspectives can help you solidify what you do believe, making your own teaching that much stronger. Information on the web runs the gambit from outstanding to awful, however, so if you're searching outside your area of expertise, be sure to ask a trusted colleague for recommendations.

Collaborative Learning Opportunities

INFORMAL TEACHING COMMUNITIES

> We would meet once a week on Wednesday afternoons for one hour, sitting around a large dining room table, void of a specific agenda except "talking about teaching." We did not discuss symphony rehearsals or our children—only teaching. Everyone brought their experiences during that week to the table: successes, frustrations, challenges, and insights. These discussions were without a doubt some of the most powerful and beneficial learning experiences of my career.
>
> LAURIE SCOTT

Private teachers tend to keep to themselves, mostly because they often teach out of their homes, and interaction with other teachers is not built into their professional circumstance. If this is your situation, don't be shy about going out of your way to meet and talk about teaching with other teachers in your community. Sometimes the best environments for learning communities are informal meetings, intended for sharing ideas and materials, working collectively to solve issues and provide inspiration.

FESTIVAL AND CONCERT COLLABORATION

You can foster a tremendous amount of energy in your studio by collaborating with other teachers to organize concerts and festivals. These festivals can be as grand or as intimate as you like and hosted on a local, state, national, or even an international level. Ideas for local collaboration might include chamber music festivals, pre-concert performances for local arts organizations, performances at daycare centers and libraries, or even combined studio performances in the lobby of an airport. Enhancing numbers of performing students through collaboration means your studio of twenty can suddenly be doubled in size. Your students will enjoy the rich sound of a larger ensemble, and such a distinctive gathering can make a powerful impression on your community.

The benefits of international music and cultural exchanges can be enormous for yourself and for your students. Professional student touring companies and international student organizations can be very helpful in making arrangements for concert venues and arranging sightseeing. If you teach independently and would like to offer this kind of experience to your students, it is wise to consider collaborating with another local teacher or director of an established program who travels with students on a regular basis. They will have experience with the logistics and liability issues that are involved with such ventures.

PROFESSIONAL ORGANIZATIONS AND TRAINING

> What I learned in the field—going to workshops, collaborating with and observing a master teacher—has been invaluable to my teaching.
> STUDIO TEACHER

Professional teaching organizations exist at every level: local, regional, state, national, and international. The mission of these organizations is to further the profession and support their members through a variety of possible services and offerings, including publications, informative web sites, sponsored events, group benefits, well-produced advocacy materials, and even project grants.

Many professionals find that the conferences are in many ways the most beneficial part of their memberships. Conferences can provide an immense amount of training and information in a few days. Conference fees and travel expenses are in addition to annual membership dues; however, the gathering of like-minded professionals to attend educational sessions and network with colleagues is considered invaluable by many. In addition, exhibit halls host music merchants and publishers, making it possible to try out instruments, browse music, and buy accessories directly from the manufacturers.

Some professional associations, such as the Suzuki Association of the Americas, the Organization of American Kodaly Educators, and the American Orff-Schulwerk Association, provide opportunities for continuing education that result in accreditation or certification. Professional organizations at the national, state and local level offer a variety of opportunities for teacher development, for example the Comprehensive Musicianship Through Performance (CMP) workshop, early childhood music training, eclectic styles programs, fiddling camps, and world drumming workshops. Most programs of this type are scheduled during summer months to make it possible for teachers to attend.

It might come as a surprise that many organizations, conferences, and workshops for professionals are not for profit and are developed and managed primarily by volunteers. Certainly this speaks to the mission of the organization and its members who work to make it strong and vital. Find an organization in whose purpose you believe, and consider your own volunteer service as part of your professional responsibility. Becoming a conference organizer, adjudicator, or presenter will increase your visibility as a professional, while contributing to the mission of shared ideals. You could serve as an officer or chair of a committee, write an article for the organization's journal, or review a new publication. Check the organization's journal or web site for the different divisions of its operation, and investigate an area of interest that will allow you to contribute productively to your community of fellow teachers and musicians.

FORMAL EDUCATION TRAINING

By enhancing the part of musical life that involves teaching—reading books or taking courses—you have already taken an important step toward broadening your career possibilities and increasing your professional viability. If teaching in primary or secondary schools is a future career possibility, you should consider a teacher certification course of study. Besides performance training, the curriculum usually includes courses related to child and adolescent development, educational psychology, classroom management and discipline, teaching students with special needs, and teaching in an urban setting. While an alternative certification option can lead to accreditation, teacher certification provided through music education degree programs provide beneficial apprenticeship opportunities and guided feedback over a longer period of time. Musicians who obtain education degrees or teaching certificates are eligible to receive state certification that allows for the possibility of teaching in a public school setting.

If you have aspirations toward college-level teaching, the job advertisements in Chapter 12 might have alerted you to the fact that many university programs require their applied instructors to teach secondary instruments and methods classes. Knowing this, you would be wise to consider taking lessons on a secondary instrument or enrolling in a methods class offered by the music education department.

These and other courses could expand your understanding of how people learn while you develop teaching skills and increase your knowledge of related subjects that would make your well-rounded abilities all that much more attractive to perspective employers.

Students in either a music performance or education degree plan can and should take advantage of learning opportunities that increase both performing and teaching skills. By looking at degree requirements and course options, education students may be able to pursue a performer's certificate, and performance majors could choose pedagogy as a minor area of study or decide to later pursue an education certificate. If you are working toward a college degree now, be sure to explore all available options toward the best possible preparation for a successful career that includes teaching.

For some musicians, teaching will always be simply a way to bring in a little extra money between gigs. However, perhaps you are discovering—or you already know—that while music is wonderful to *do*, it can be even more gratifying to *share*. Combine the excellent training you've received with lots of practice, thoughtful approaches to both performance and teaching, and an open mind, and you'll have many more opportunities for both employment and gratification.

Your influence can expand far beyond the stage or your studio, so make it positive, and extend it to as many students and situations as possible. Your best teaching won't be reserved for your best students, but generously offered to every student; the events you plan needn't be exclusively for your studio, but offered to all the studios in your community; ideas can be exchanged not just locally, but nationally and internationally; and new ideas won't emerge only from the field of music, but drawn from and linked with other arts, humanities, and sciences.

So read a book, create a handout, attend a master class, meet with a colleague, schedule a student recital; write an article, offer an outreach concert at the elementary school, register for a workshop, and smile at that little violinist waiting for her lesson in your big music school. It expands you, you expand others, and it all matters.

In a completely rational society, the best of us would aspire to be teachers and the rest of us would have to settle for something less, because passing civilization along from one generation to the next ought to be the highest honor and the highest responsibility anyone could have.

LEE IACOCCA

Conclusion

WHEN YOU THINK about the people you most admire, you recognize not only great passion for their vocation, but also the respect and genuine care with which they treat other people, and the earnest and infectious way that they share their passion. From early in your musical journey, and all along the way, a series of teachers invested in you as a musician and cared about you as a person. To help you become a performer, they've nurtured virtually every part of your being: physical, mental, psychological, philosophical, spiritual, and emotional. Now it's your turn to embrace the opportunity to bring passion and excellence not only to the stage, but to your students as well.

At some point, music becomes second nature to us, so integrated into our lives we forget the importance of explaining it. Doesn't everyone understand this the way we do? The answer is no. It's the role of a teacher—you—to reflect on what you do and what you know, and to pass it along. Music teaching is no small undertaking, though. Just like any art, excellence in teaching requires more than brief consideration—it requires ongoing analysis, exploration, and practice. Be confident in your ability to make positive changes in yourself as a teacher, just as you have in your development as a performer. Yet unlike performing, where you alone demonstrate your proficiency, your expertise will be revealed not by what you do, but what your students do.

By all means, continue nurturing your artistry: practice and perform as much as possible. Renew your passion for music every day, be gratified by your work, and bring joy to your audiences. At the same time, remember to see yourself and your musical life in the big picture, and be willing to extend your influence beyond your immediate situation. No matter what your position in the music world, your nurturing presence in people's lives will carry more weight than the most substantial performance resume, and your magnanimous sharing of what you know and love will resonate far beyond the last note you play—beginning with those who now call you "teacher."

How to Use This Book

For the Pedagogy Teacher

The premise of this book is to demonstrate the synergy between pedagogy and performing. Part I thoroughly examines the elements and concepts central to becoming a well-rounded musician: musicianship, listening, technique, practicing, and performance. Because this text does not advocate any specific approach, readers are asked to explore their own technique and musicianship, and should be strongly encouraged to seek guidance from their applied teachers when questions arise. Once these concepts have been examined, Part II asks the reader to consider the interaction between teacher and student—how knowledge, skills, and musicianship are communicated effectively and transferred through sequencing, fostering independent thinking in students, and a comprehensive approach, all guided by the best principles of good teaching. After considering these important aspects of teaching, the reader can create a teaching philosophy that brings together what he or she considers to be the most significant aspects of music performance with the important teaching approaches and ideals

Part III then examines specifics of life as a professional teacher: setting up and teaching in a private studio situation, involvement in a variety of teaching situations as a "freelance teacher," and emphasizing through actual job advertisements the more unexpected responsibilities of college level teaching. Common problems and ethics issues are discussed in a separate chapter. The final chapter focuses on the cycle of teachers and students in the music world, making the case for mutual respect, cooperation, and intersection of all musicians whether the focus is more on performance or more towards education. All must make a conscious choice to continue to develop as a performer, teacher, and advocate of the highest ideals in the profession.

Throughout this book are "Personal Inventory" sections that prompt the reader to generate some kind of self-reflective response, usually in writing. (In fact, the "Personal Inventory" sections in Chapter 10, *Your Teaching Philosophy*, are designed as progressive steps toward creating a philosophy statement by the end of the chapter.) The "Consider This" sections are interesting asides related to the text that could be used to stimulate class discussions. At the end of most chapters you will find "Ideas for Further Exploration." These directives can carry the reader into a deeper experience of topics mentioned in the chapter, and can be used as weekly assignments or developed into semester projects. Finally, the appendices contain teaching ideas and tools for both you and the pedagogy student, guidance for graduating students who will soon begin their job searches, as well as more information for those who have already secured employment.

For the Applied Teacher

This book is designed with performers in mind—not to distract musicians from practice and study, but to optimize the ability to self-analyze, self-assess, and think pedagogically about how learning happens best. You can expect that your students' active participation in that which increases their understanding and fosters their own best playing will be of great benefit to their work with you. This book discusses universally important issues of technical efficiency and physical freedom, as well as approaches to teaching complex areas such as intonation and musicianship, but it does not espouse a "right" or "wrong" way to learn or teach a technique, nor the best way to make music. As the applied teacher, you will be an important part of your students' exploration of these areas, because your students will be seeking your guidance and expertise throughout the course. Your personal experiences, insights, and ideals about music and teaching will provide valuable input to the performers and teachers of the next generation.

Course Proposal

Presumably the benefits of offering such a course are self-evident. However, if further justification is needed to ensure it is added to your school's curriculum, you might wish to include the following cogent reasoning with your proposal:

1. Most musicians, including those whose primary profession is performance, will teach during their careers. Since it is the school's mission to turn out well-prepared, employable graduates, we have an obligation to prepare all music majors for this likelihood.

2. Students' awareness of their own technique, musicianship, and performance will be heightened through "how" and "why" questions related to their own development as musicians. When questions arise, students will be encouraged to turn to their applied teachers for advice and clarification.

3. Because the course is designed to increase students' awareness and understanding of their own musicianship, their performing can become more refined and meaningful *while* they learn skills related to effective teaching—therefore, students can learn to teach while progressing toward their primary performance goals.

4. By demonstrating the essential connections between music performance, history, theory, composition, and other disciplines, the course will help coalesce information that tends to be compartmentalized in students' lives—thereby increasing students' awareness of the larger picture of a complete performing musician.

5. Since the course is intended for all performance majors, including conducting majors, it will foster the sharing of ideas between students from different studios whose contact might otherwise be limited.

6. While students continue to grow and flourish through their applied teachers' instruction, this course will foster each student's individual sense of what is significant about what he or she has to offer, and help each musician establish a distinct voice as a performer and a teacher.

7. (Optional) Faculty will be invited to reflect on the significance of what they do as teachers and musicians and speak about their philosophies, allowing students to benefit from the knowledge and experience of many more of the faculty than the normal curriculum usually allows.

8. (Optional) Videotaped and archived faculty lectures could be a valuable resource for the student body at large.

Two-Semester Companion Syllabus

The following sample two-semester syllabus outlines topics presented in the book and suggests assignments, topics for faculty lectures, and discussion points. This syllabus is only a model from which you can structure a syllabus that is appropriate for your course sequence, length of study, and students' development level. Both semesters' descriptions and objectives are listed first for overview purposes, and the two fourteen-week syllabi follow.

Overview of Performance-Based Pedagogy

Course rationale. The ability to analyze and reflect on one's musical skill is essential to growth as a performer, and provides a basis for ongoing development in technical facility and musical maturity. The ability to communicate instrumental technique and musical concepts to others prepares the musician for a multifaceted career that is likely to include teaching.

SEMESTER 1: APPLIED CONCEPTS

The first semester is focused on the performer's ability to self-reflect, explore and explain the most significant aspects of being a musician, thereby creating a foundation for teaching musicianship, listening skills, technique, practicing, and performing. (You might want students fill out a questionnaire about their current major, any teaching experience they may have had, their previous background as precollege students, and what they want to gain from the class. This will give you a baseline understanding of where they are and how to focus class discussions and projects.) By the end of the semester, students will be able to do the following:

1. Identify and articulate musical concepts.
2. Explain the underlying principles behind effective technique specific to an individual's performing area, and demonstrate practical pedagogical understanding of those techniques.
3. Describe a variety of effective practice techniques and processes, and explain the physical and cognitive basis for optimum learning.
4. Describe the role of listening in the development of musical thought and performance and ways to teach listening skills to students.
5. Make insightful connections between their own musical development and those of parallel fields, such as other musical styles or instruments, or divergent fields, such as philosophy, psychology, neurology, and musicians' health.
6. Develop and compose a teaching philosophy.

SEMESTER 2: TEACHING PRINCIPLES AND PRIORITIES

(Prerequisite: Performance-Based Pedagogy: Applied Concepts) The second semester helps translate the performer's musical and technical self-awareness into effective teacher–student relationships and learning environments. By the end of the semester students will be able to do the following:

1. Sequence technical and musical growth with well-chosen repertoire and an understanding of cumulative skill development.
2. Communicate effectively with students to foster meaningful progress in a variety of teaching situations.
3. Demonstrate an understanding of basic teaching principles at various stages of development.
4. Organize lesson materials and demonstrate a practical understanding of everyday matters in private lesson and small group settings.
5. Demonstrate effective master class teaching.
6. Thoughtfully answer interview questions for a teaching position through clarified priorities and a refined teaching philosophy.

Syllabus for Performance-Based Pedagogy: Applied Concepts, Semester 1 (28 Classes)

Required Textbook: Watkins, C., and L. Scott. (2012). *From the Stage to the Studio: How Fine Performers Become Great Teachers.* New York: Oxford University Press.

1. *Introduction.* Read the introduction out loud. What does a young musician need to learn before going to music school? (Write as much as possible in ten minutes.) Are these skills part of your background? What does an undergraduate need in four years to be prepared for a career in music? Course materials: Create a notebook for class/teaching with sections on musicianship, technique, practicing, performing, philosophy, practical info (handouts for students, lesson policy, contact info, notes on lessons, etc.). Discussion

about ongoing development of teaching philosophy—suggestions for recruiting students, practical needs of setting up a studio. Syllabus, semester projects, and short-term assignments discussed. Assignment: Read Chapter 1, *Musicianship* and find a succinct statement—a quote from a teacher, composer, performer, or music lover—that describes music. Be ready to read the statement in class and discuss the elements of it with which you are in agreement *or* disagreement.

2. *Musicianship*. Defining musical playing—do we need one statement or many? How do you describe a musical performance when you hear one? Unpack meanings of descriptions. What do you hear, see, feel, experience? Connecting the ethereal to the visceral when communicating about music. What was the best communication of music you have been offered by a teacher, conductor, or colleague (specific or general)? How did it affect the way you played—has the idea been applicable in unexpected ways? Assignment: Write a definition of musicianship, and explain how it is manifest in a performance.

3. *Musicianship*. Share definitions. What do you need to know to be a musician? Language of music, such as playing with appropriate articulations, dynamics, colors of sound, understanding notation, terminology, historical, biographical, theoretical knowledge, and how it informs musicianship. Relating moods, situations, spoken language, physics, and other natural phenomena to meaningful musical sounds. What happens when one of these aspects is lacking in a player? Assignment: Further Exploration 1—create a very short (thirty seconds or less) performance of a familiar piece that is lacking one of the aspects of musicianship discussed—be prepared to play for next class.

4. *Musicianship*. Sharing "lacking" performances—discussing how to "fix" a musical problem. The connection between musical playing and technique. Which comes first, or is there any separation? Are there techniques specific to musical performance, and others that are only skill-oriented? How listening is essential to musicians—different ways to listen: Assignment: Read Chapter 2, *Listening*.

5. *Listening*. Watch Dame Evelyn Glenny's TED lecture on listening. Discuss what it means to listen, how heightened awareness of all senses affects what we do as musicians. How did we learn to listen? How do we teach students to listen? Assignment: Choose your semester project and bring necessary book, repertoire, or proposal for approval at next class. Teacher observation 1 due next class.

6. *Listening*. Discussion of listening skills, how to develop pitch recognition, intonation, tone production, self-evaluation. What does it mean to play in tune? Developing a multi-level approach to intonation: sound, vibrations, singing, measuring, looking, feeling. How does this involve instruments with fixed intonation? Essential singing skills, developing listening/singing habits. Working with physical issues: measurements, fine muscular adjustments, embouchure. Visual approach? Practice techniques for developing intonation skills. Understanding/hearing perfect and nonperfect intervals. Assignment: Read first section of Chapter 3, *Technique*. Observe your own technique, and make notes on the chart about how each of the foundational items (posture, balance, breathing, muscular release) are essential to the way you sing, conduct, or play your instrument.

7. *Technique*. Discussion of elements of fundamental setup. Positioning feet, body, arms, and hands; examining efficiency and freedom in movements—use of imagery. Exercises/ stretching that help posture from start. (Show a web-based teaching video for ideas.) Assignment: Describe in written words and/or pictures a basic set-up exercise and

explain how it helps. (One or more of these can be developed as handouts for semester assignment.) Read the *Instrumental Acoustics* and *Mechanics of Sound Production* sections of Chapter 3. Be prepared to talk about the sound production and acoustics of your instrument at the next class, answering the questions in the book.

8. *Instrumental acoustics, fundamental technique, and tone production.* Discuss, compare, and contrast basic acoustics of instruments. Making a sound: Tone production and basic articulations. In what way is your playing a cooperative effort between you and your instrument? In what ways do you make the sound happen, and in what ways do you have to get out of the instrument's way and let it do what it does? What is the difference between a musician who understands the acoustics and someone who just sings, plays, or conducts without awareness? Assignment: Prepare your approach to teaching basic set-up, including posture, positioning, balance, and muscle release to a new student. Be ready to teach a member of the class in one week.

9. *Guest lecturer on sequencing fundamental skills: Dalcroze (or other early childhood music) specialist.* Movement and sound first; then connect to instrument and music on page. Developing coordination. Implementing images, vocabulary, and associations that help students understand gestures, shapes, feelings in body when playing. Assignment: Describe in written words and/or pictures a basic set-up exercise and explain how it addresses fundamental issues while developing the ability to create a good tone on the instrument. (One or more of these can be developed as handouts for semester assignment.) Make final preparations for your five-minute (maximum) "basic setup lesson" at next class.

10. *Technique.* "Basic setup lesson" taught to other members of class with no previous experience of playing, singing, or conducting. Did the lecture on childhood music help you sequence your basic learning skills for this lesson? Share stretching/posture exercises, images, ideas—compare and contrast techniques of different instruments. Begin looking at how efficiency, strength/stamina, freedom/flexibility/fluidity, and control directly affect technique of your instrument. Assignment: Teacher observation 2 due next class.

11. *Technique.* Explore how more expressive technique is manifest on instrument. Articulations, dynamics, techniques that color sound, etc. What is required physically to learn these techniques? How does a musician's basic physical approach to their instrument affect their ability to play with dynamics, color, and articulation? The role of listening in these techniques. Are there other approaches besides listening that heighten awareness of these techniques? Assignment: Read the *Movement and Accuracy* section of Chapter 3. Observe your own playing, and make notes on chart about each topic. Make notes of common physical pitfalls in the technique of your discipline, and potential long-term problems.

12. *Physical health specialist: technique, musicians' health.* Explore and discuss areas of efficiency, strength/stamina, freedom/flexibility/fluidity, and control in your own playing. Specialist's advice about balance, muscle efficiency, overuse problems, and so on. Assignment: Observe your own playing, considering ideas from today's class, and make notes on chart about how each of the components mentioned above influence your technique. Read the *Cognitive Processes Essential to Technique* section and begin to observe your own mental approach to playing. Make notes into chart, and add topics if you utilize another approach that is not listed here.

13. *Cognitive processes connected to effective physical technique*. Discussion of the ideas—how directly connected to the physical are they? Do you think they are appropriately categorized as techniques? Are they more related to practicing or performing? How do teachers contribute to or inadvertently inhibit fluid mental processes in lessons? Assignment: Read Chapter 6, *Teaching Principles* to preview ideas about teaching. Jot ideas about a different order for these principles, as proposed in Further Exploration 4.

14. *What happens at the first lesson*. What makes a good teacher? Establishing a working relationship with your student. Getting to know your student—how teacher and student benefit. How much should the teacher assign a beginning student versus one who has studied for a few years? Seeing the big picture of student development. Is there such thing as "beginner technique"? Student instrument—is it playable or not? Integrating musical playing from the beginning. Assignment: Continue to work on semester project.

15. *Applied faculty guest lecturer (1)*. Assignment: Write one- to two-page personal reflection on faculty lecture/discussion. Read Chapter 4, *Practicing*. Think about favorite practice technique, why you think it works, and best recent practice session. Teacher observation 3 due next class.

16. *Practicing*. Share favorite practice techniques and best practice sessions. Why do they work? What allows learning to happen best—working with the awareness of both brain and body. Understanding why repetition is necessary. Practicing to change old habits. Establishing a universal process for applying practice techniques; creative practicing. Pros and cons of practice charts and clock time. Variety in practicing, limiting parameters for making corrections. Should students practice only what they can't do? Assignment: By next week be ready to present thoughts about how listening directly and indirectly effects your best playing/conducting/singing.

17. *Guest lecturer: personal or research-based lecture on practicing*.

18. *Practicing*. Continue sharing thoughts and ideas about practicing. How should students be taught how to practice? Begin discussion of importance of listening for self-evaluation of tone production, dynamics, intonation, ensemble. Assignment: Vocalists and wind and string players: describe a minimum of three approaches to develop and practice intonation. (Piano, organ, harp, and conductors: choose one challenging aspect of your performance area that requires refined listening skills.) Explain each technique in written form—additional pictures or diagrams may be used if they support and clarify written words.

19. *Applied faculty guest lecturer (2)*. Assignment: Write one- to two-page personal reflection on faculty lecture/discussion. Read Chapter 10, *Your Teaching Philosophy*. Teacher observation 4 due next class.

20. *Philosophy*. Discussion of what makes a philosophy based on ideals effective and realistic. Class observations from listening to the faculty lecturers up to this point. What is the driving force in each teacher's desire to help students? What do you know or are you discovering about yourself and your energy toward teaching? What do you envision will be the most challenging aspect of teaching? What is the most important thing a student receives from you? Assignment: Work on philosophy statement—rough draft to be handed in for review next week. Read Chapter 5, *Performing*.

21. *Performing.* What enables you to perform your best? Practice process, attitude, clarity, focus on what is important. What are the distractions from these things? What do you do about it? What would you say to a student who is nervous about an upcoming performance? Does "staying out of your own way" help you? How does competition help and/or hinder your ability to play well? Assignment: Think about how the cognitive processes connected to physical technique affect your ability to perform. Reminder about upcoming semester project presentation.

22. *Performing.* Explore and discuss the role of mental foundation of technique and how it affects our ability to perform. What else makes a good performance possible? (Responsiveness, flow, thinking, *not* thinking, deeply felt expressiveness, and . . .) Assignment: Complete the sentences at the end of Chapter 5, *Performing.*

23. *Applied faculty guest lecturer (3).* Assignment: Write one- to two-page personal reflection on faculty lecture/discussion. Continue honing philosophy statement.

24. *Transferring what we know to students—what we want our students to learn.* Setting priorities and choosing an approach that offers students a fertile environment for growth. Discussion about expectations, motivation, inspiration, and trust.

25. *Transferring what we know to students.* Efficiency and goal setting—envisioning where each student is going. The aural standard: defining excellence—how to expect it at every level. Environments and attitudes conducive to learning. How to supplant student's bad habits with good ones—that is, remedial teaching—helping students make lasting changes for the better. Overview of learning styles: verbal, kinesthetic, aural, visual approaches to any teachable element. Assignment: Be ready to present your semester project next week.

26. *Class presentations.* Composed etudes based on repertoire passage, journal of semester progress on technical or musical development, or review of book from booklist—how has this book shaped your thinking about playing, teaching, learning, practicing, musicianship, and so on.

27. *Class presentations.*

28. *Presentation of philosophy statements.*

FINAL: Completed semester notebook due—Evaluation/grade based on level of competence, scholarship, and professional presentation and organization.

Semester Assignment Ideas

1. Create a notebook with sections to keep notes on musicianship, listening, technique, practicing, performing, philosophy, and practical teaching information. Generate two handouts: one that describes a series of steps that lead students to learn a basic concept or skill that you will be teaching (such as an exercise, diagram, scale fingerings, or practice techniques); and one that is more business oriented, such as lesson policy, student roster with lesson notes, or flier to advertise your availability to teach lessons.

2. Observe four lessons (two on your primary instrument, two in other studios), taking notes on teacher's demeanor, relationship with student, approach to teaching, and effective strategies.

3. Write a one-page teaching philosophy.

4. Choose one for class presentation: (a) Write an etude (minimum thirty-two bars) based on a challenging passage from a piece you are currently practicing. Be prepared to perform your etude for the class, as well as the targeted passage. (b) Choose one aspect of your own technique or musicianship that you wish to improve this semester. Create an initial proposal for your plans for improvement (you may wish to discuss this with your applied teacher), keep a practice log or videotaped demonstrations of your progress for a minimum of eight weeks, and assess at the end of the semester. Present your work for the class. (c) Read one book from the recommended reading list at the end of the chapters and present a review that describes the relationship between the topic and any current aspect of your playing or teaching.

Syllabus for Performance-Based Pedagogy: Teaching Principles and Priorities, Semester 2 (28 Classes)

1. *Introduction to second semester.* Overview of course: daily work, semester assignments, videotaping lessons, master class teaching. Teaching with the big picture in mind. What happens at the first lesson; reviewing priorities from last semester; seeing the big picture of where each student is going; a continuum of learning; prioritizing and clarifying the steps to move students toward big-picture goals. The aural standard: defining excellence, how to expect it at every level. Assignment: Read (or reread) Chapter 6, *Teaching Principles*, and be prepared to discuss Further Exploration 2 about motivation in class.

2. *Teaching principles.* Ways to guide your everyday interactions with students and your attitude toward the teaching process. Motivating students. What makes them want to practice and improve? What motivates you? Assignment: Schedule an interview with your teacher, and review questions in Chapter 10, *Your Teaching Philosophy*. If you know your pedagogical lineage, do some advance research on your teacher's teacher, and prepare additional questions for the interview.

3. *Learning styles and age-appropriate teaching.* Creating verbal, kinesthetic, aural, and visual approaches to any teachable element. Age-appropriate guidance and expectations: preschoolers, primary grades, adolescents, precollege, college, special needs students. Assignment: Choose one aspect of technique or musicianship from your Semester 1 notes and create four different approaches to teaching that element using the four learning styles: verbal, kinesthetic, aural, and visual. (Further Exploration 3) Also decide how you might alter your approach depending on the age of the student, and be ready to alter your ideas accordingly.

4. *What actually happens in lessons.* Do you focus on only what needs fixing? Do you say "Good" even if it's not? Environments and attitudes that foster learning—motivation, inspiration, and trust. Imitation and "right/wrong" versus hearing, exploring, and so on. Brain-based pedagogy: enhancing learning by understanding how the brain/body learns best. The teacher's responsibility that learning happens in a lesson. Presentation of learning styles assignment. Assignment: Attend (or know date of) first master class you will attend this semester. Compose the letter proposed in Further Exploration 1 of Chapter 6.

5. *What actually happens in lessons.* Student–teacher relationship, psychological factors. Getting stuck in teaching ruts—how to get out of them. Is it appropriate to modify expectations? Assignment: Read Chapter 7, *Sequencing*. Make a list of repertoire you studied as a prep student, from earliest memory to present. Conductors: list important pieces for young orchestra, band, or choir in pedagogically logical order. Avoid student arrangements wherever possible.

6. *Sequencing learning.* Create a logical sequence for learning technique and musicianship utilizing repertoire list. Overview of skills—which techniques are required at each stage? (Refer to technique chart from previous semester.) What musical concepts can be taught with each piece? Beginners: What do they need to know? Why beginners tend to be tight; minimum tension in playing/singing. Sort repertoire and supplemental materials into logical order. Assignment: Finish work on repertoire list, making notes of skills needed. Fill in gaps with pieces you might not have learned but could be added to your repertoire. Choose etudes and studies that support technical and musical elements.

7. *Sequencing learning.* Learning situations: Long-term, interim, and short-term teaching. Sequencing musical experiences, knowledge, other supporting facets of developing musicianship. Challenges of remedial teaching and strategies that help. Assignment: Bring in book chosen for review. Read Chapter 8, *Fostering Student Independence*.

8. *Guest lecturer: Suzuki specialist.* Assignment: Write a one- to two-page essay discussing the following points: What are the key points of the Suzuki philosophy and method? Strengths/advantages for the student of the Suzuki approach? Strengths/advantages for the teacher? Do you see any disadvantages or missing elements important to musical development? Would you consider taking Suzuki training?

9. *Fostering student independence.* Why students are dependent, what teachers inadvertently do to perpetuate it; student-centered learning activities: how to increase student awareness, self-observation, instilling self-confidence. How to motivate students from within themselves—connecting life to music. Assignment: Make a list of your best practice techniques, and what students need to know to make their practicing effective. Think about how you will teach these concepts and techniques to students of different ages and developmental levels.

10. *Fostering student independence.* Sharing practice techniques; teaching students how to practice and troubleshoot. Assignment: Teacher observation 1 due next class. Read Chapter 9, *Comprehensive Teaching*.

11. *Comprehensive teaching.* Planning for learning: being a musician is not all about technique—knowledge and expression are always a part of it. How to incorporate and integrate all facets into teaching. Teaching the best repertoire, knowing the music from the inside out. Examples of great teaching plans from great repertoire. Assignment: Complete Further Explorations 2 or 3 at the end of Chapter 9, *Comprehensive Teaching*, using a short but substantial piece that you know well, perhaps having studied it in high school.

12. *Comprehensive teaching.* Developing teaching goals from your piece—choosing strategies for learning, incorporating experiences that foster musical understanding and growth. Assessing skills and musical understanding. Assignment: Further Exploration in Chapter 9.

13. *Applied faculty guest lecturer (1).* Assignment: write one- to two-page personal reflection on faculty lecture/discussion. Read Chapter 11, *Establishing a Teaching Studio.*

14. *Setting up a private studio.* Practical matters/organization. The business of running a studio; recruiting students; teaching at schools; lesson policies; student rosters; setting fees payments; what it means to be self-employed. Assignment: Begin writing a lesson policy. Include information about fees, scheduling, cancellation policies, what you expect of the student (practicing, preparation, outside activities, etc.) and what the student and parents can expect of you. Read Chapter 13, *Daily Considerations and Challenges.*

15. *What really happens in lessons.* How's it going? Addressing common problems in studio teaching—efficiency, scheduling, talking too much, "problem" students. Discussion of specific/current concerns. Parental involvement versus parental interference; ethics issues. Discussions addressing current concerns, self-evaluations. Assignment: Continue work on your lesson policy. Schedule or attend your second master class.

16. *Applied faculty guest lecturer (2).* Assignment: Write one- to two-page personal reflection on applied faculty presentation. Read the first half of Chapter 12, *Groups, Ensembles, Classrooms, and Other Teaching Situations*, up to and including the section on master class teaching.

17. *Master class teaching.* Discussion on master class setting—acknowledging work, best aspects of playing. How to choose a focus for work. Appropriate and inappropriate comments. Sampling of recorded prep student performances—what would you say to the student? Assignment: Be prepared with short solo for next two classes, ready to act in the role of both teacher and student in a master class practicum.

18. *Master class teaching.* Student-to-student master class practicum. Assignment: Attend or secure date for second master class observation, if not already completed.

19. *Master class teaching.* Student-to-student master class practicum. Assignment: Consider differences between an ideal performance experience for a beginner and a highly a competitive audition for an advanced performer. Review Chapter 5, *Performing*, and notes from your first reading. Jot down ideas about how best to prepare students for performing through all stages of development.

20. *Preparing students for performance.* Establishing performance goals. Helping students develop the focus and clarity needed to perform without recurring issues of stage fright, stopping for mistakes, memory problems, and so on. Helping students understand the difference between "knowing" a performance piece and from other forms of "knowing." Creating informal performance situations within regular teaching schedule, using recording devices, and so on. Assignment: Review Chapter 10, *Your Teaching Philosophy.* Outline thoughtful responses to each interview question—be prepared to answer questions "interview-style" in class. Be sure your philosophy statement and answers are in alignment.

21. *Philosophy/interview questions.* Discussion about setting priorities, personal goals for students based on philosophy—sharing ideas and ideals. Your heritage and your legacy—who were your teacher's teachers, and what has been passed to you? What will you pass along to your students? Specific ways that teaching and teaching life will reflect your philosophy. "The Studio as a Community"—the culture created within a

studio is shaped by the way teachers deal with master classes, recital attendance, and so on. Reminder: Finish reading book and begin preparing book review. Assignment: Read Chapter 14, *The Cyclical and Reciprocal Nature of Teaching and Learning*. Reminder: Teacher interview essay is due in one week.

22. *Applied faculty guest lecturer (3).* Assignment: write one- to two-page personal reflection on faculty lecture/discussion. Finish reading Chapter 12, *Groups, Ensembles, Classrooms, and Other Teaching Situations.*

23. *Future teaching situations.* Group classes, adjudicating, coaching larger groups, adult students. College teaching often include methods classes, remedial teaching (nonmajor music students). Do you choose your students or do your students choose you? Being an effective adjudicator—solo and ensemble situations, chair tests, competitions, examinations, and juries. Assignment: Student handout is due at next class.

24. *The teacher-student-teacher cycle.* Circles of influence, how teaching everyone well matters. Teaching communities, ideas for continued learning. Professional memberships and service. Research related to teaching and learning. Conferences; presenting ideas; publishing. Assignment: Book review presentations begin next class.

25. *Presentation of book reviews.*

26. *Presentation of book reviews.* Assignment: Master class observations due next class.

27. *Observations and interviews.* What has been most significant about your observations? What are the best teaching strategies you learned from these experienced teachers? What do you now know about your teachers themselves that you didn't know before?

28. *Successful teaching.* You're teaching well not because *you're* doing the right things; you're teaching well because your *students* are doing the right things. Fostering your own personal growth and improvement as musician and teacher—observations of yourself and other teachers, student evaluations of your teaching.

FINAL: Notebook due for final evaluation.

Semester Assignment Ideas

1. Videotape yourself teaching four lessons with one student—these can be sequential or spread out over the semester. Watch the tapes and write a reflection paper that answers the following questions. How did you improve as a teacher over the course of the semester? Did the student improve? What else did you learn from observing yourself?

2. Attend two master classes—make notes on observations, and write a paper comparing and contrasting the style of teachers, their rapport with students, and effective teaching strategies. Include your thoughts and experiences from our master class practicum sessions.

3. Interview three teachers: your current applied teacher, a former (precollege) teacher, and another teacher (preferably of a different instrument) you admire. Use the questions in Chapter 10, *Your Teaching Philosophy*, for a starting point, reword, or add others as seems appropriate. Write a paper about what you learned, comparing teachers' approaches, including notable quotes, and your own thoughts and observations and how (if) these interviews have influenced your thinking. You may also include ideas from applied teacher lectures in class.

4. Create one helpful handout for your students, describing a technique regularly taught, practice suggestions, an exercise for stretching or positioning, or other helpful information that you find yourself repeating to most students.

5. Read a book from one of the recommended reading lists at the end of each chapter and write a review on its relative merit when applied to teaching and playing.

6. Design a resume, cover letter, and updated curriculum vitae over the course of the semester. Write the cover letter highlighting your strengths as they relate to the job for which you are applying. Take some time near the middle of the semester to discuss your documents with a classmate. Give each other feedback related to the clarity and organization of your documents. Make necessary changes and complete the project by the end of the semester.

Grading

Grades will be based on the completion of all assignments and course requirements. It is expected that each student complete all assignments with competence and accuracy. Assignments will be graded for exceptional competence or understanding ($\sqrt{+}$), competence or understanding ($\sqrt{}$), or lack of competence or understanding ($\sqrt{-}$).

A: Course requirements and/or assignments completed with competence and accuracy, scholarly integrity, and exceptional quality.

B: Course requirements and/or assignments adequately completed.

C: One or more course requirements and/or assignments not completed.

F: Anything worse than the aforementioned scenarios.

Each absence over two absences will result in a lowered final letter grade.

No grade of Incomplete will be allowed.

The use of cell phones, texting, or responding to email is strictly prohibited during class time.

Americans with Disabilities Act (ADA) Compliance Statement: The University provides upon request appropriate academic accommodations for qualified students with disabilities. For more information, contact the Office of the Dean of Students.

The Fully Prepared Music Student

Use a table like this one (table I.1) to list the aspects of your instrument or performance area that you believe a student should have studied in preparation for entering a college or conservatory as a music major.

TABLE AI.1 The Fully Prepared Music Student: Skills, Repertoire, Concepts, and Experiences

Etudes and technical studies	Concertos	Sonatas and miscellaneous pieces	Techniques	Music theory concepts	Concepts related to stylistic performance	Concepts related to understanding the instrument	Other musical experiences and functional skills

Connecting Expressive Sound to Bow Technique

1. Name the three bowing variables that contribute the most to creating a variety of sounds on a stringed instrument.
2. With your instrument, explore the variables in the tables (tables A9.1–3) and write a description for each sound created, avoiding "good/bad" and "loud/soft" labels. Use colorful and expressive adjectives.

TABLE A9.1.1 Placement of Bow on Strings: Near Fingerboard

Weight → Speed ↓	Light	Medium	Heavy
Slow			
Medium			
Fast			

TABLE A9.1.2 Placement of Bow on Strings: Middle (Between Fingerboard and Bridge)

Weight → Speed ↓	Light	Medium	Heavy
Slow			
Medium			
Fast			

TABLE A9.1.3 Placement of Bow on Strings: Near Bridge

Weight → Speed ↓	Light	Medium	Heavy
Slow			
Medium			
Fast			

APPENDIX 9.2

Student Assessment Form

Student should fill out the form first—teacher will follow up with consultation. The student should enter a number from 1 to 5 for each item in the table (table A9.2.1).

Student Name _____

Teacher _____

TABLE A9.2.1 Student's and Teacher's Assessments of Progress

Please rate progress: 5 = excellent 4 = good 3 = fair 2 = poor 1 = deficient		
	Student's assessment	Teacher's assessment
Follows through on assignments		
Responsive in lessons		
Practices with attentiveness to the following specifics:		
Posture/positioning		
Intonation		
Musicianship		
Rhythm		
Control/accuracy		
Vibrato		
Tone production		
Memorization		
Total: overall progress this semester (maximum score 50)		

1. How many hours did you practice each day? Was this amount enough to achieve your goals? If it wasn't enough, what prevented you from practicing as much as you needed?

2. Are you satisfied with your lessons? Can you suggest anything that would make them better?

3. Please add any additional constructive comments you would like to make about our work together.

Applying for (and Securing) a University Teaching Position

It may be a common assumption that a great performer will also be a great teacher, but is that the view of college search committees? In 2008, 142 college teachers who participated as a member of a faculty search committee were surveyed regarding their priorities when screening candidates.[1] The results indicate that 97 percent of respondents ranked teaching ability as "very important" when hiring new faculty. Second in that category was the interview, receiving a top rank from 89 percent of those surveyed, and third was teaching experience, selected by 73 percent. Performance ability was a close fourth, rated very important by 72 percent. Finishing this category were recommendations and references (62 percent) and performance experience (54 percent).

You might be surprised that teaching ability ranked as a higher priority than performance ability, and that teaching experience outranked performance experience. However, remember that while great performers are revered on the concert stage and appreciated for their artistic contributions to the performing vitality of colleges, the primary function of a music school is to be sure their music majors receive the training they need to succeed as professionals. So, very simply, in order to be desirable to a college or university, you must be able to demonstrate your ability to teach as well as perform.

Music teaching positions are acquired through a series of events. Initially, most positions require an application, cover letter, curriculum vitae, and list of references. You might also be asked to supply a recording and occasionally a philosophy statement. Once the application date is closed, the search committee members read the material and typically invite three candidates to visit the campus for a series of interviews, solo or collaborative chamber music recitals, and master class presentations. Every aspect of the interview process is important; however, the master class is the primary way for you to demonstrate you expertise in teaching your instrument as well as your ability to relate to the students. You will want the master class you teach to reveal your highest standard of musicianship and your interview to be a true reflection of yourself as a teacher, scholar, musician, and colleague. Applying for a job is a full-time job in itself, so set aside plenty of time to prepare your materials professionally.

Cover Letter

While it might be tempting to use a computer template for cover letters, every letter needs to be specifically crafted to suit each individual position. The letter needs to be in your voice rather than a stilted one-size-fits-all language. Explain why you are the right person for the job by connecting your qualifications with the requirements outlined in the position posting. Let the search committee know that you are truly interested in the position by showing evidence of extra research you have done on the school and/or the department. Because your accompanying curriculum vitae will be long and comprehensive, keep the cover letter brief (one page if possible), calling attention to distinguishing or particularly impressive entries, and explain how you would be a useful addition to the faculty.

Before you send your materials, check for grammar and typographical errors, making certain that everything is spelled correctly, especially the name of the institution and the person to whom the letter is directly addressed. A good cover letter can help your application stand out among the many they will receive for this position (sometimes two hundred or more), and can increase the likelihood that you will be considered on their short list of the most qualified applicants.

Curriculum Vitae

Your accompanying curriculum vitae will include your myriad qualifications. Keep an ongoing list of awards, honors, recitals, teaching positions, grants, special concerts, studies abroad, master classes, published articles, and conference presentations. Add to it regularly before you forget important details, including dates and names of people, schools, publications, or organizations associated with the job or event. Even if each entry is not fully formatted initially, at least the information will be there when you need it.

Preparing for an Interview

Before you attend an interview at a teaching institution, you may want to think about the questions that a search committee or administrator may pose to you. Study the vision statement of the institution and be familiar with its student and faculty demographics, traditions, and special programs and projects. Read the biographies of the faculty members you are most likely to meet, especially in your specific area of expertise. Reflect on what you have to offer the institution as a colleague, performer, scholar, and teacher, and how you see your skills fitting in to the existing department in terms of projects and vision.

The Actual Interview

If you are applying to teach at a university or independent music school, your interview makes a significant impact on the possibility that you will get the job. The importance of the interview and the quality of the master class eludes many performing musicians, who are understandably focused on the recital presentation. Do remember, however, that a teaching institution's primary task is to hire someone who will be an effective teacher and a contributing colleague as well as a skilled performer.

You will be asked questions related to your approach to teaching (from philosophical to specific) and your sense of mission or personal contribution to the world of music. If you have already written a philosophy statement, many of your answers can be based on those thoughts. The committee might ask you more personal questions concerning what you view as your weaknesses, your strengths, and the most significant moments in your career as a performer and teacher. They might want to know how you would handle certain common teaching challenges. If you have had experience with some of these situations and have written a lesson policy, you might already know how to answer them—but if you're still new to this, it is important to think in advance about what your ideal responses would be, based on your core beliefs.

It's wise to be prepared for an interview with your thoughts well formed and clarified. Consider the following questions and then put your answers in writing. Use full sentences, because that is how you would answer the questions in the real interview situation. Wrestling with fluent and meaningful word choices now is much smarter than sounding inarticulate at your interview.

Potential Interview Questions

1. Tell us about yourself.
2. What are your responsibilities in your current position and what prompted you to look for another teaching situation?
3. What do you see as your strengths? Challenges?
4. What do you look for in a student? What do you think makes a good student?
5. How do you prepare your students for professional life? How do you balance, differentiate, and teach the various aspects of performing (solo, chamber, orchestral)?
6. Do you use a defined sequence of studies for your students or a different sequence for each student?
7. Do you have specific goals or plans for the time your students will be spending with you (planning repertoire, competitions, auditions, recitals, etc.)?
8. How do you motivate your students toward productive practice?
9. How often do you schedule studio classes? Are the students separated into different levels, or do you meet with all students at the same time?
10. Do you have a hierarchy of issues to fix (e.g., musical issues before technical issues, setup before sound, sound before rhythm, etc.)? Related to that, do you have a basic practice process that you have found to be particularly efficient and effective?

11. Do you recommend the use of metronome? How, when, for how long, and to what purpose?

12. Do you recommend "team teaching" with another colleague? Are you a good collaborator? Can you give us an example?

13. How often do your students perform? How important is solo performance in your studio?

14. How do you help students deal with performance stress and stage fright? Have you personally dealt with such issues? Have you encountered students who have had performance anxiety in ways that were totally different from yours?

15. Do you include techniques like yoga, Feldenkreis, Alexander Technique, or any other body awareness approaches in your teaching?

16. Do you recommend that your students enroll in pedagogy classes? Why or why not?

17. Have you ever had students that did not do what you asked of them—students who did not practice enough, skipped lessons, or didn't follow through on related assignments? If so, how did you handle the situation?

18. What specifically do you have to offer to our campus/department?

19. What have been some of your most gratifying teaching experiences? Where do you see yourself in five years?

Further topics specific to a preparatory program interview:

20. How many students do you have, what levels do you teach, and what ages?

21. Do you have any special requirements for a students to be part of your studio, such as previous years of study, or a level of accomplishment?

22. What are the criteria that would prevent you from teaching someone (e.g., lack of motivation, lack of practice)?

23. Do you use the Suzuki method or other sequenced methodology? Why or why not?

24. If you use the Suzuki method, do you use supplementary material in addition to the Suzuki repertoire? Are there certain supplementary pieces and technique exercises that all your students play in a specific order?

25. If you don't use the Suzuki repertoire, how do you choose a progressive repertoire for your students?

26. Do you have experience starting a student on your instrument?

27. When do you introduce note reading? Why do you choose that point in skill development?

28. What do you expect in terms of parent involvement?

29. Do you have parent education classes? If so, do you require class attendance only when children begin lessons, or throughout the child's time in your studio?

30. What is your policy on makeup lessons?

31. How do you prepare students for music school auditions?

32. Do you recommend that your students attend a summer festival or music camp?

Topics specific to primary or secondary teaching positions:

33. What is your process for planning lessons?

34. How would you describe a "good" lesson?

35. How do you manage classroom behavior? Can you offer an example of one of your classroom rules?
36. What might your classroom look like?
37. Describe for us the culture you envision for your classroom.
38. What has been your most challenging teaching moment so far?
39. How would you deal with a very angry parent?
40. What is your view of competitions and contests? How do you prepare students for these events?
41. Do you have any interest in sponsoring an after-school activity?

Topics specific to how you see yourself as a teacher:

42. What makes a good teacher? What would make you a better teacher?
43. How would you define your style of teaching? How has it evolved from "teaching what your teacher taught you" to a style that is your own?
44. What do you think has made your studio successful?
45. Are you the teacher you want to be? Are you the teacher you imagined you would be?
46. Do you have any questions for us?

The last question is important, because you want to be as interested in them and the position as they are in you. Questions for them should be based on having done your homework: study their web site and be familiar with school's philosophy; peruse their catalogues and curriculum, especially in your area; look over their promotional materials, recent concert programs, important fundraising events, and so forth. Know important names, such as those of the dean and other key people, special grants the school may have received, and projects of which they are particularly proud. You will also want to be prepared to talk about how your professional aspirations connect to those of the institution.

Do not discuss salary, vacation time, or any other aspect of the job that takes the focus away from your intent to be a dedicated faculty member. These topics can be discussed after you have been offered the position.

Most institutions have a career services office that provides a full range of resources associated with writing resumes, cover letters, and curriculum vitae. If you are still in school, take advantage of the services that can assist you with professional development and other issues related to job searches and interviews.

The Master Class

Your solid technical and musical understanding combined with clear ideas related to good teaching will make you a strong master class teacher. You can increase your skills as a master class teacher through practice and assessment. Any teaching experience helps, but if you have the opportunity, practice teaching a master class, either with real students or with the students of colleagues. More information specific to a master class teaching is provided in Chapter 12.

Audition/Recital

Choose music that reflects your highest standard of musicianship, and create interesting program that can be performed well with limited time to rehearse with an unfamiliar accompanist. Consider introducing each piece by mentioning why you enjoy performing that particular literature.

Note

1. Strietelmeier, A. (2011, January). *Profiling the Performer/Teacher: Preparation, Livelihood and Reflections of Working Musicians*, based on the Scott, L., and Watkins, C., *Performance Pedagogy Survey*, February 2008, University of Texas at Austin.

Sample Course Objectives
for a Methods Class

Depending on the area of focus, the following objectives could be included in a syllabus to describe expectations for semester accomplishments. Your chosen objectives will guide the planning of your class activities, assignments, and assessments.

By the end of the semester students will

- Understand basic performance principles essential to {string, brass, woodwind, percussion, choral, elementary general music classroom} teaching, demonstrated through performance, peer teaching, and written evaluation.
- Demonstrate basic performance skills on secondary instruments.
- Demonstrate an understanding of the fundamentals of performance on all (woodwind, brass, percussion, orchestral stringed) instruments.
- Diagnose and remediate the most common technical problems associated with a specific area of performance.
- Demonstrate the basic components of advanced techniques and a sequence of study specific to skill development of each technique through written work and verbal explanation.
- Increase knowledge of terminology unique to each area of study.
- Increase knowledge of successful techniques used to organize elementary and secondary music programs through observation and written expression.
- Observe successful teaching in heterogeneous group settings.
- Demonstrate a verbal sequence of instruction that establishes basic fundamental posture for voice and instrumental performance.

- Review current method books and become familiar with graded solo and ensemble literature in a specific area of study. (See "Method Book Review Considerations" below)
- Self-assess video recordings of their own teaching episodes.
- Lead the class during music learning and performing episodes that simulate group instruction in school settings.
- Compose, arrange, and simplify music for the purpose of instructing students of diverse skill levels in group settings.
- Participate in supervised field experiences with local teachers.
- Compile a notebook that can serve as a professional resource and reference for further development of competence and understanding.

Method Book Review Considerations

Thoroughly review your assigned texts using the following criteria:

1. *Logical sequence of instruction.*
2. *Technical exercises that encourage repetition and skill development.* Are exercises present that allow the student the opportunity to practice the introduced skill? Are charts included? Are there suggestions for repetition and drill?
3. *Balance of technical exercises and musical selections.*
4. *Quality and functional merit of the musical selections.* Are the selections tunes that would prompt the players to memorize or perform often? Are there pieces that include techniques covered earlier in the book, and is this made apparent?
5. *Visual appearance.* What does the book look like? Is it interesting to view? Are pages too cluttered or too stark? Is it colorful or visually captivating? Are there pictures of actual performers in the book? Are these pictures up-to-date? Do pictures or drawings of position set provide good models for imitation?
6. *Glossary of terms.* Are foreign terms translated and explained?
7. *Well-defined parameters for mastery of skill.* Is it clear how students or the teacher assess whether they are ready to move on?
8. *Printing and binding quality.* Is the book sturdy? What is the binding like? Is the cover laminated and waterproof?

Suggestions for Effective Middle
and High School Rehearsals

- *Call students by name.* Using their names from the very beginning of instruction is powerful in gaining and maintaining attention. Hang signs on music stands or have students make nametags when they arrive, and be sure to address every student by name at least once during your time with the group.
- *Tune the group efficiently.* There are many different ways to tune ensembles, but decide on a system ahead of time. If you don't like the results, try another approach the next time.
- *Start on time and end on time.* Running overtime can be frustrating to families that have other commitments, or to festival organizers who have limited time to reorganize and lock up the facilities.
- *Call on individuals rather than asking for volunteers.* Keep everyone engaged in the process of making change. Involve students in assessment as well as small group performances within the large rehearsal setting.
- *Model graciousness.* In festival settings, publicly acknowledge the individuals responsible for logistics, including scheduling, auditions, and programs, and expect students do the same.

For all directors and future directors of youth ensembles
"You're asking for trouble if you . . ."

Program music that is too difficult
Choose music that is uninteresting

Have incomplete folders and no extra parts
Fail to teach listening skills
Fail to teach principles
Try to repair an instrument during a rehearsal

For suggestions pertaining to *all* ensembles and groups irrespective of level or size, see Chapter 12, *Groups, Ensembles, Classrooms, and Other Teaching Situations*.

Musician's Universal Rubric

The goal of a rubric is to

- Categorize specific performance areas for the purpose of assessment
- Facilitate agreement among judges by defining competencies in categories
- Provide an outline of different aspects of performance in a graded continuum
- Provide a means to assign an overall score or points for each category
- Share competencies with students so they know how their work will be judged
- Provide descriptors that define a final grade

This rubric (table A12.1) was designed to suggest appropriate, categorized terminology to suit a variety of situations. It should be modified to suit each separate context.

TABLE A12.1   Universal Rubric for Musicians

	Superior	Excellent	Average	Below Average	Poor
General descriptors	Exemplary Exceptional Superb	Very Good Above average Distinguished	Good Satisfactory Ordinary	Unsatisfactory Substandard Minimal	Inferior Deficient Unacceptable
Tone	Consistent Focused Resonant Superior tone throughout entire range Artistic control of vibrato	Minor imperfections Mature tone with occasional flaws Dynamic contrast usually evident Secure and consistent vibrato	Unstable tone in outer ranges Inconsistent tone Occasionally thin or weak Vibrato evident through most of performance	Thin Forced Weak Immature Underdeveloped Inconsistently applied vibrato	Lack of fundamental tone throughout Deficient quality Unfocused sound No dynamic contrast No evidence of vibrato
Technique	Full command of all aspects of technique Manual/vocal dexterity Near perfect facility in all areas Clear articulation throughout	Played all correct notes Minor imperfections and inconsistency Minor lapses in precision Mostly consistent articulations	Played mostly correct notes Satisfactory posture, clarity, and precision Inconsistent attacks and releases Inconsistent articulation	Some incorrect pitches Substandard posture Lack of clarity and precision Substandard articulation	Numerous incorrect pitches Poor fundamental posture Repertoire is not matched to the student skill level No discernable articulation

Musicianship/ expression	Consistent evidence of phrasing, musical line, and musical meaning Expressive Dynamic contrast throughout Performed with accurate style, tempo, dynamics, phrasing, and interpretation	Musical understanding evident with attention to phrase shapes Appropriate style with minor inconsistencies Dynamic contrast mostly evident Correct style and tempo but some inconsistencies	Satisfactory phrasing but showing little evidence of musical understanding Satisfactory tempo and style Occasional dynamic contrast Fair energy and emotion	Musical line or phrases are not evident Nominal evidence of style Inconsistent tempo Mechanical performance and minimal dynamics throughout Weakness in fundamental skills inhibits almost all musical expression
				No evidence of style Inaccurate tempo Lack of dynamic contrast No fundamental performance skills to allow any evidence of musicianship
Accuracy	Outstanding facility in all areas of technique Artist-level intonation Pitch adjustments made immediately Rhythmic stability and fluidity throughout	Excellent facility with minor inconsistencies Minimal intonation problems Pitch adjustment obvious but successful Excellent sense of rhythm and tempo with minor inconsistencies	Demonstrates some technical facility but flaws are evident Some pitch problems Slow or unsuccessful pitch adjustments Stable sense of rhythm	Poor facility causing major disruptions to performance Many inaccurate notes and unstable pitch Pitch adjustments attempted but unsuccessful Weak sense of pulse and obvious problems in technical passages
				Lack of facility Inaccurate notes and intonation problems throughout No attempt to adjust pitch Unclear tempi and barely recognizable rhythms

Disability Law, Accommodations, and Resources

Laws Most Pertinent to Music Teaching and Learning

1. The Americans with Disabilities Act is civil rights legislation that protects individuals with disabilities in the areas of employment, public facilities and accommodations, and state and local governments. The Act's accessibility guidelines require handicap access to most existing buildings and in all newly constructed or renovated buildings.
2. The Individuals with Disabilities Education Act (IDEA) was originally written in 1975. This law specifies conditions under which students from birth to the age of twenty-one with documented disabilities can receive early intervention, special education, and related services. The Act requires that children will receive a free appropriate public education (FAPE) in the least restrictive environment (LRE).
3. Section 504 of the Rehabilitation Act of 1973 states: "No otherwise qualified person with a disability in the United States shall, solely by reason of a disability, be excluded from the participation in, be denied the benefits of, or be subjected to discrimination under any program or activity receiving federal financial assistance."

The Individualized Education Program

Public schools have dedicated staff to ensure that every child in the school is, whenever possible, educated in inclusive classroom settings. Special education staff members, teachers, parents, and when appropriate, the student are part of the team that designs the Individualized Education Program (IEP) for every student with a documented disability. This document outlines goals, accommodations, modifications, and related special education services for the student. Your attendance at the IEP meetings will allow you to learn more about the student from those present, to designate specific musical goals, and to request assistance, if appropriate, in music classroom or ensemble settings. Often, because of schedule conflicts or lack of information, music teachers do not attend IEP meetings. However, valuable information related to teaching and behavioral strategies will most likely be communicated during that meeting. Your attendance could help you and your student be successful in the music classroom. If you have a student with a disability in your ensemble, private studio, or music classroom, stay in close contact with special education staff members and most definitely with the parents of the student. Make sure you receive notification regarding support, resources, and the scheduling of the IEP meeting.

Accommodations for Individuals with Disabilities at the University Level

The designated campus office for students with disabilities may suggest the following or similar accommodations.

- Access to syllabi and calendars before the semester begins to aid students in semester planning and time management
- Video or audio recording of lessons or master classes
- Braille services
- Flexible attendance requirements due to disability-related absence
- Course substitutions
- Permission to take breaks from instruction
- Course load reductions
- Use of a service animal

Additional accommodations such as the following may require the completion of specific application through the university.

- Priority registration to ensure enough time to get from class to class
- Sign language interpreters
- Extended time for exams

Additional Resources Related to Disabilities

- U.S. Department of Education, Institute of Educational Science, National Center for Educational Statistics
- National Endowment for the Arts' Office for AccessAbility, Statewide Forums on Careers in the Arts for People with Disabilities

- National Center for Educational Statistics and Office of Special Education Programs, part of the U.S. Department of Educational and Rehabilitative Services data analysis system: statistics related to disabilities; Office of Civil Rights and Americans with Disabilities Act Accessibility Guidelines: additional information related to accessibility standards
- Disability Information Pages found through the Online Resources link, Center for Music Learning, University of Texas, Austin (www.cml.music.utexas.edu): more information about specific laws and services

Seek out campus and community resources for additional information and support.

Index